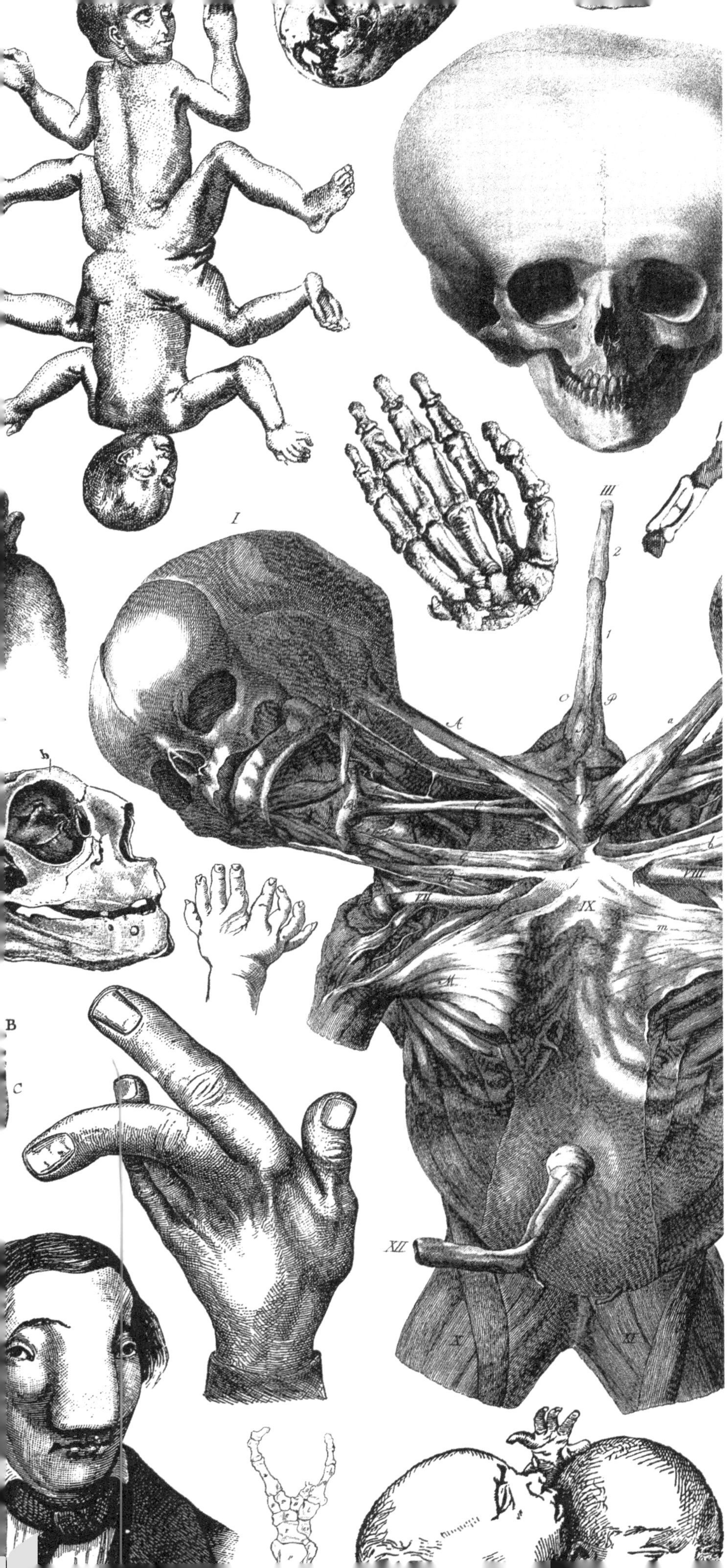

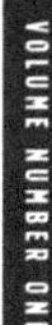

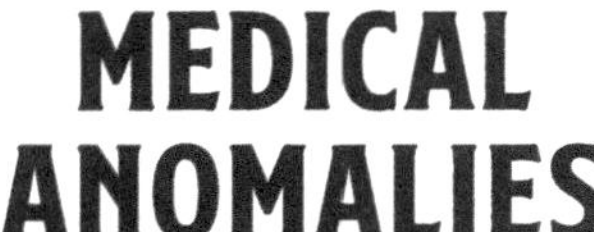

MEDICAL ANOMALIES

AN IMAGE ARCHIVE FOR ARTISTS *And* DESIGNERS

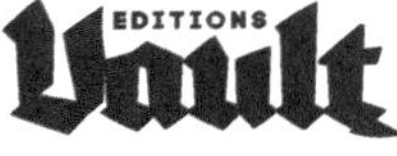

INTRODUCTION

Medical Anomalies from Vault Editions is a resource of 240 downloadable illustrations documenting defects, deformities and medical anomalies as represented from the 15th to 18th-century. It is a powerful resource for tattoo artists, illustrators, designers and fine artists looking for rare and unusual sources of reference material. Categories include conjoined twins, supernumerary limbs, giants, cyclopia, leprosy, elephantiasis, deformities of the skull, congenital abnormalities, spina bifida, hydrocephalus and much more. This book is designed for creative practitioners to introduce unusual and little known medical anomalies into their visual references and take their designs to the next level.

Features:
This book comes with a unique download code giving you access to all 240 high-resolution images featured.

About the author:
This book was curated and authored by the creative director of Vault Editions, Kale James. Kale has published over 30 acclaimed books within the art design space and has worked with Nike, Samsung, Adidas and Rolling Stone. Kale's artwork is published in numerous titles, including No Cure, Semi-Permanent, Vogue and more.

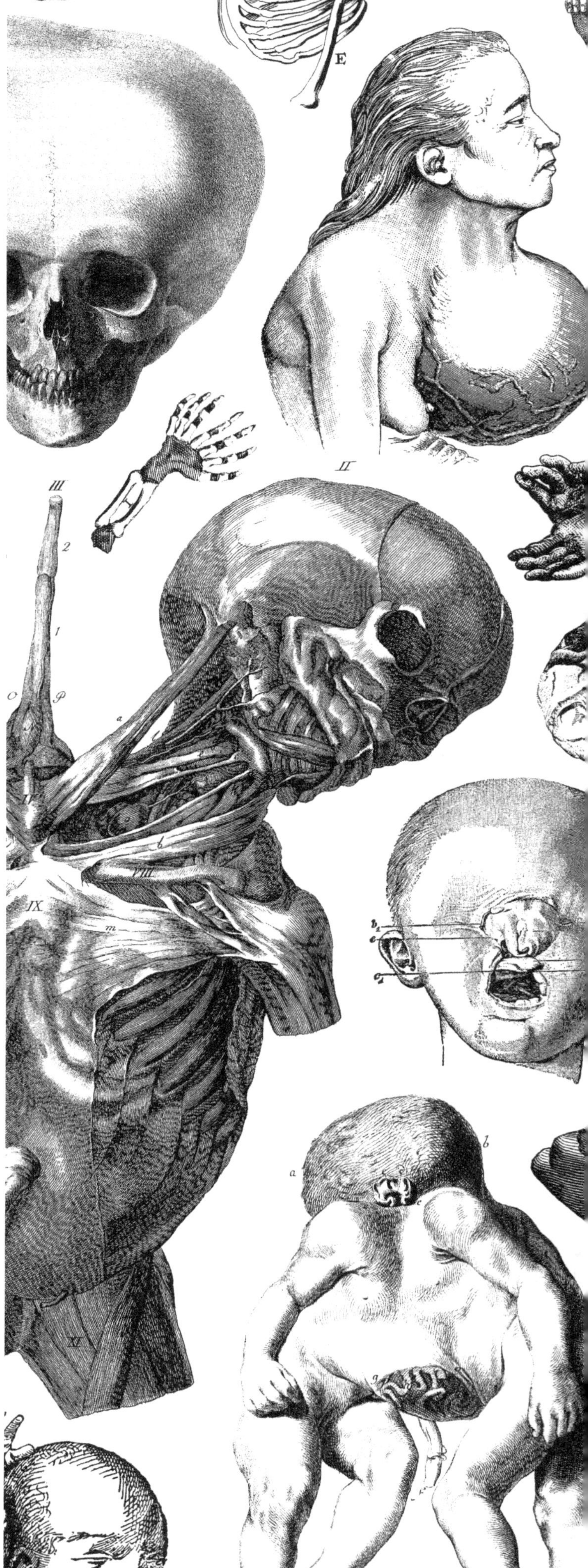

TABLE OF CONTENTS

DOWNLOAD YOUR FILES

Downloading your files is simple. To access your digital
files, please go to the last page of this book and follow the
instructions.

For technical assistance, please email:
info@vaulteditions.com

Copyright
Copyright © Vault Editions Ltd 2021.

Bibliographical Note

This book is a new work created by Vault Editions Ltd.

ISBN 978-1-925968-73-6

MEDICAL ANOMALIES

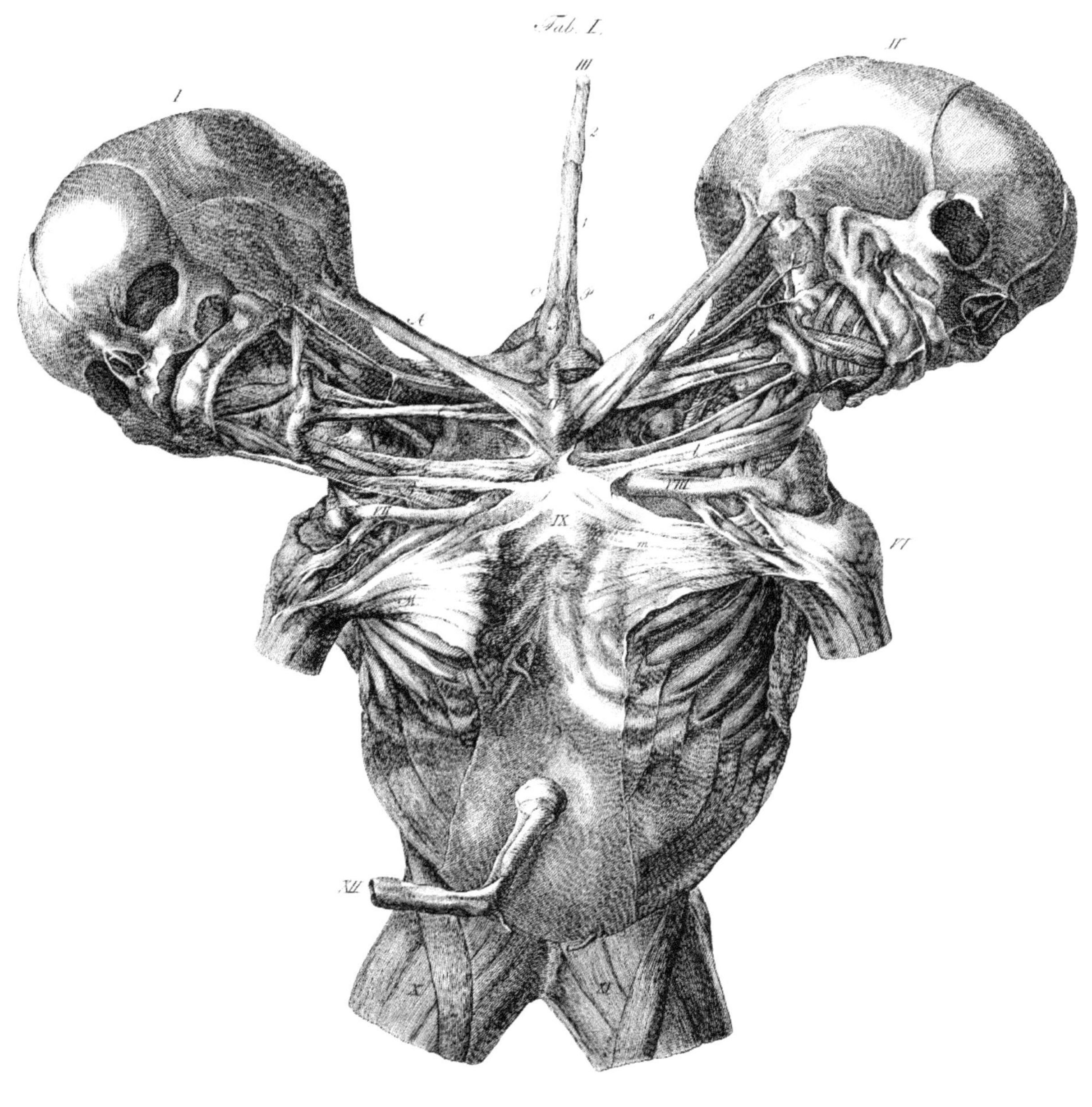

01: Abdominal viscera formed outside the peritoneum, considered reclined liver, Anterior view.

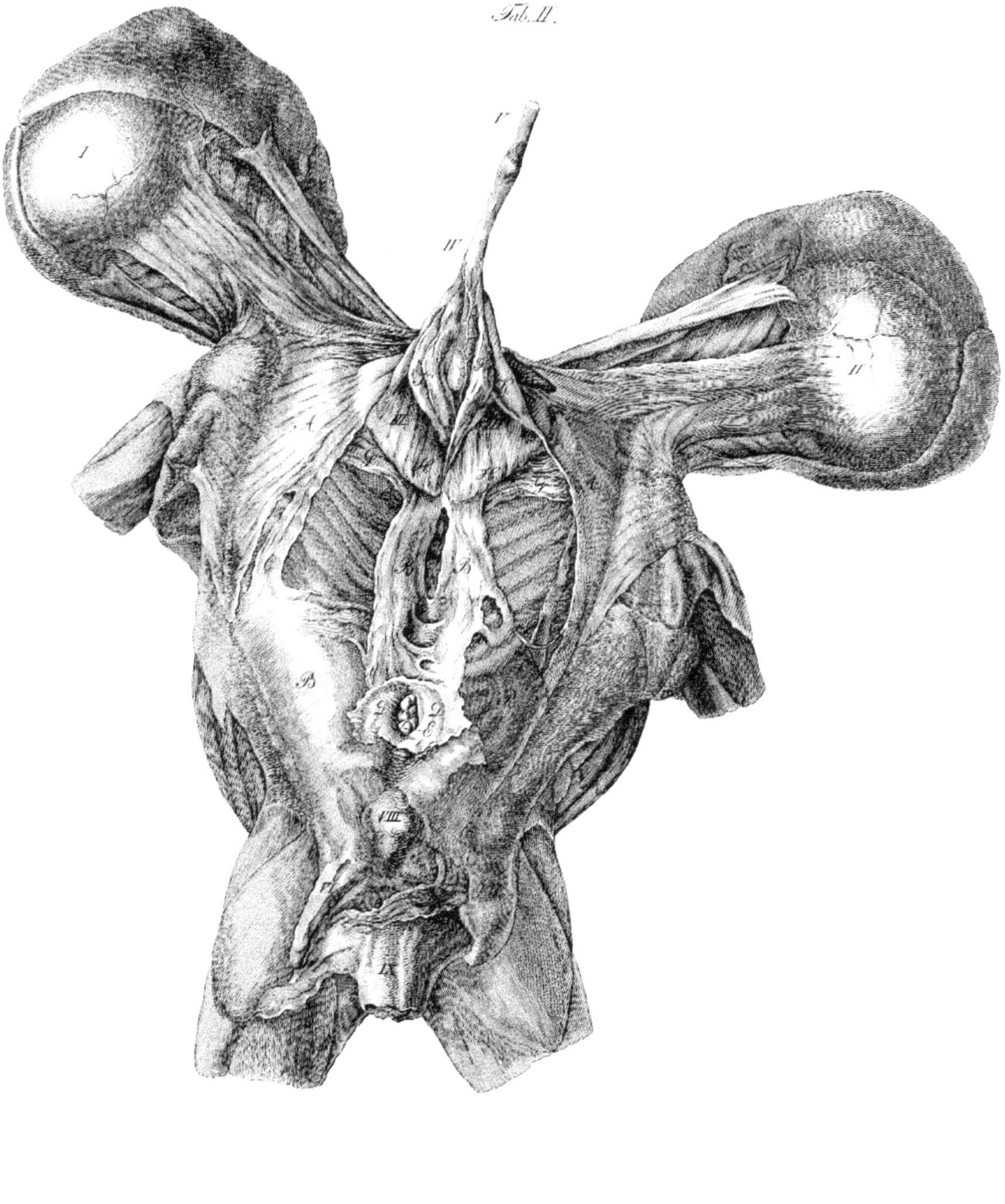

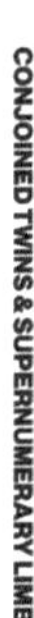

02: Abdominal viscera formed outside the
peritoneum, considered reclined liver, posterior
view.

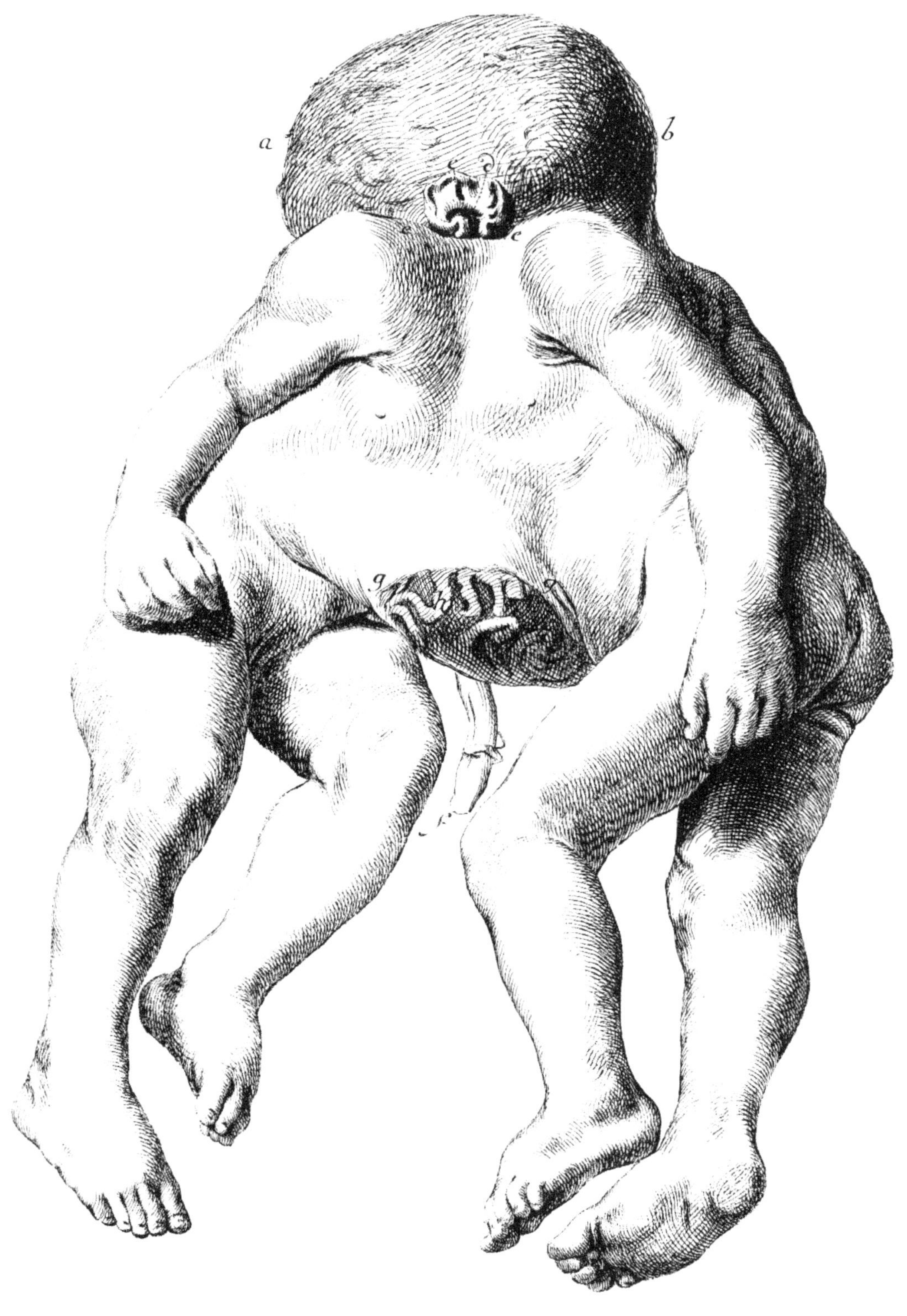

03: Craniopagus twins.

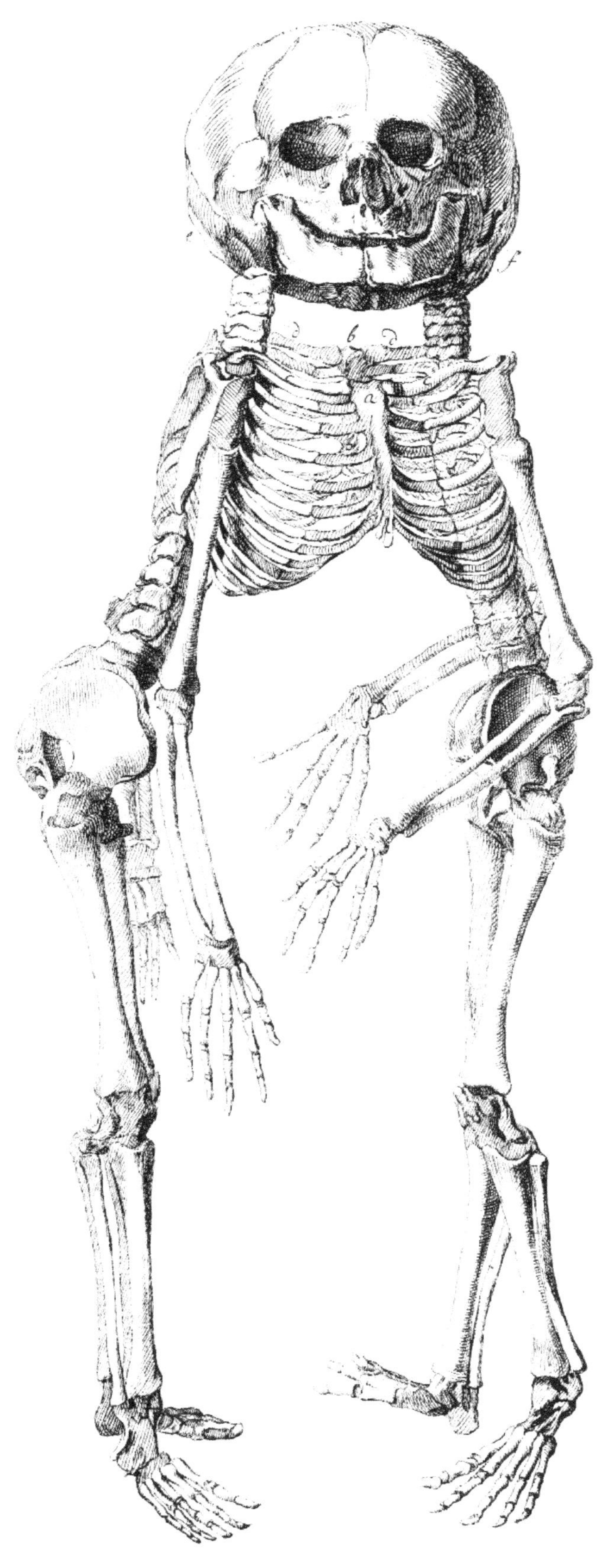

04: The skeleton of craniopagus twins.

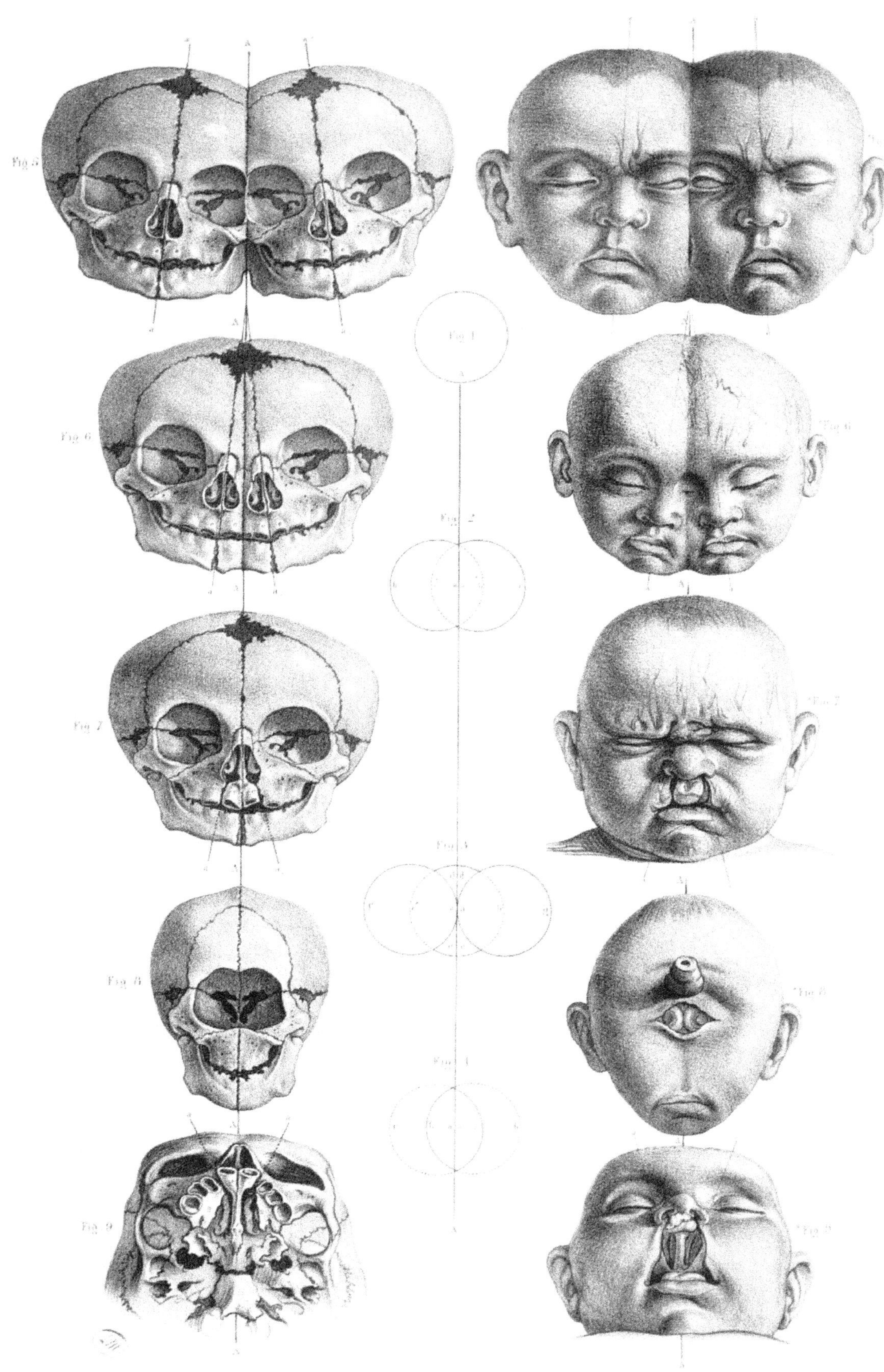

05: Head and skull of malformed infants;
conjoined twins, bilateral cleft lip and
holoprosencephaly.

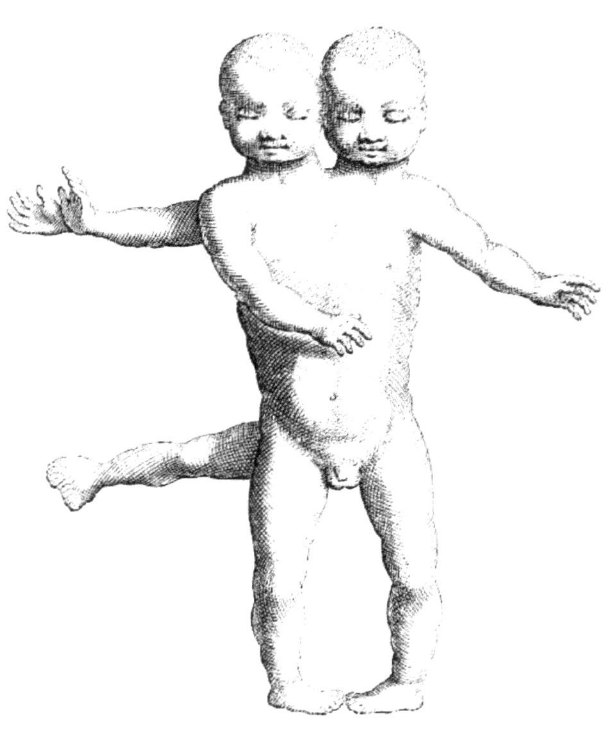

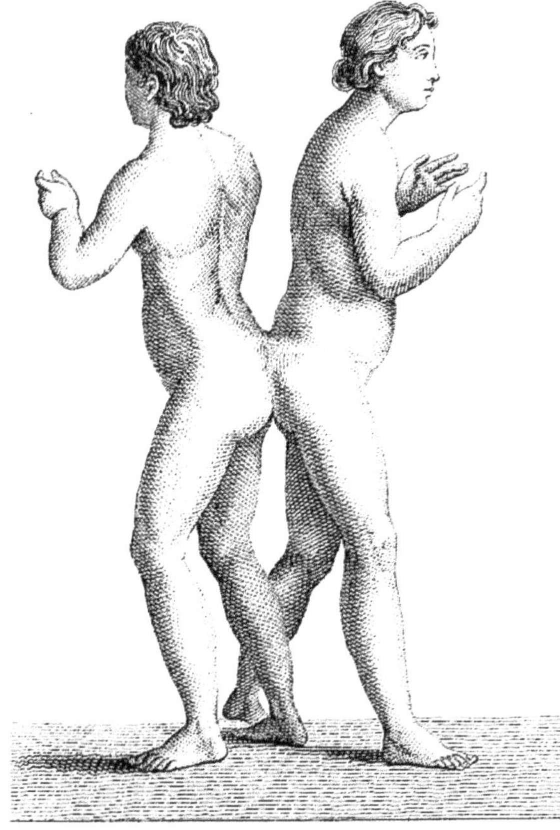

08

09

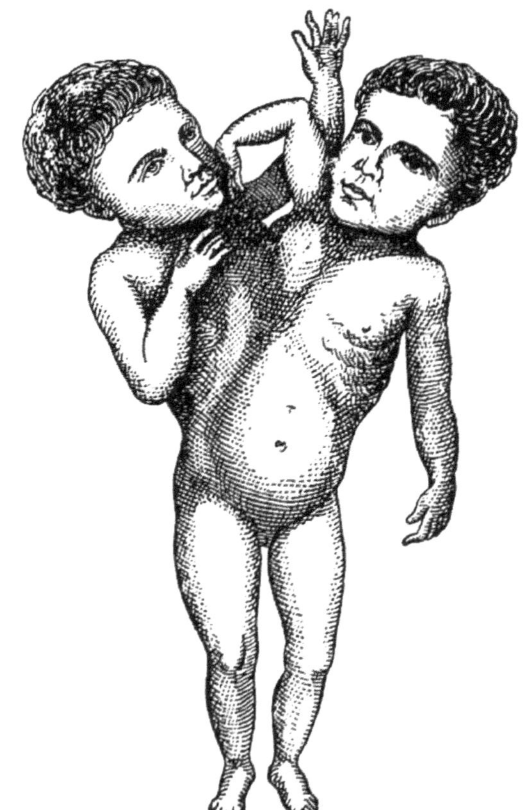

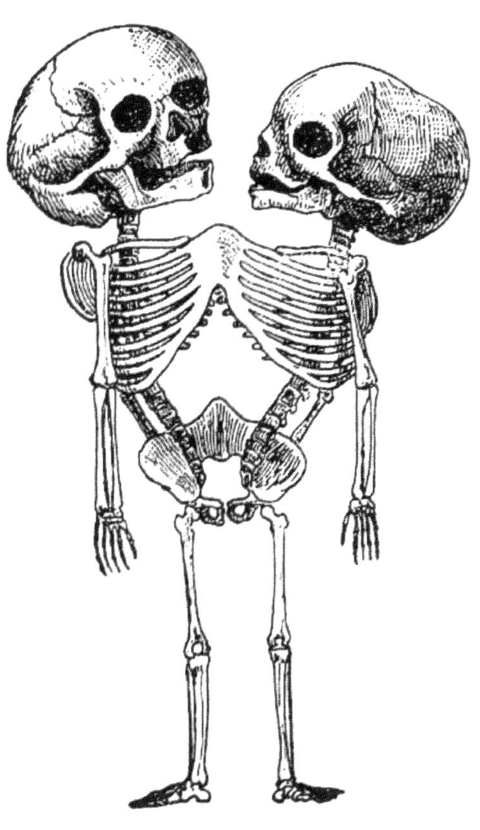

06: Conjoined–twins–Tulp, Nicolaas, 1593–1674.

07: Female conjoined twins, joined at the small of the back. Etching with watercolour, 1818.

08: Conjoined twins Ritta–Christina.

09: Skeleton of Ritta–Christina.

10

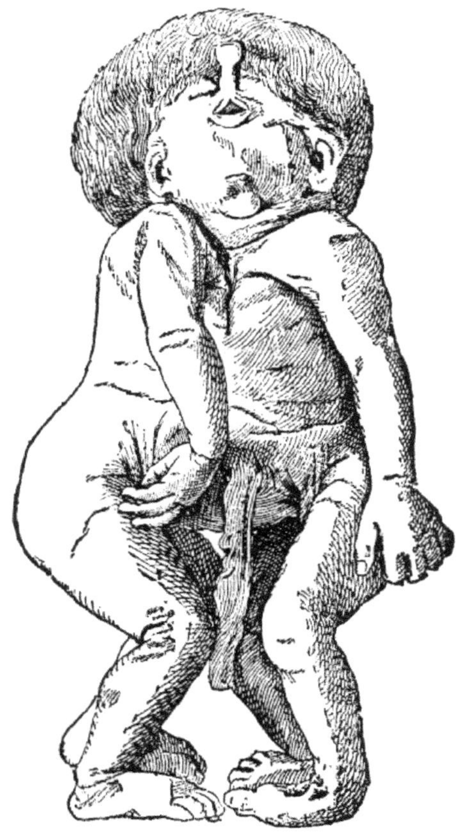

11

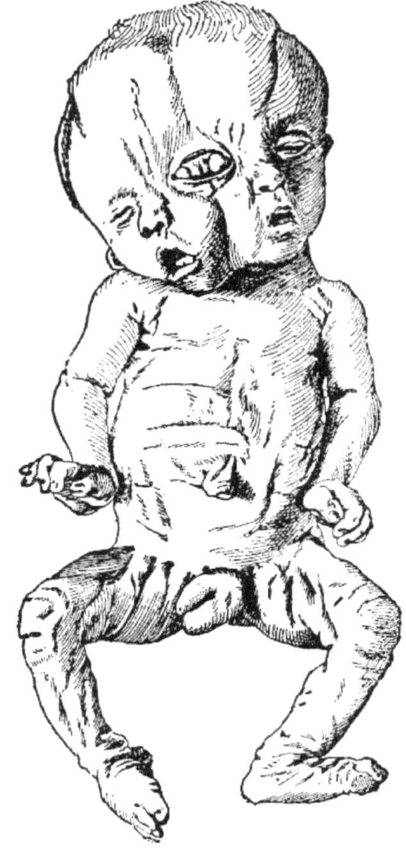

12

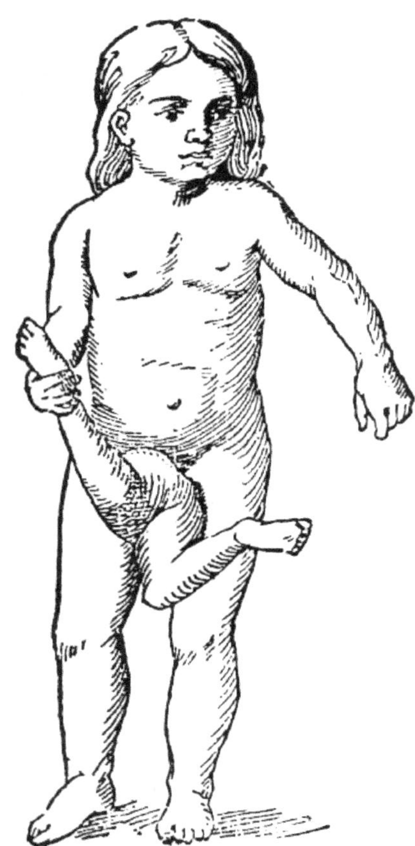

13

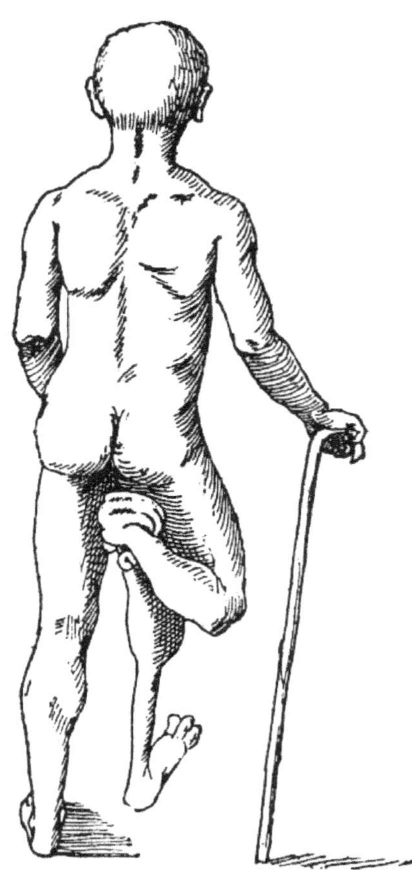

10: Cephalothoracopagus or syncephalus with Janus–head.

11: Diprosopus distomus tetrophthalmus diotus.

12: Dipygus parasiticus (After Lancereaux).

13: Dipygus parasiticus (After Liesching).

14

15

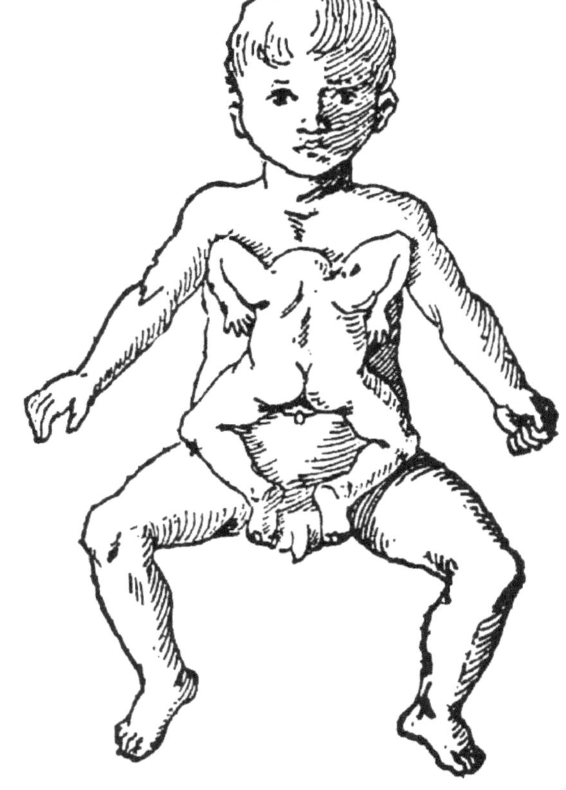

16

17

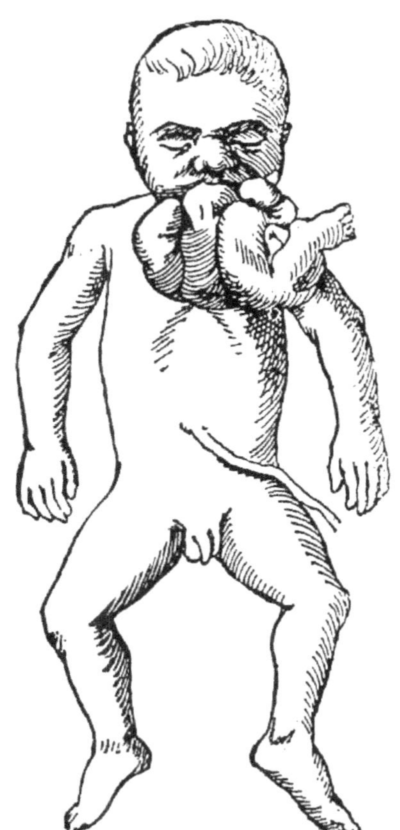

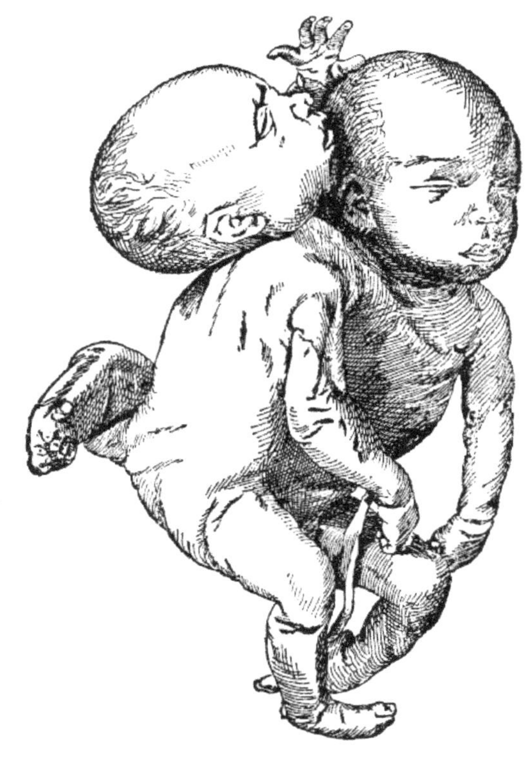

14: Ischiopagus twins.

15: Dipygus parasiticus (After Schenk von Gräfenberg).

16: Epignathus (After Lancereaux).

17: Thoracopagus tribachius tripus.

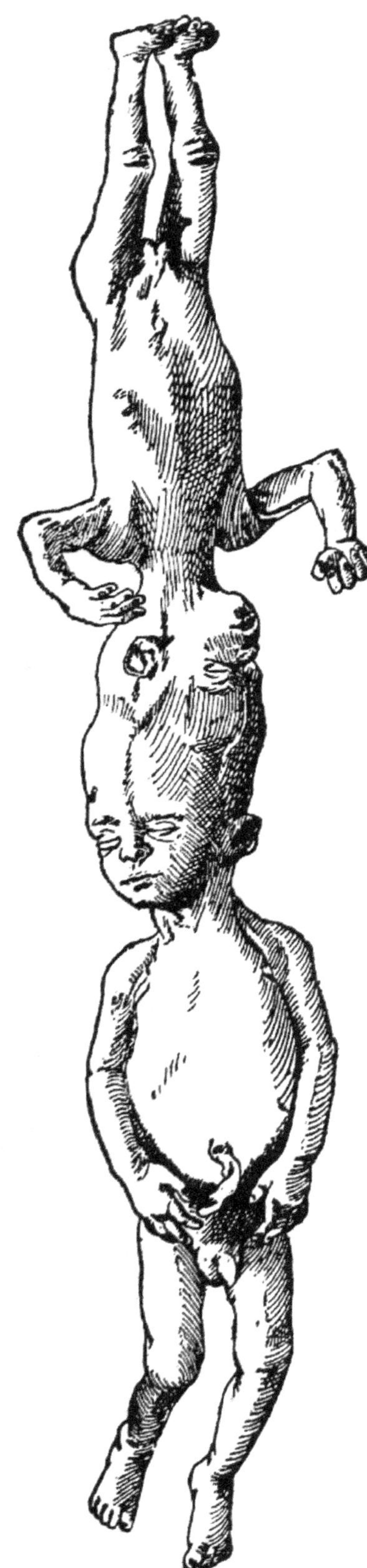

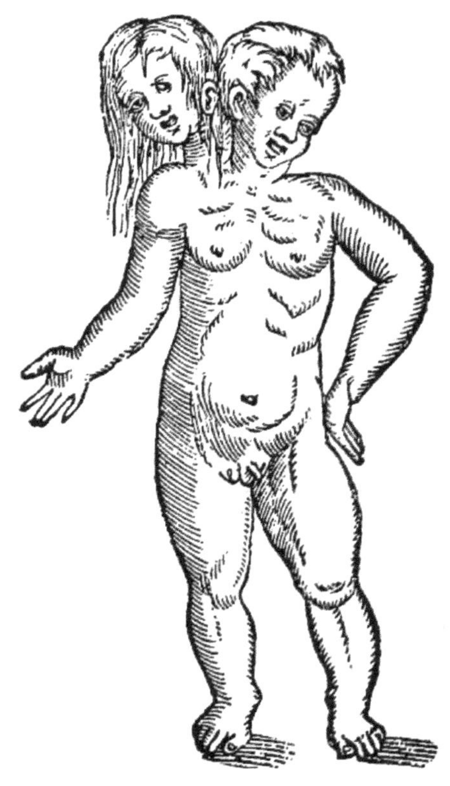

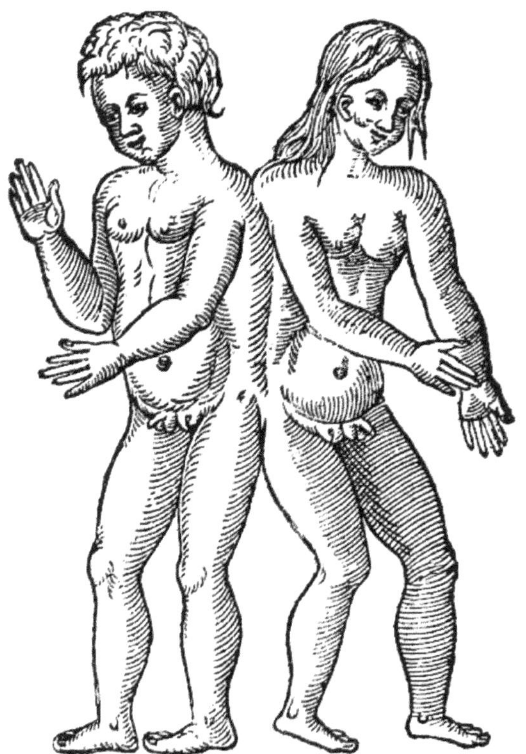

18: Cranipogagus parietalis.

19: Bicephalic and hermaphroditic monster (after Paré).

20: Double hermaphroditic monster (after Paré).

21

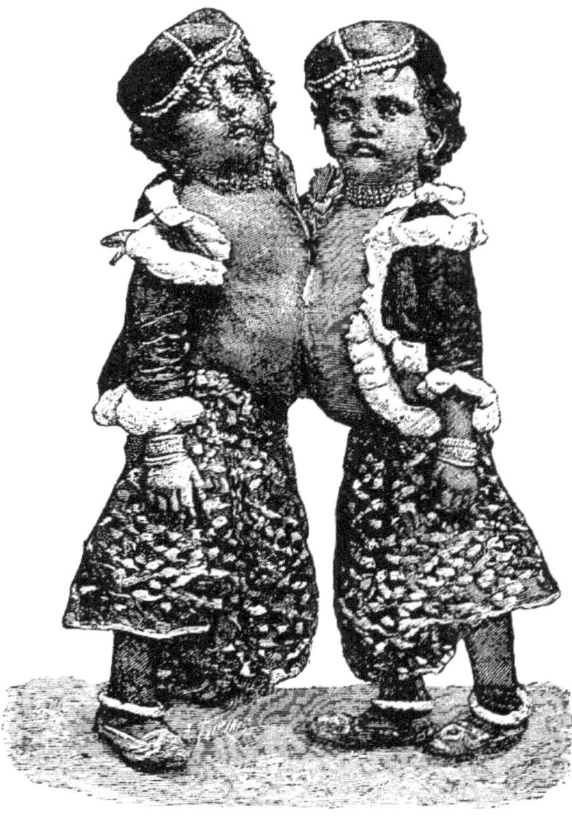

22

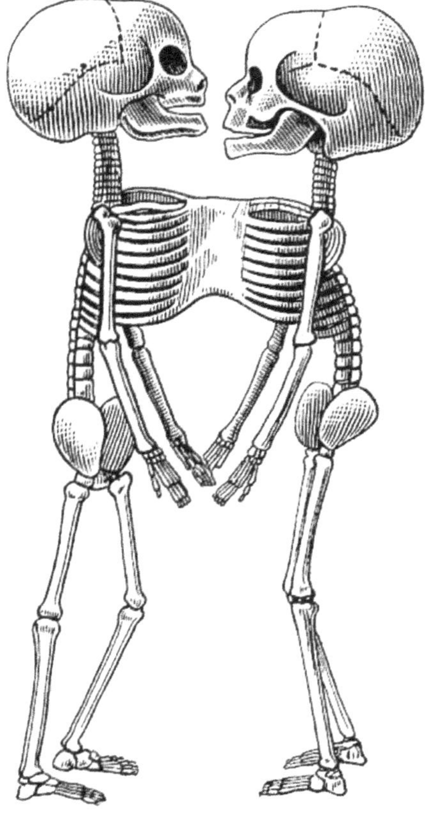

23

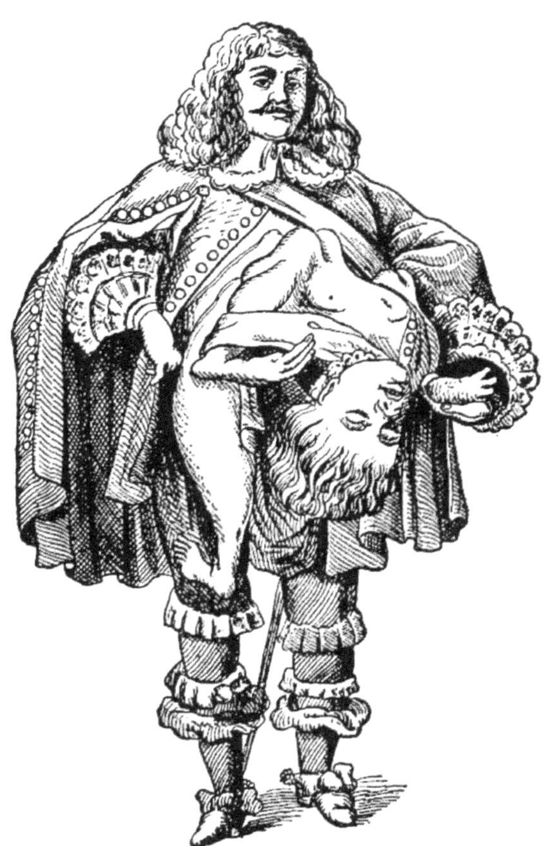

24

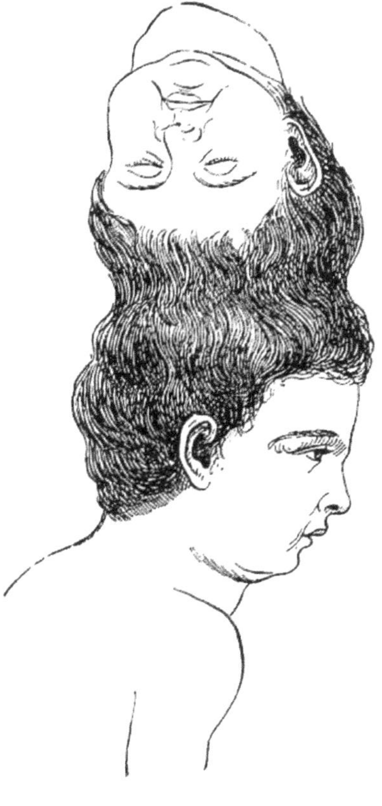

21: Radica–Doddica, the "Orissa Sisters".

22: Skeleton showing a mode of conjunction of independent double monsters.

23: Thoracopagus. Lazarus–Joannes Baptista Colleredo.

24: Two-headed boy (Home's case).

25

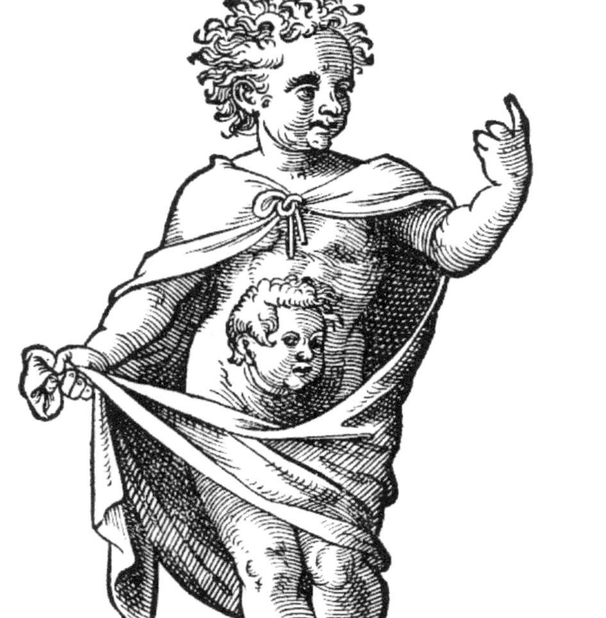

26

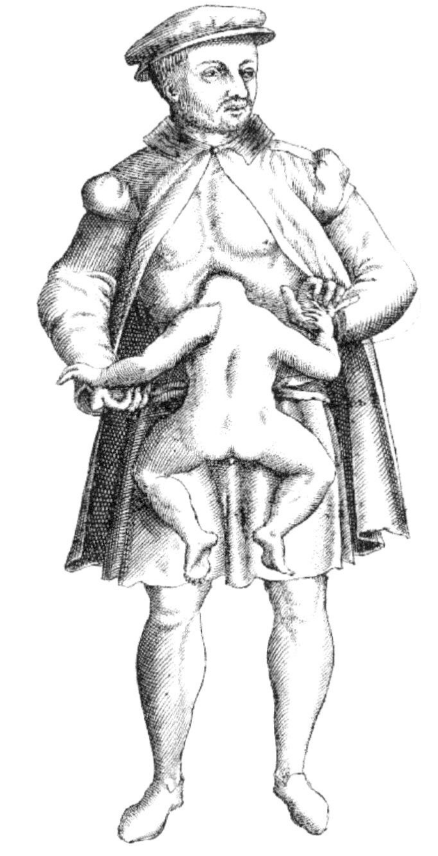

27

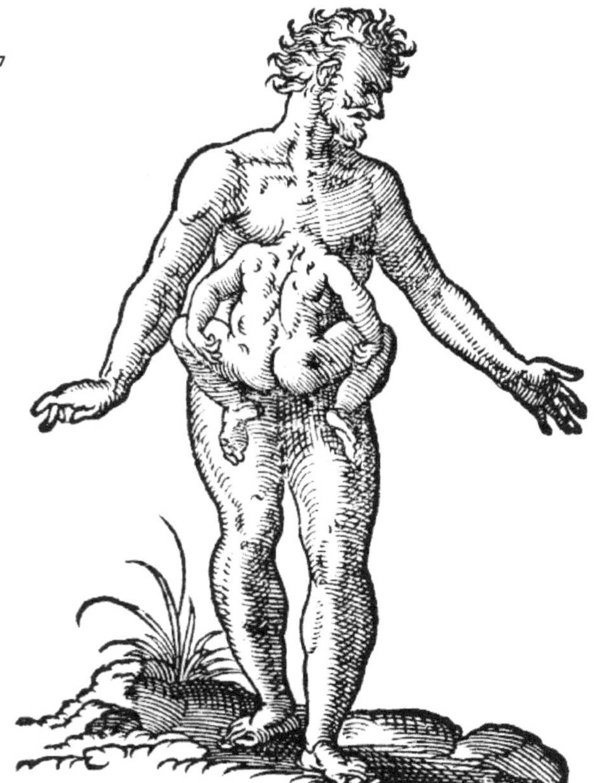

28

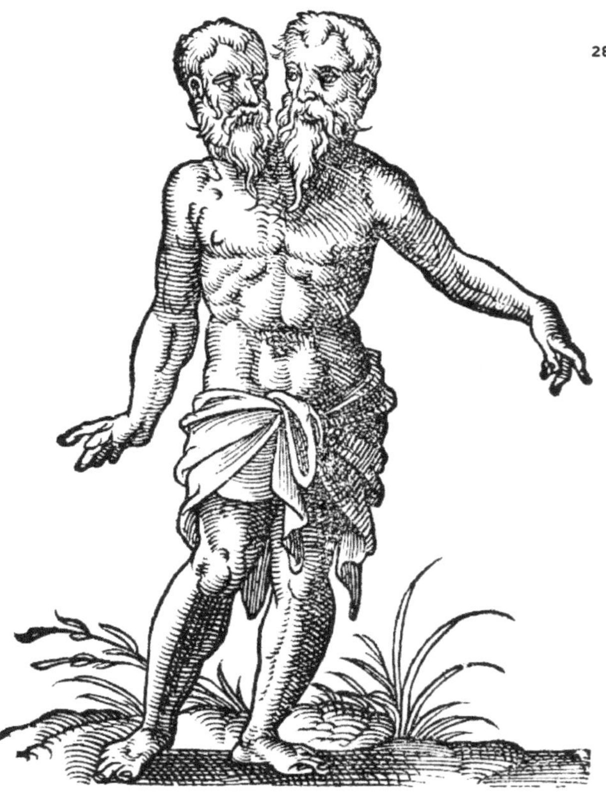

25: A man with a second head protruding from his abdomen.

26: A man with an additional body protruding from the abdomen.

27: A man with an additional body protruding from the chest.

28: A man with two heads.

29

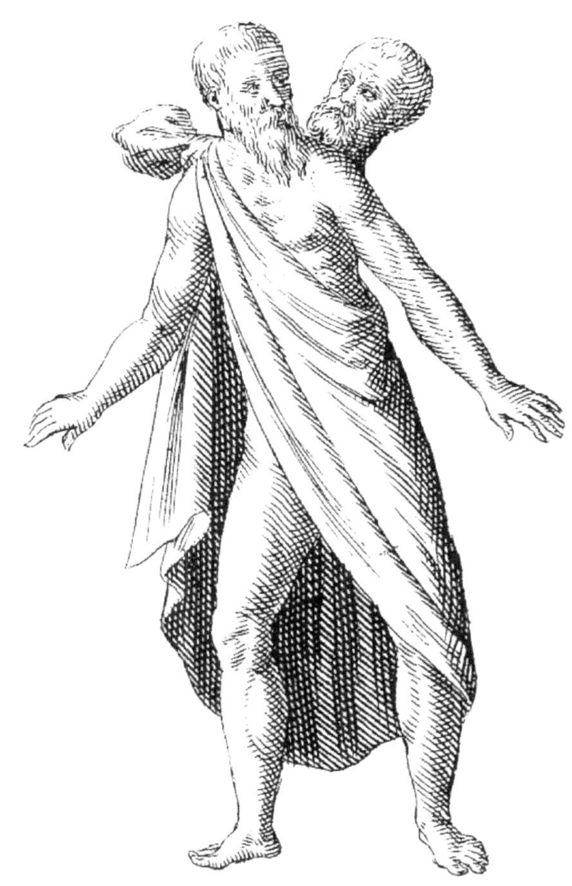

30

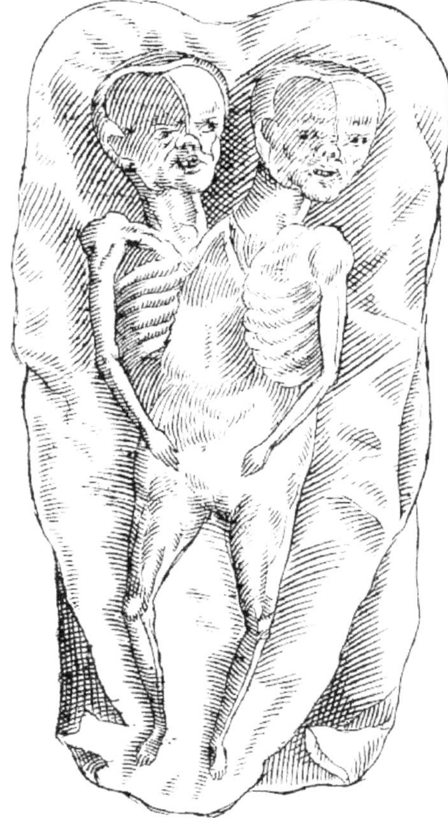

31

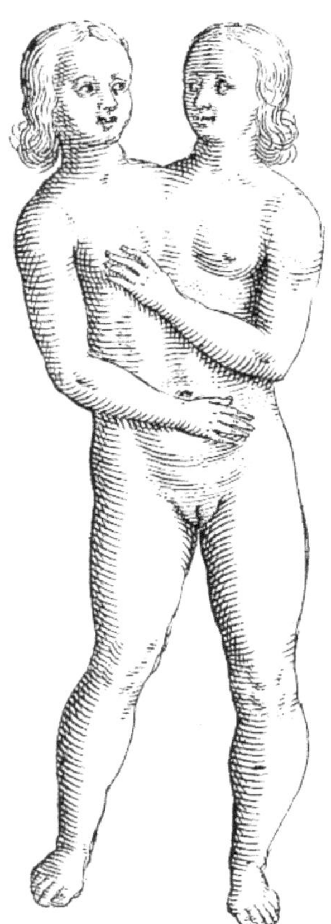

32

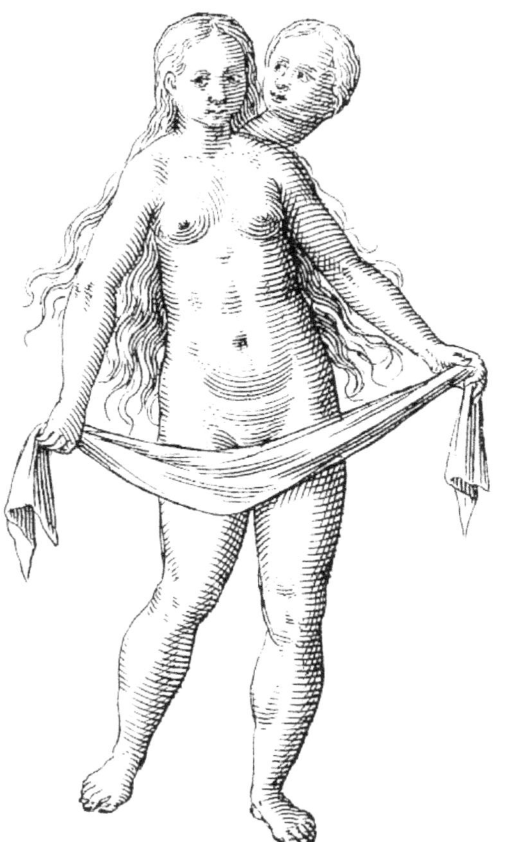

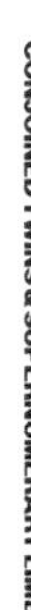

29: A man with two heads.

30: A skeletal cadaver of an infant born with two heads and both sexes.

31: A woman with two heads.

32: A woman with two necks and heads.

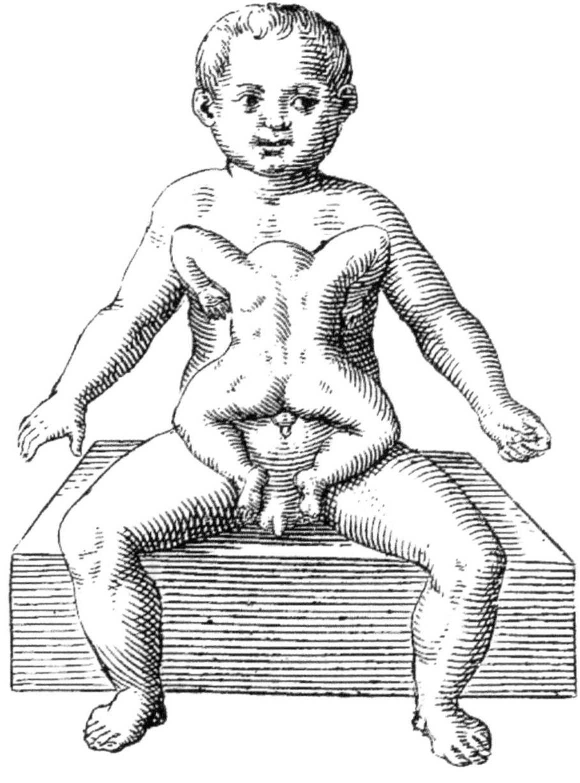

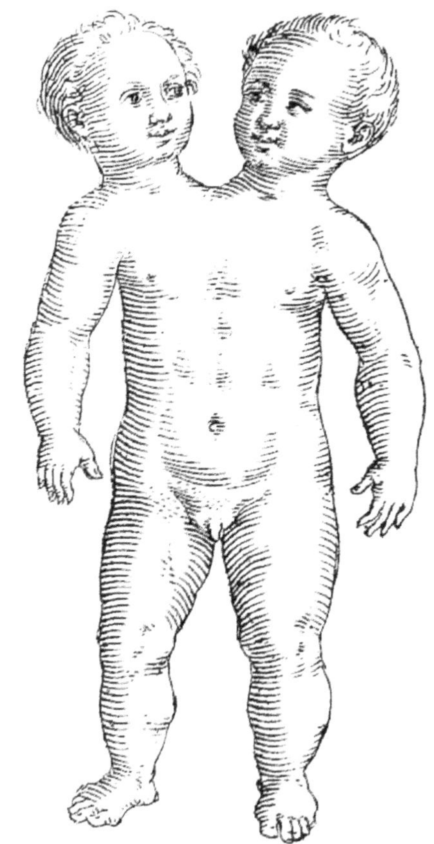

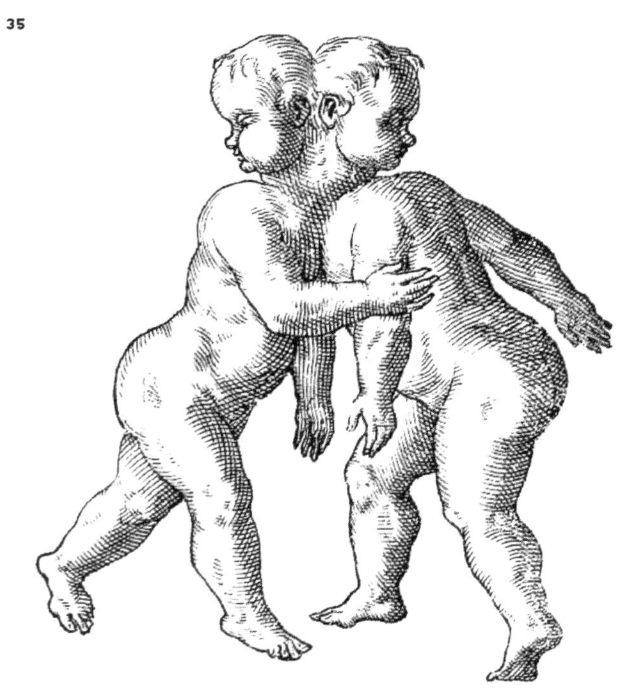

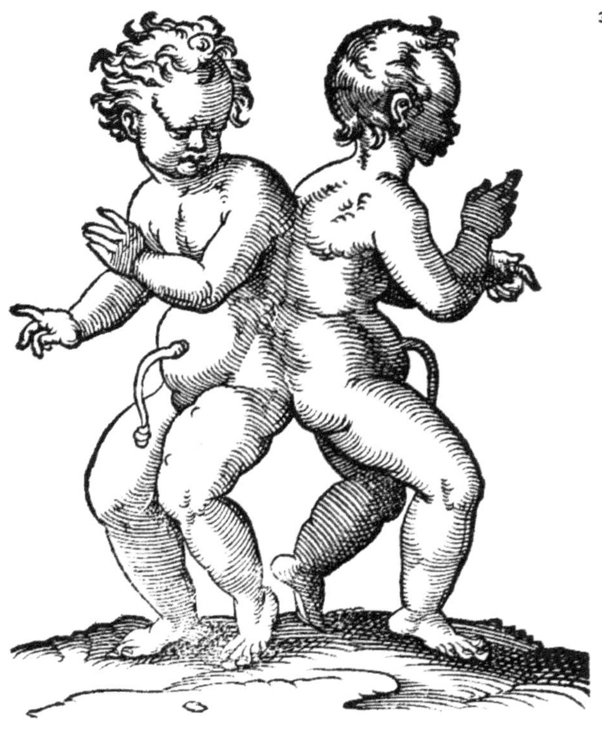

CONJOINED TWINS & SUPERNUMERARY LIMBS

33: An infant with an additional body protruding from the upper torso.

34: An infant with two heads.

35: Conjoined twins facing one another joined at the upper torso.

36: Conjoined twins joined at the back.

37

38

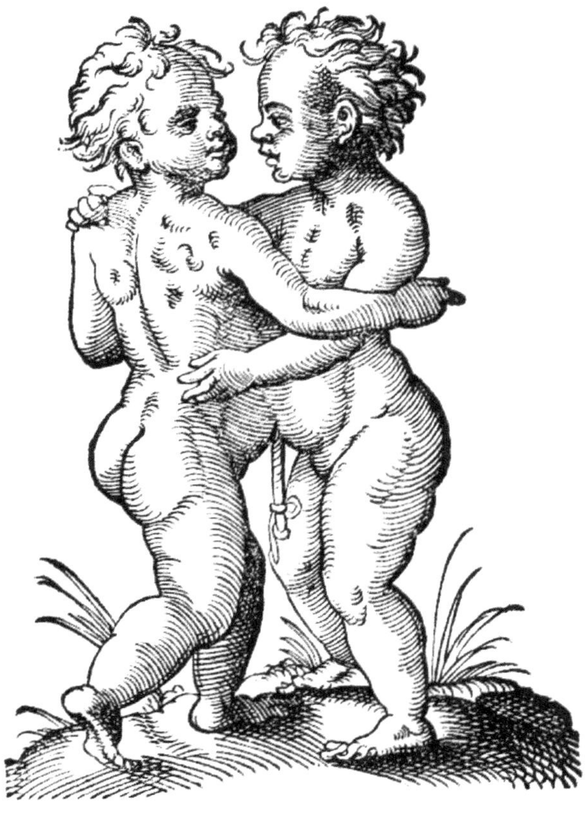

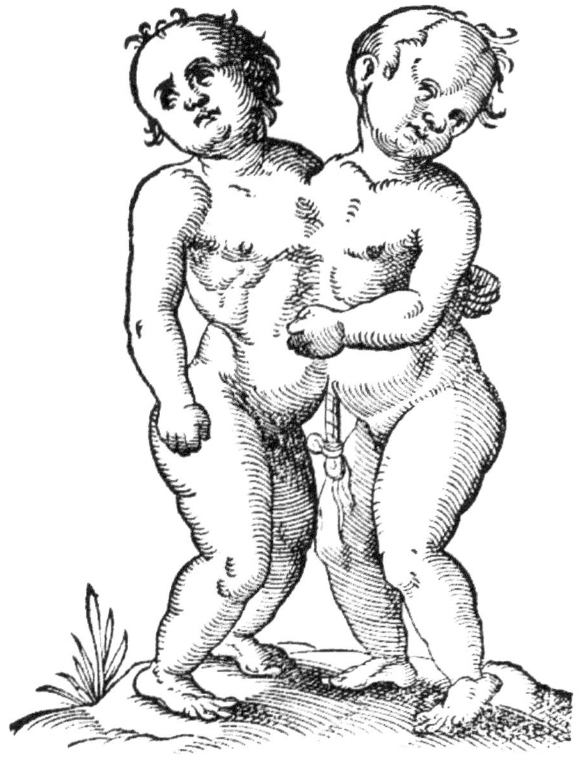

39

40

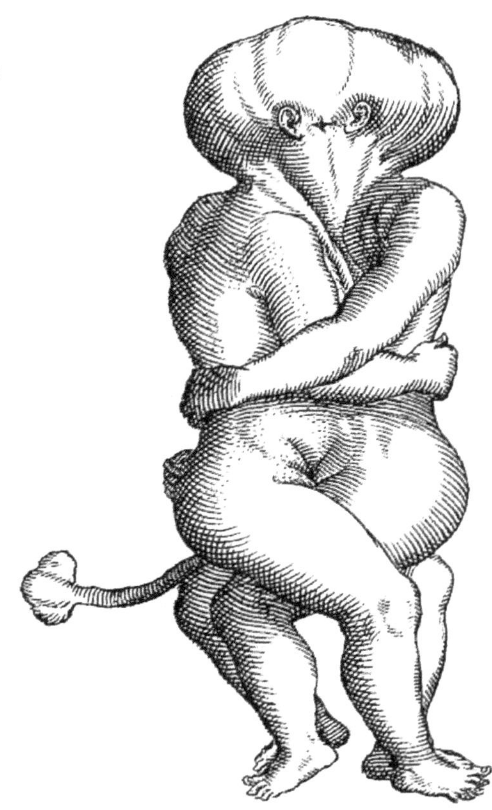

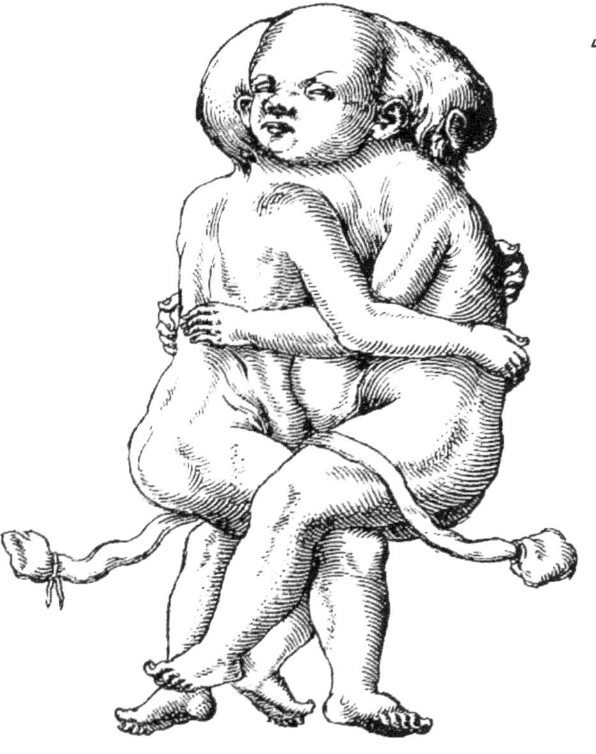

37: Conjoined twins joined at the abdomen.

38: Conjoined twins joined at the chest and abdomen.

39: Conjoined twins joined at the head and torso.

40: Conjoined twins joined at the head and upper torso.

41

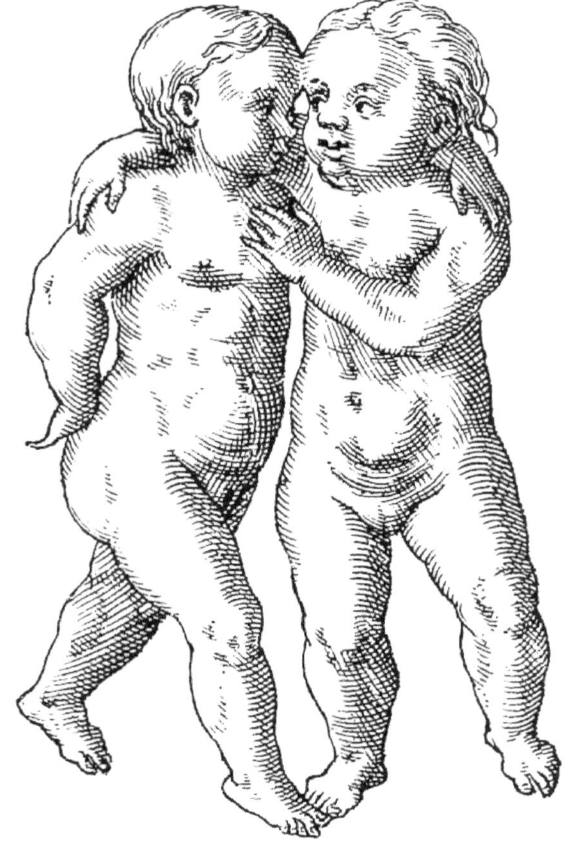

42

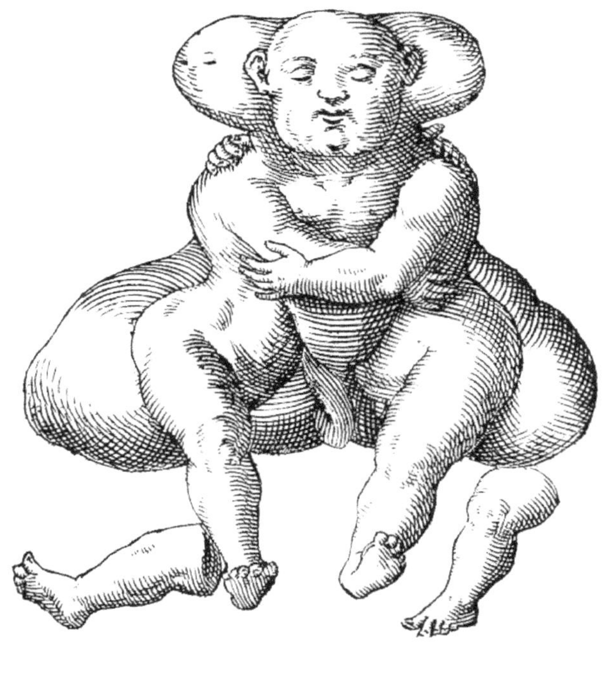

43

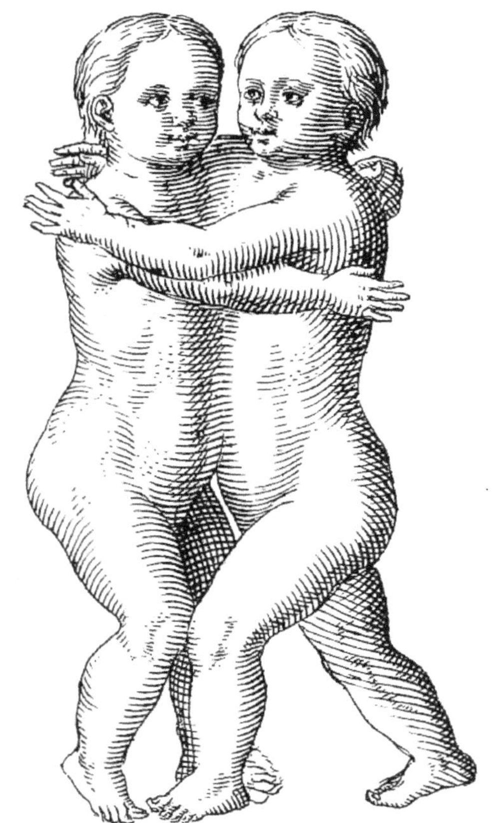

44

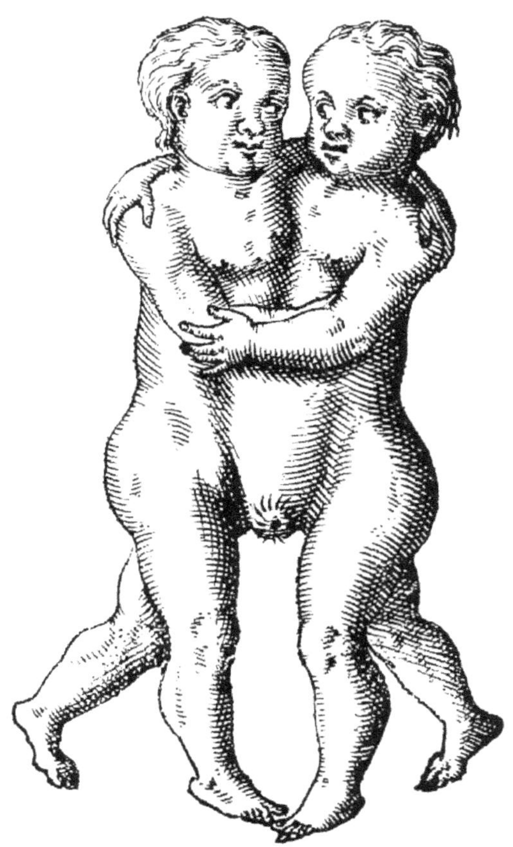

41: Conjoined twins fused at the shoulder in an embrace.

42: conjoined twins with severe deformity of the lower limbs.

43: Female conjoined twins fused along the torso.

44: Female conjoined twins fused at the abdomen.

45

46

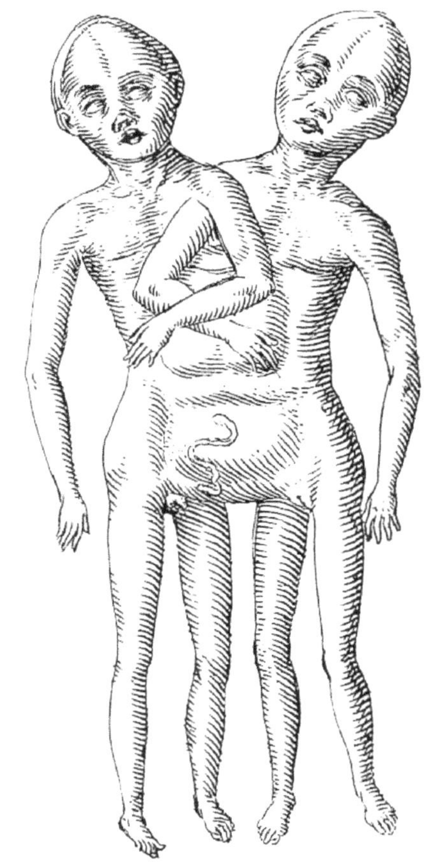

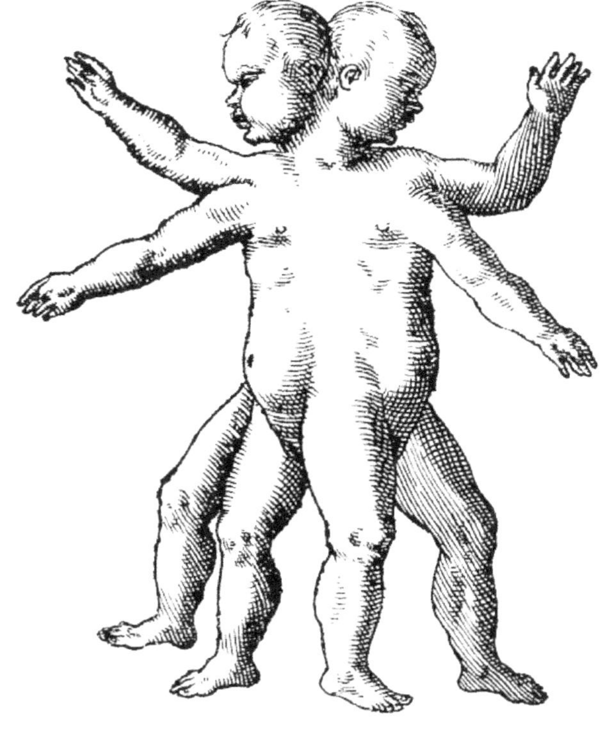

47

48

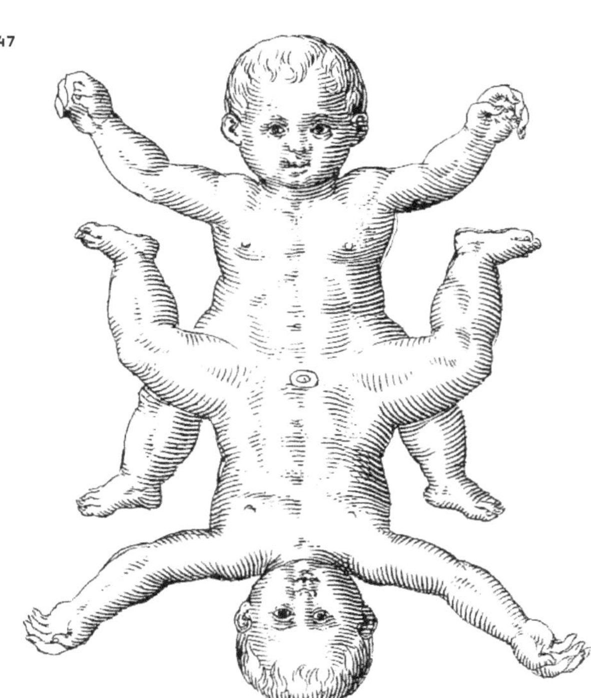

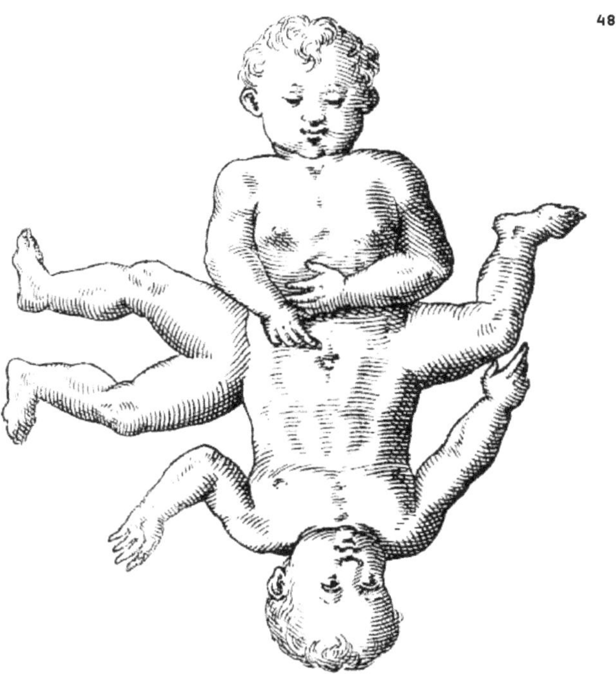

45: Female conjoined twins fused at the torson with malformed heads.

46: Male conjoined twins fused at the back and neck.

47: Male conjoined twins fused at the groin.

48: Male conjoined twins with legs protruding from the side of the abdomen.

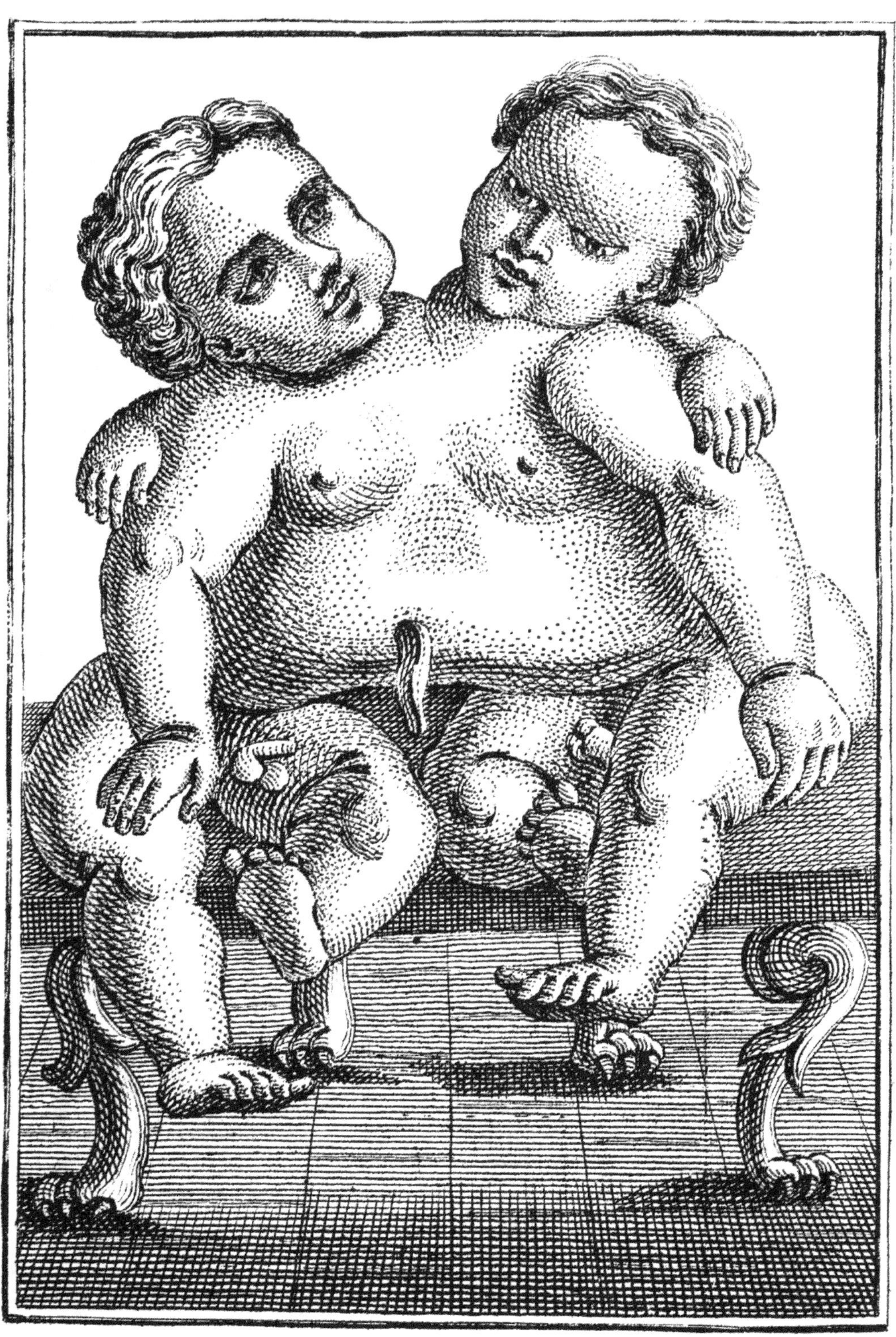

49: Conjoint twins born at Palermo in 1755.
Engraving by J. Aveline.

50

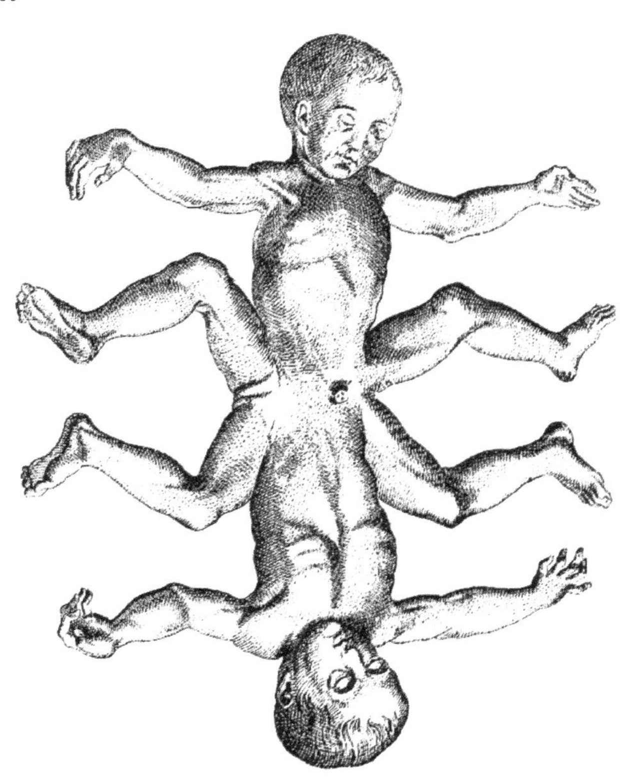

51

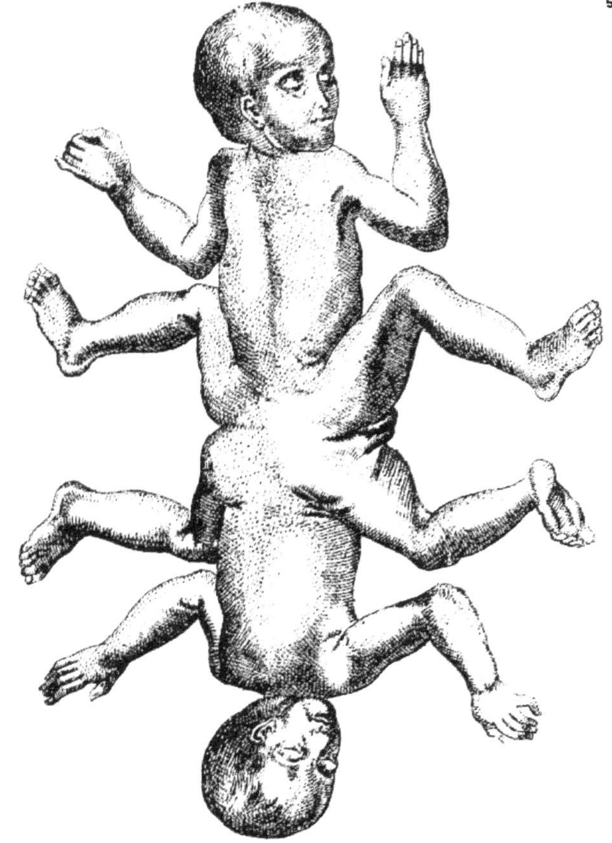

52

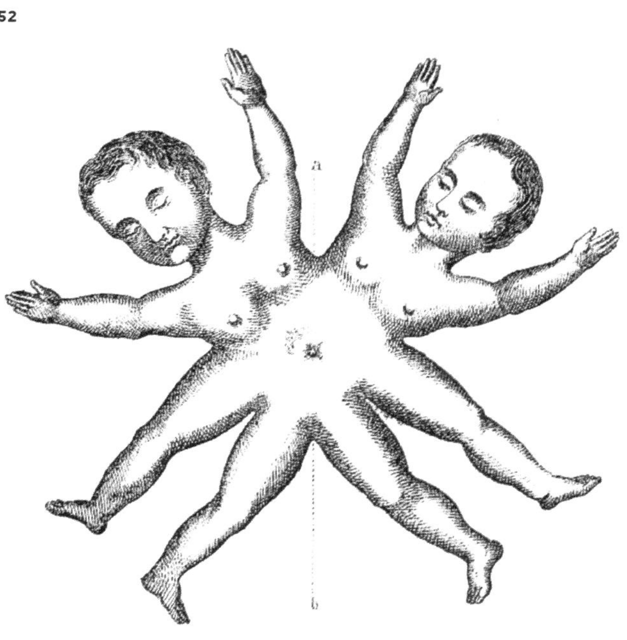

53

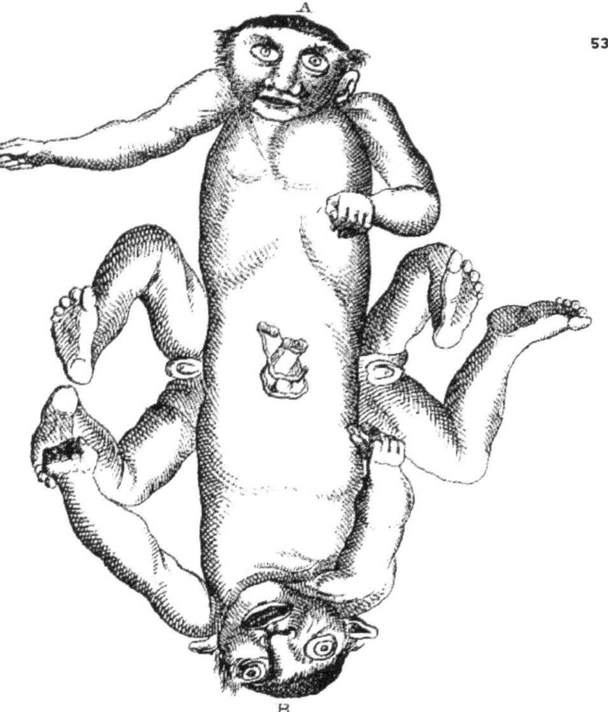

50: Ischiopagus tripus conjoined twins.　　　51: Ischiopagus tripus conjoined twins.　　　52: Ischiopagus twins.　　　53: Ischiopagus twins.

54

55

56

57

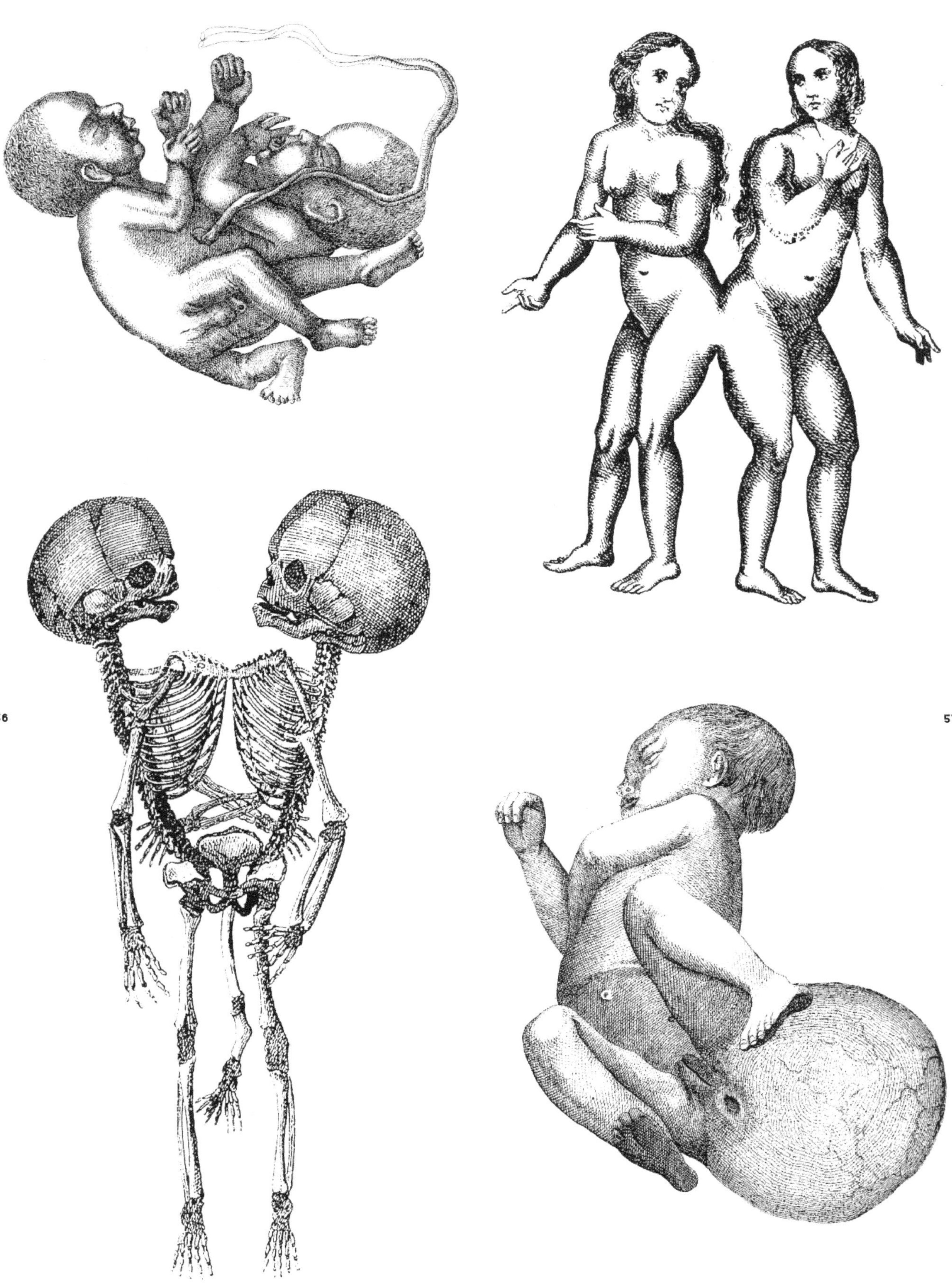

54: Conjoined twins joined at the pelvis.

55: Conjoined twins, joined at the upper lower limb.

56: Skeleton of conjoined twins, joined at the pelvis.

57: Subcutaneous Pygopagus, in which foetal rudiments are found in a tumor like mass.

58

59

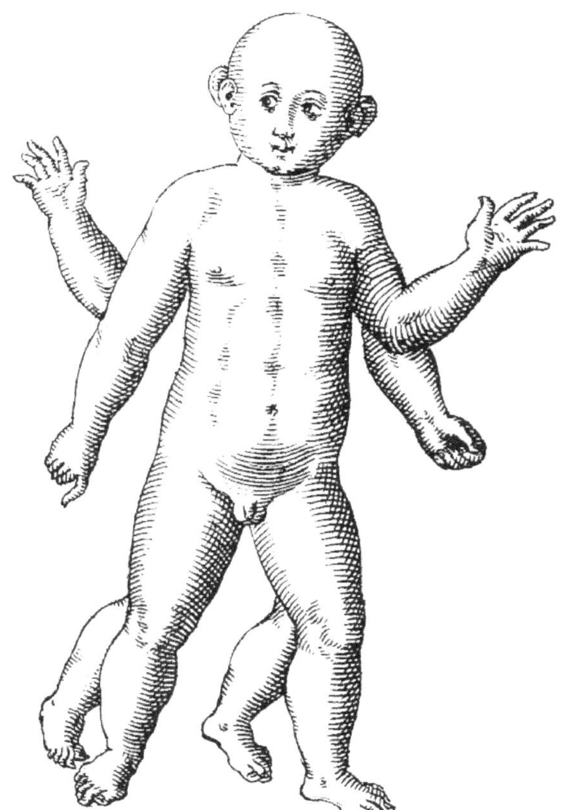

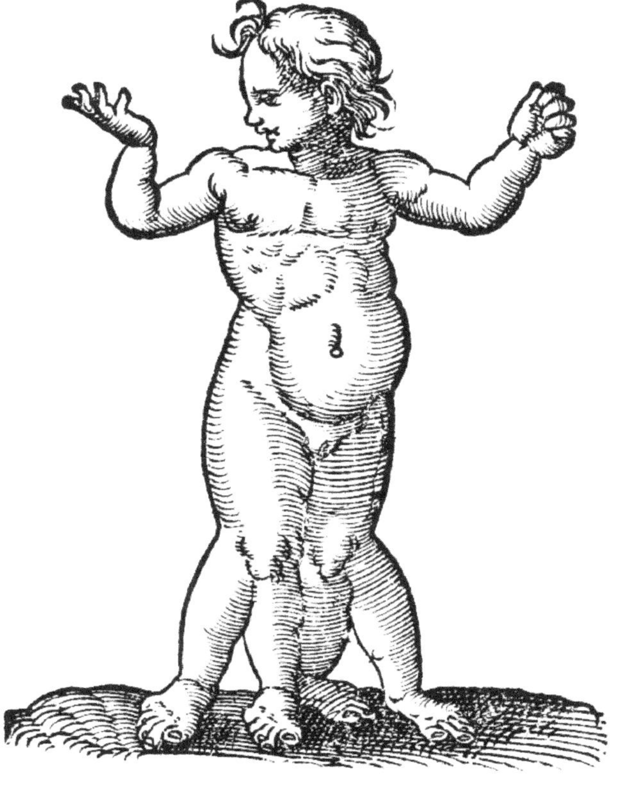

60

61

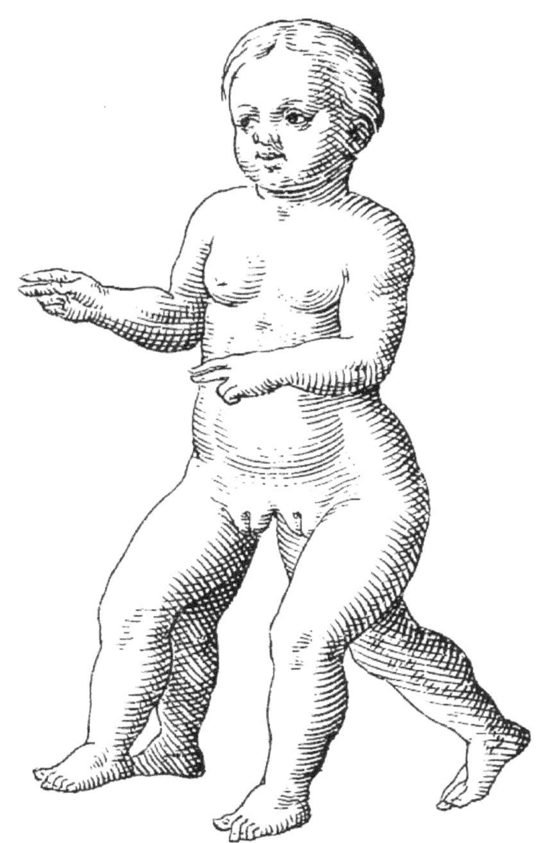

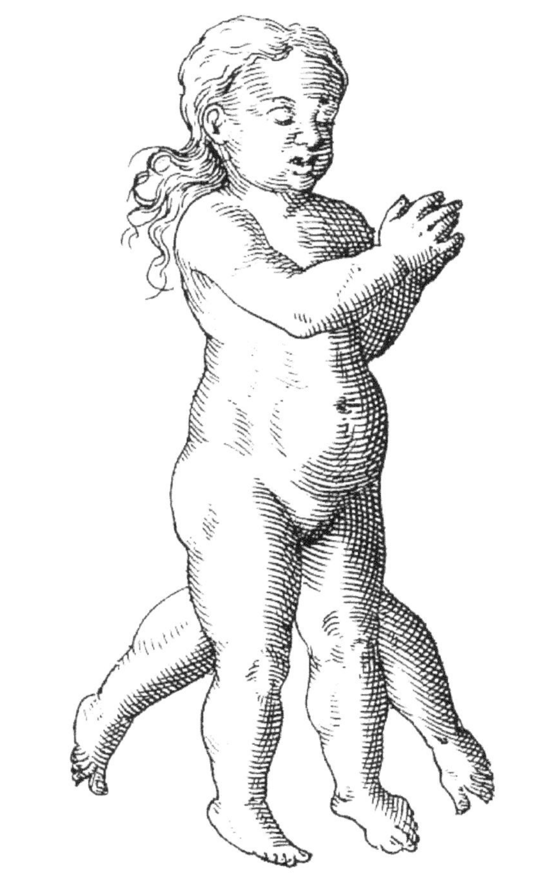

58: A child with supernumerary limbs.

59: A female infant with supernumerary limbs.

60: A female with supernumerary limbs.

61: A younf female with supernumerary lower limbs.

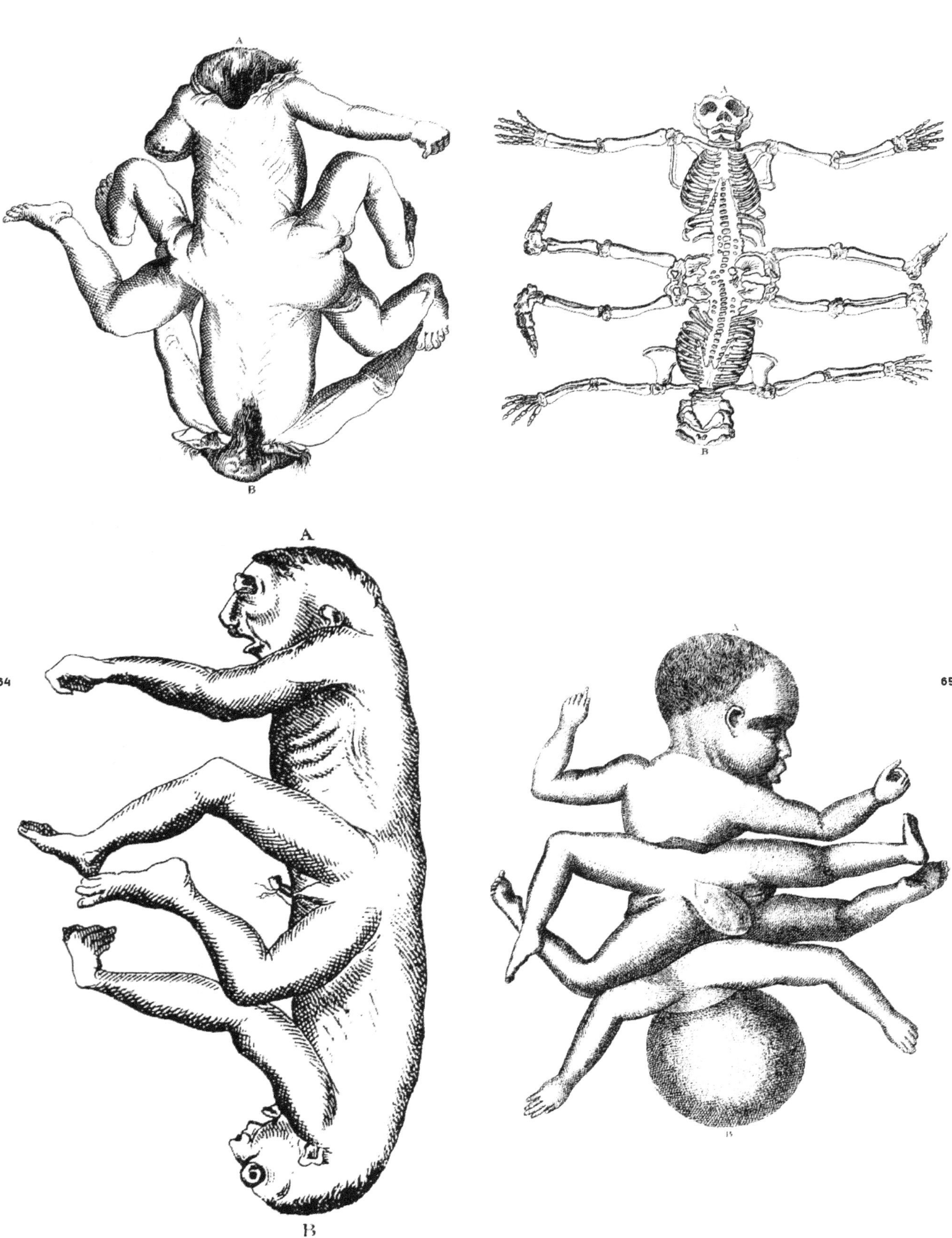

62: Ischiopagus twins, posterior view.   63: Skeleton of ischiopagus twins, anterior view.   64: Ischiopagus twins, profile view.   65: Ischiopagus twins.

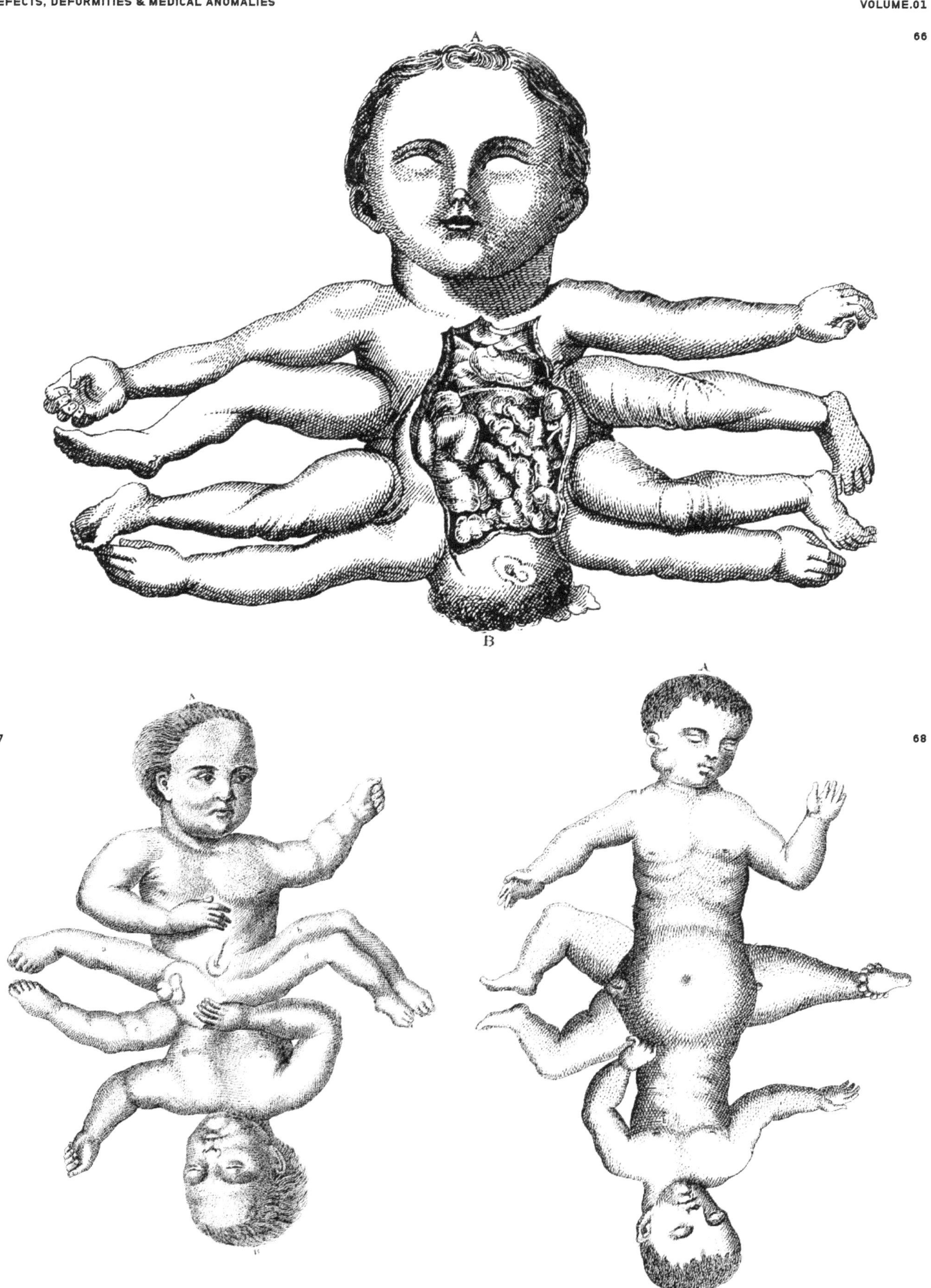

66: Ischiopagus twins with internal organs exposed.

67: Ischiopagus twins.

68: Ischiopagus twins joined at the lower pelvis.

69

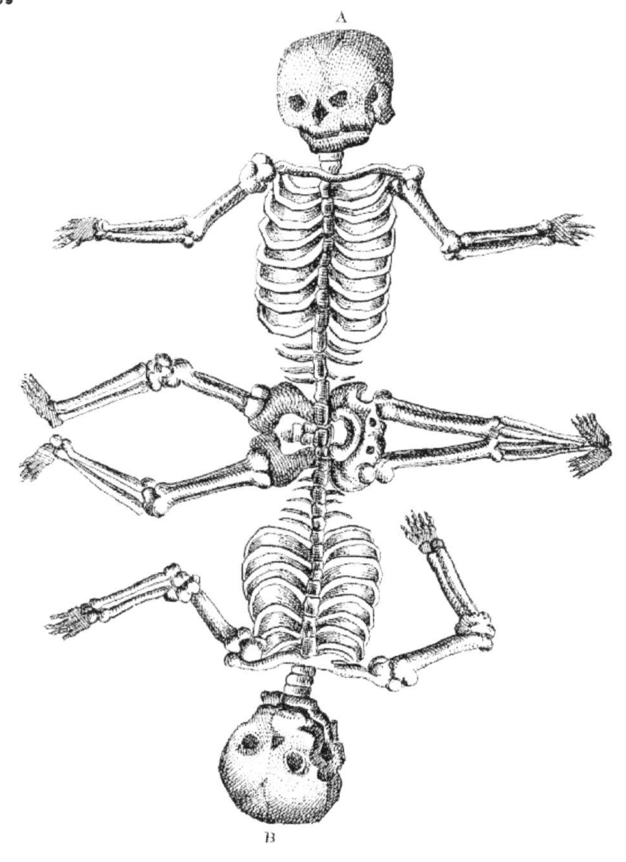

70

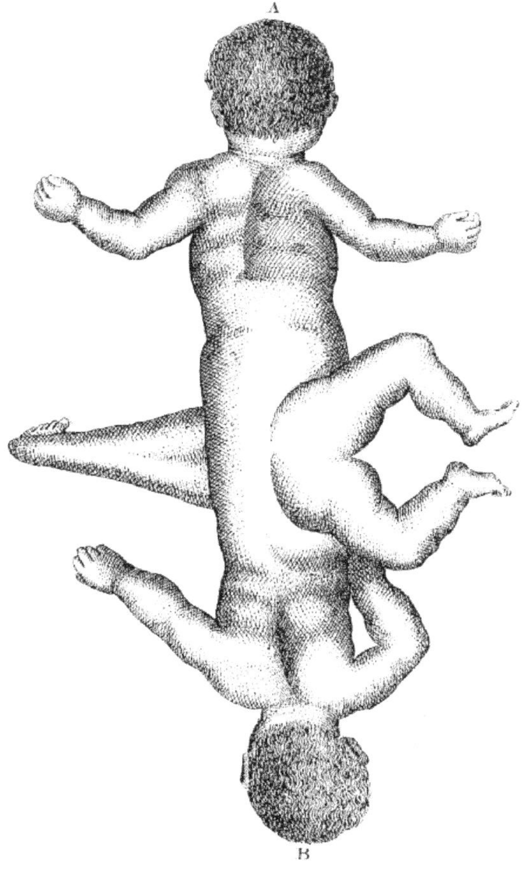

71

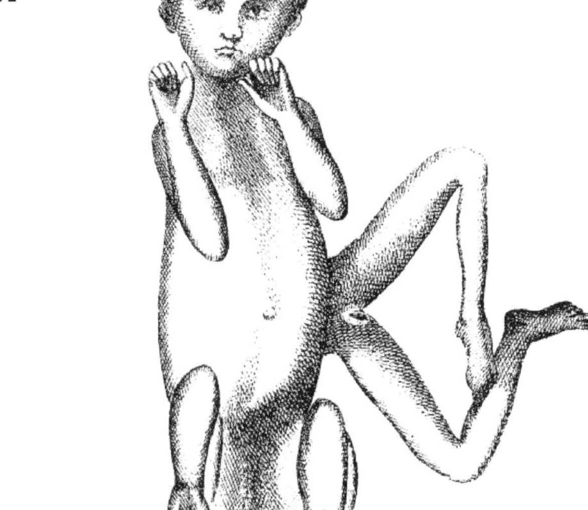

72

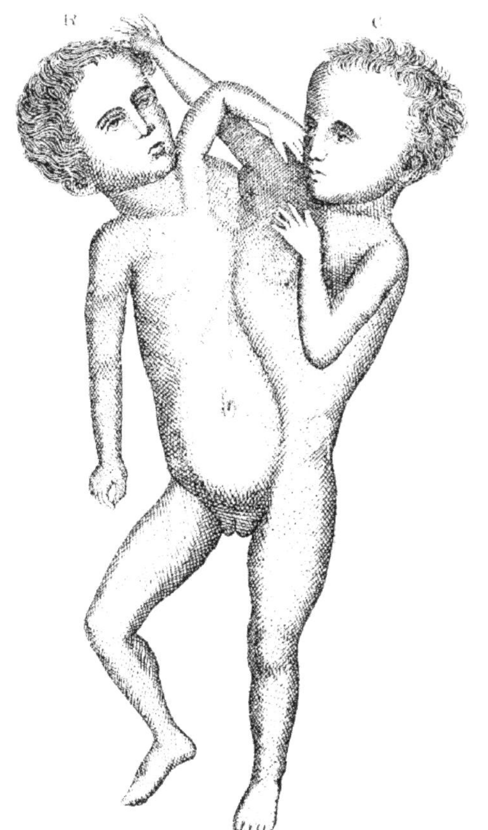

69: Skeleton of ischiopagus twins joined at the lower pelvis.

70: Ischiopagus twins joined at the lower pelvis, posterior view.

71: Ischiopagus twins.

72: Conjoined twins.

73

74

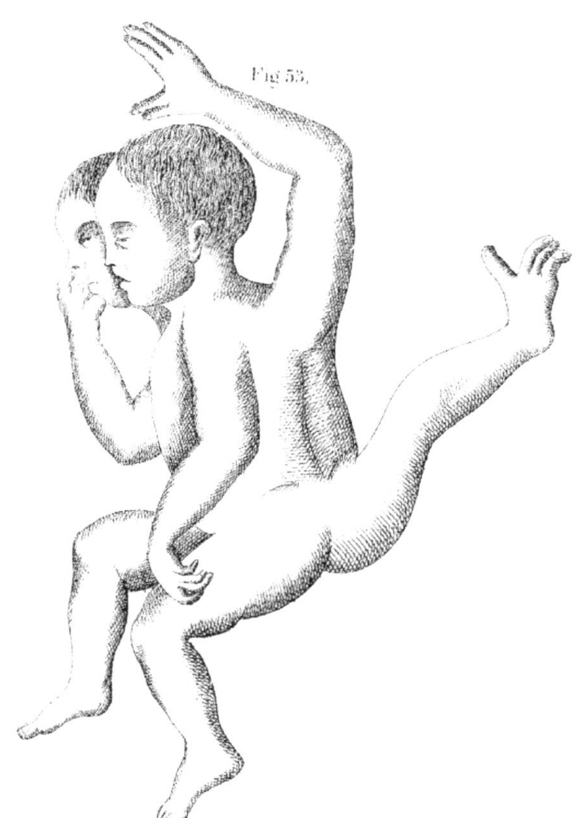

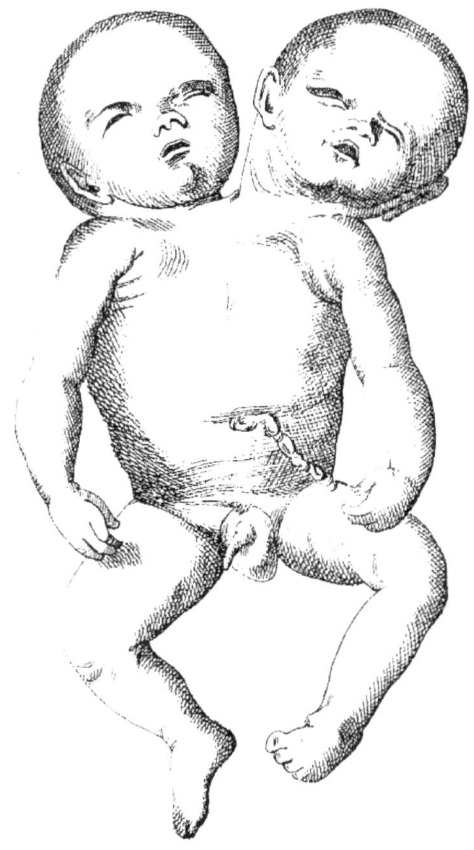

75

76

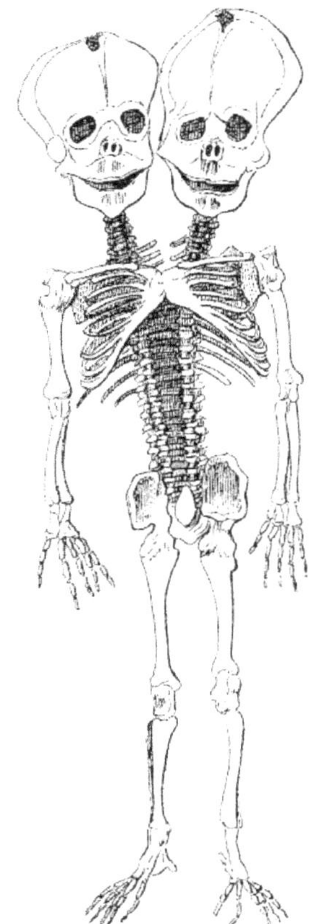

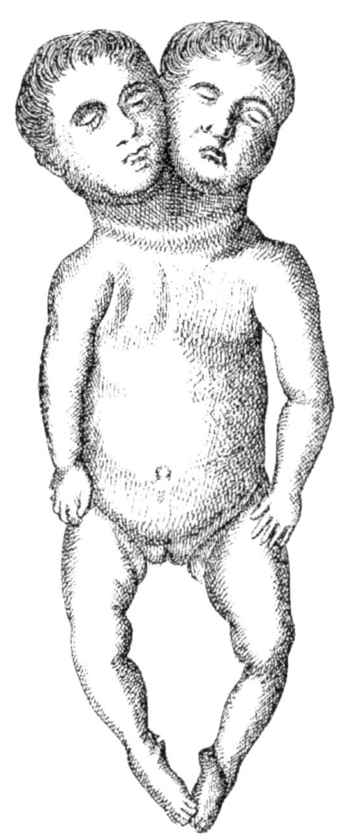

73: Conjoined twins with malformation of the hands and feet.

74: Dicephalic parapagus twins.

75: Skeleton of dicephalic parapagus twins.

76: Dicephalic parapagus twins.

77

78

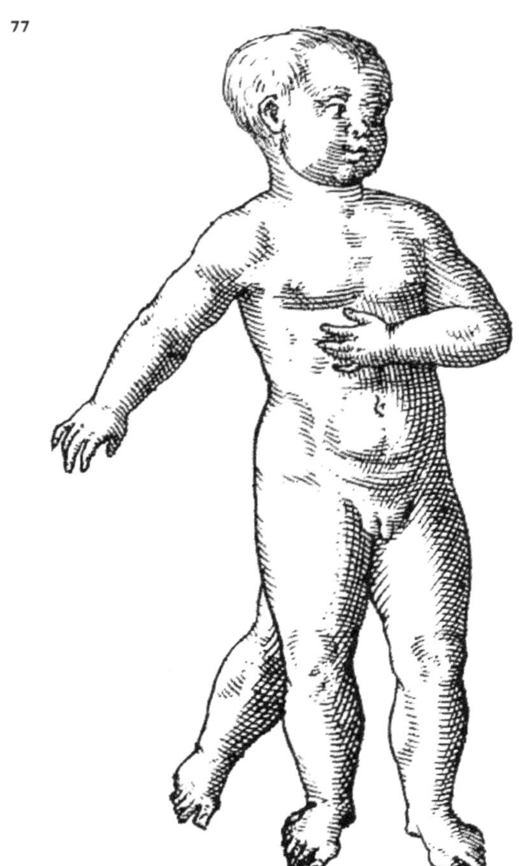

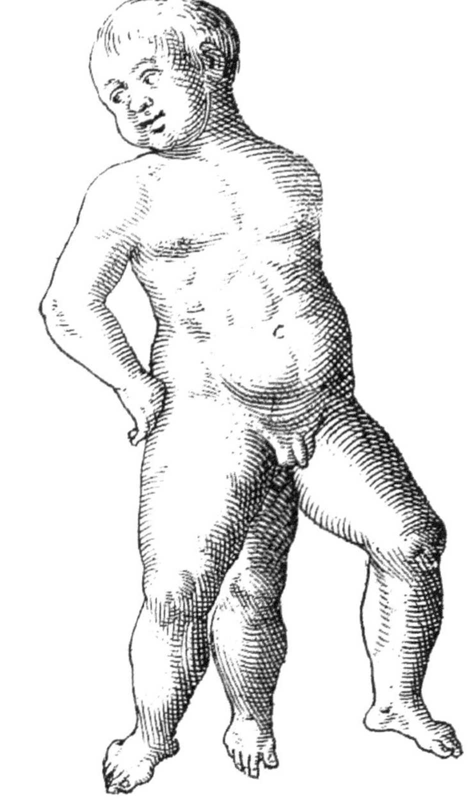

79

80

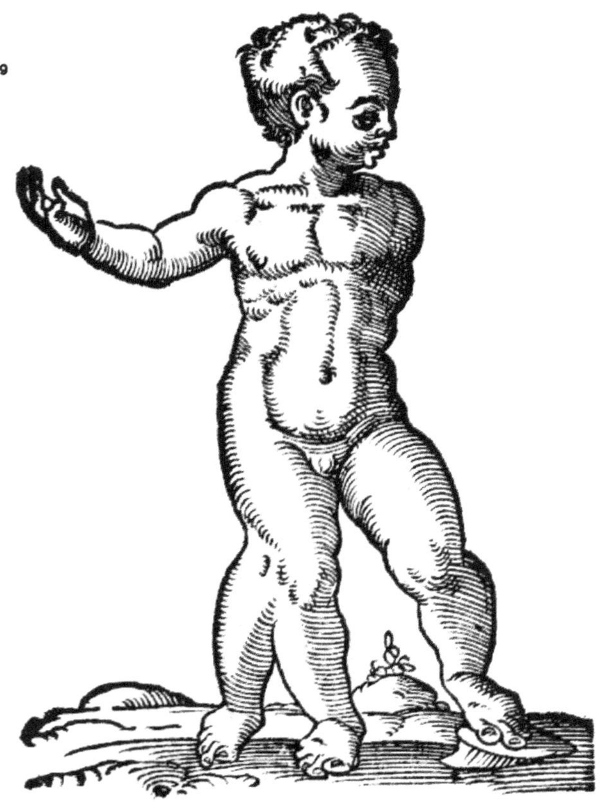

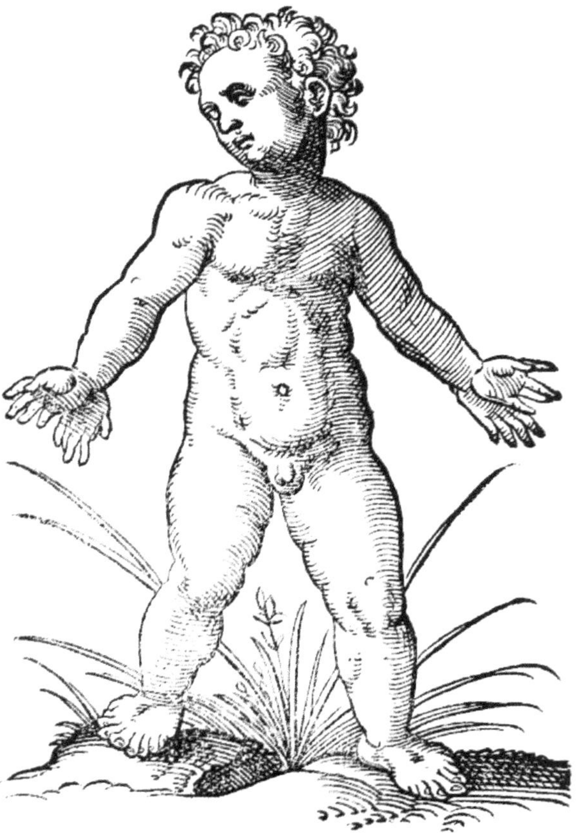

77: A young male with supernumerary lower limbs.

78: A young male with supernumerary lower limbs.

79: An infant with one arm and supernumerary lower limbs.

80: An infant with supernumerary hands.

81

82

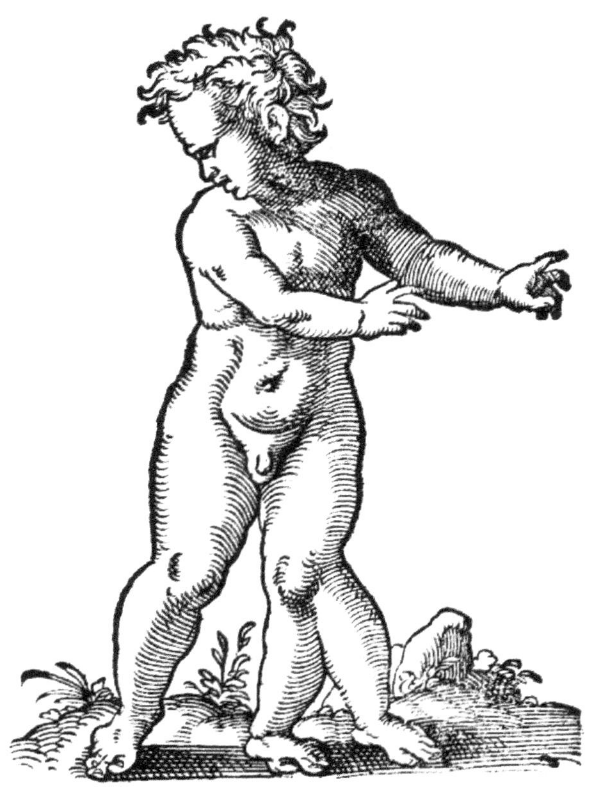

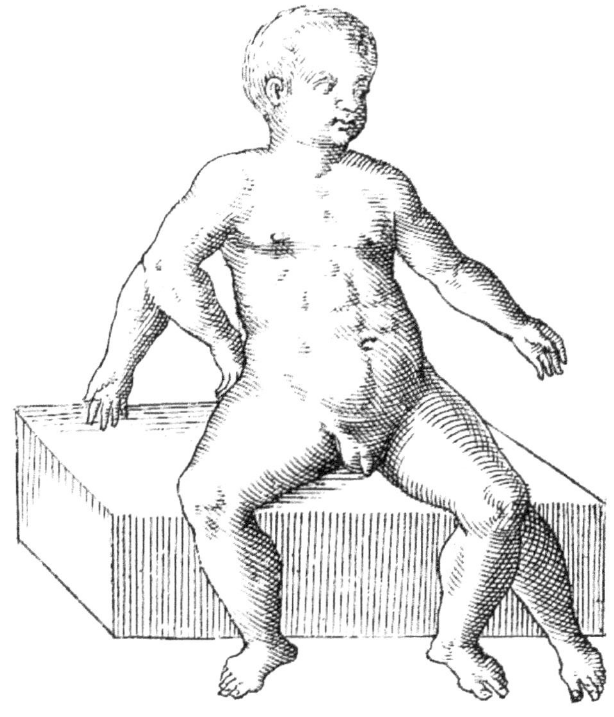

83

84

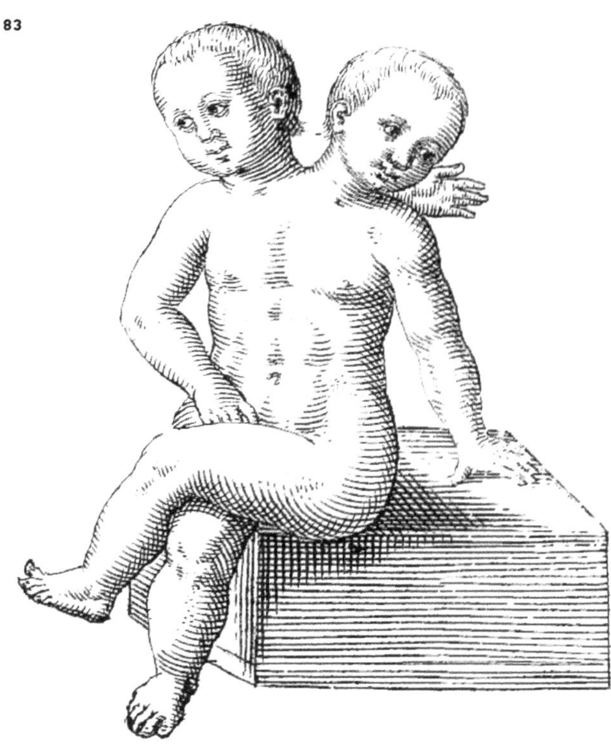

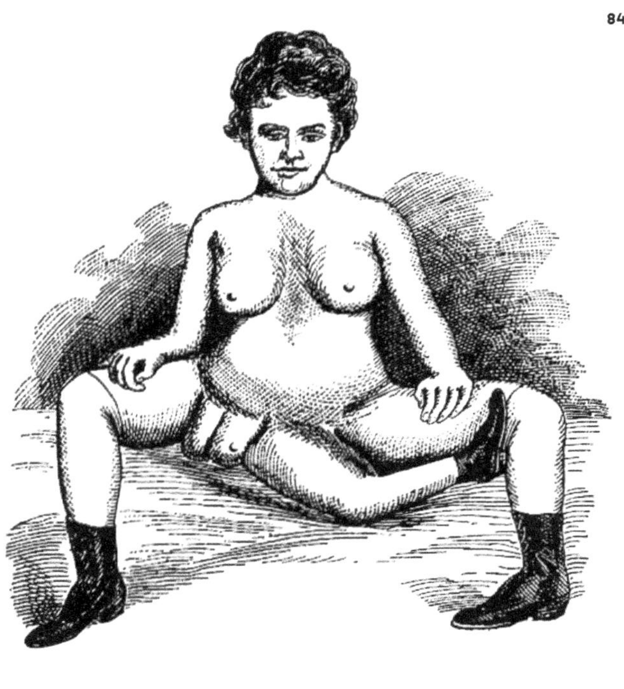

81: An infant with supernumerary left lower limb.   82: An infant with supernumerary limbs.   83: Infant with supernumerary arms and two heads.   84: Dipygus.

85

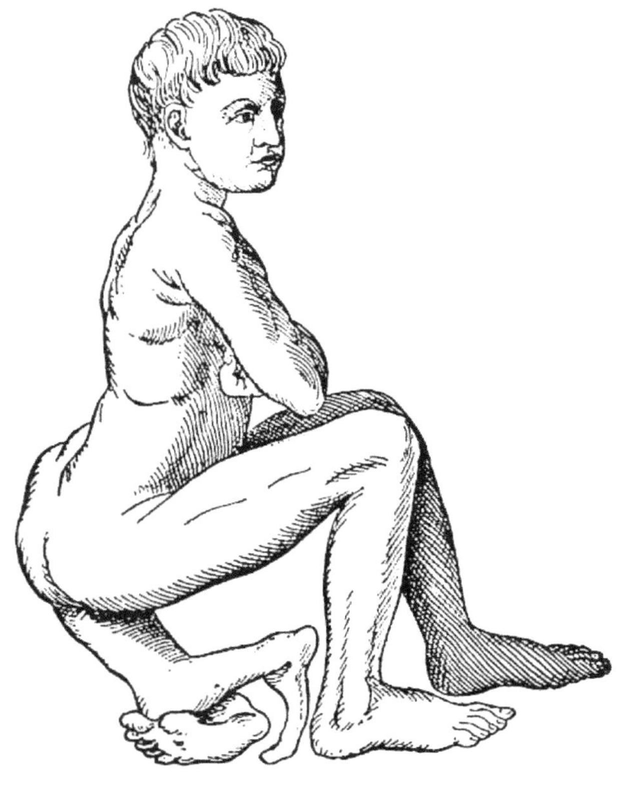

86

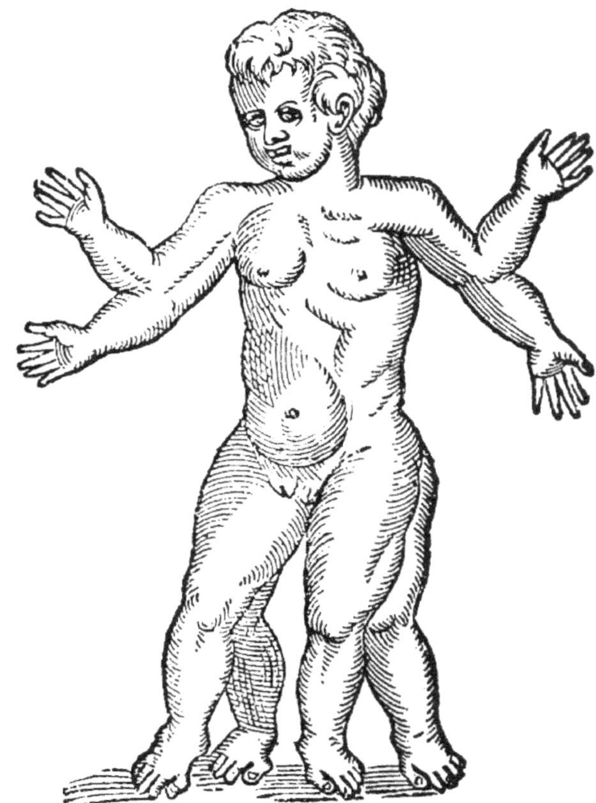

87

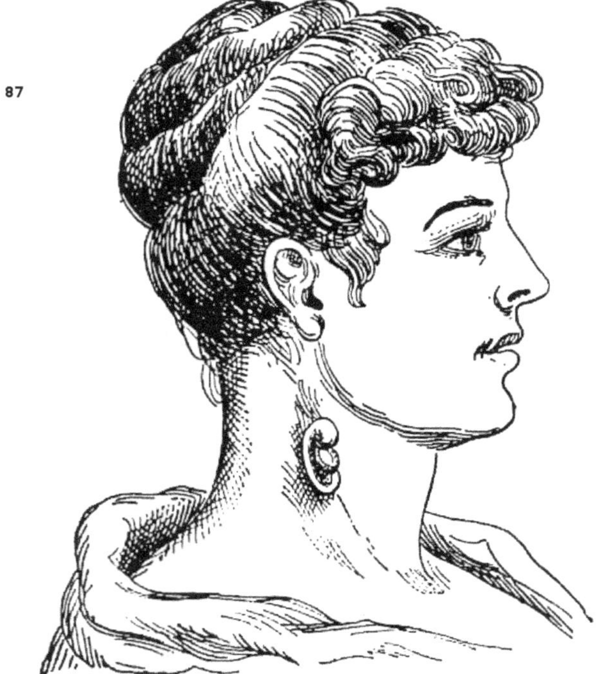

88

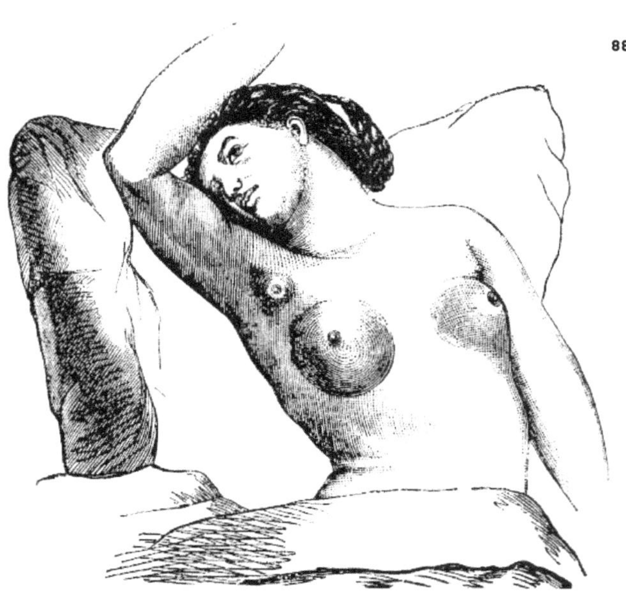

85: Supernumerary legs.   86: Supernumerary limbs.   87: Supernumerary auricle in the neck.   88: Woman with two axillary mammary.

89

90

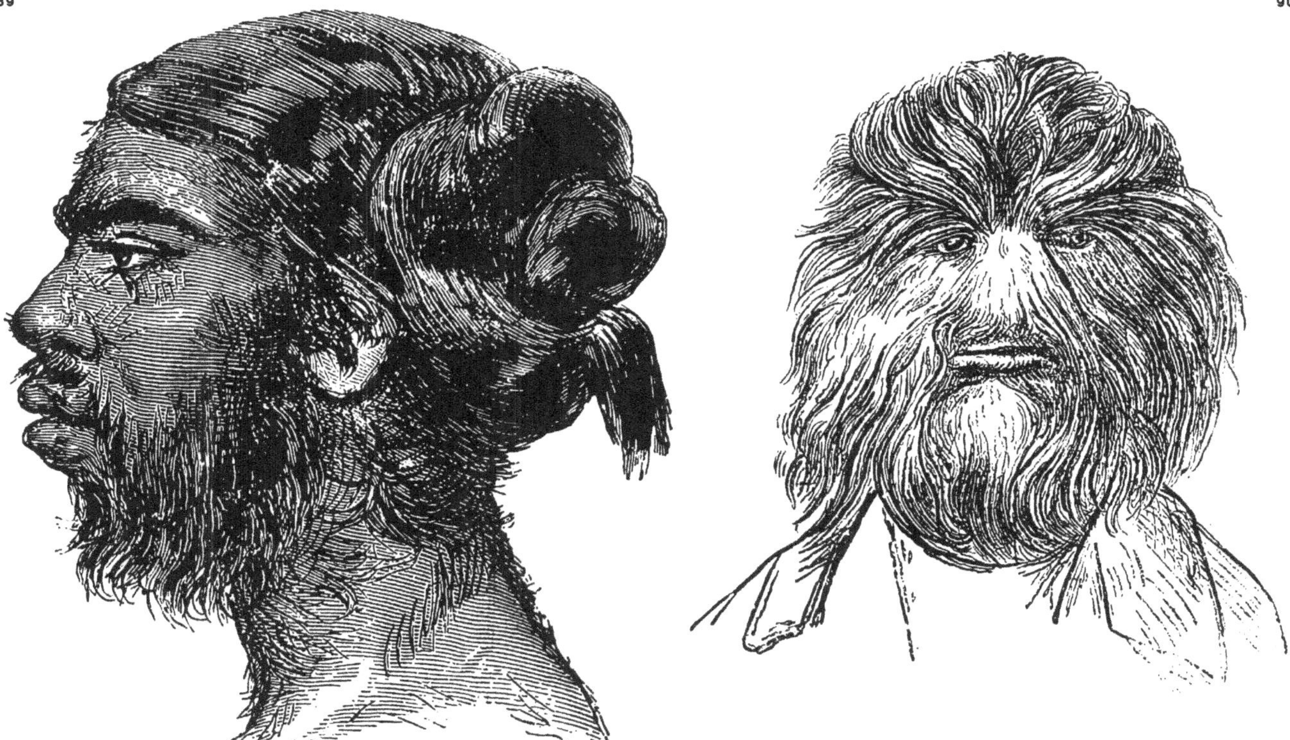

91

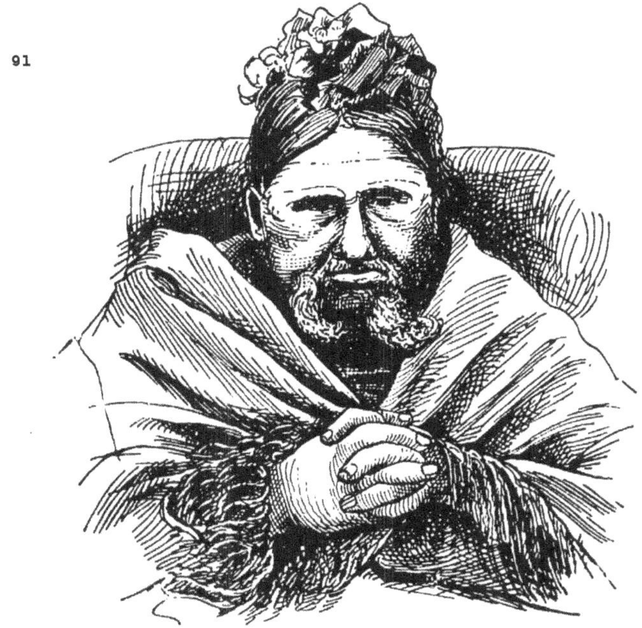

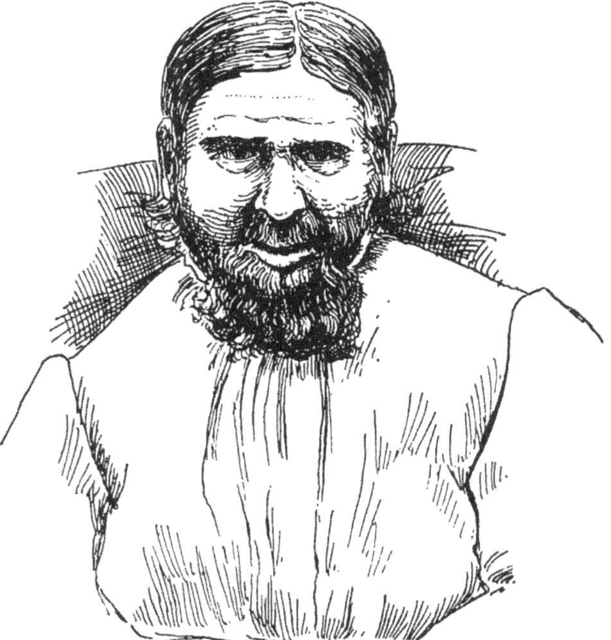

89: Bearded woman.   90: Face of an excessively hairy woman.   91: Bearded insane women (Harris).

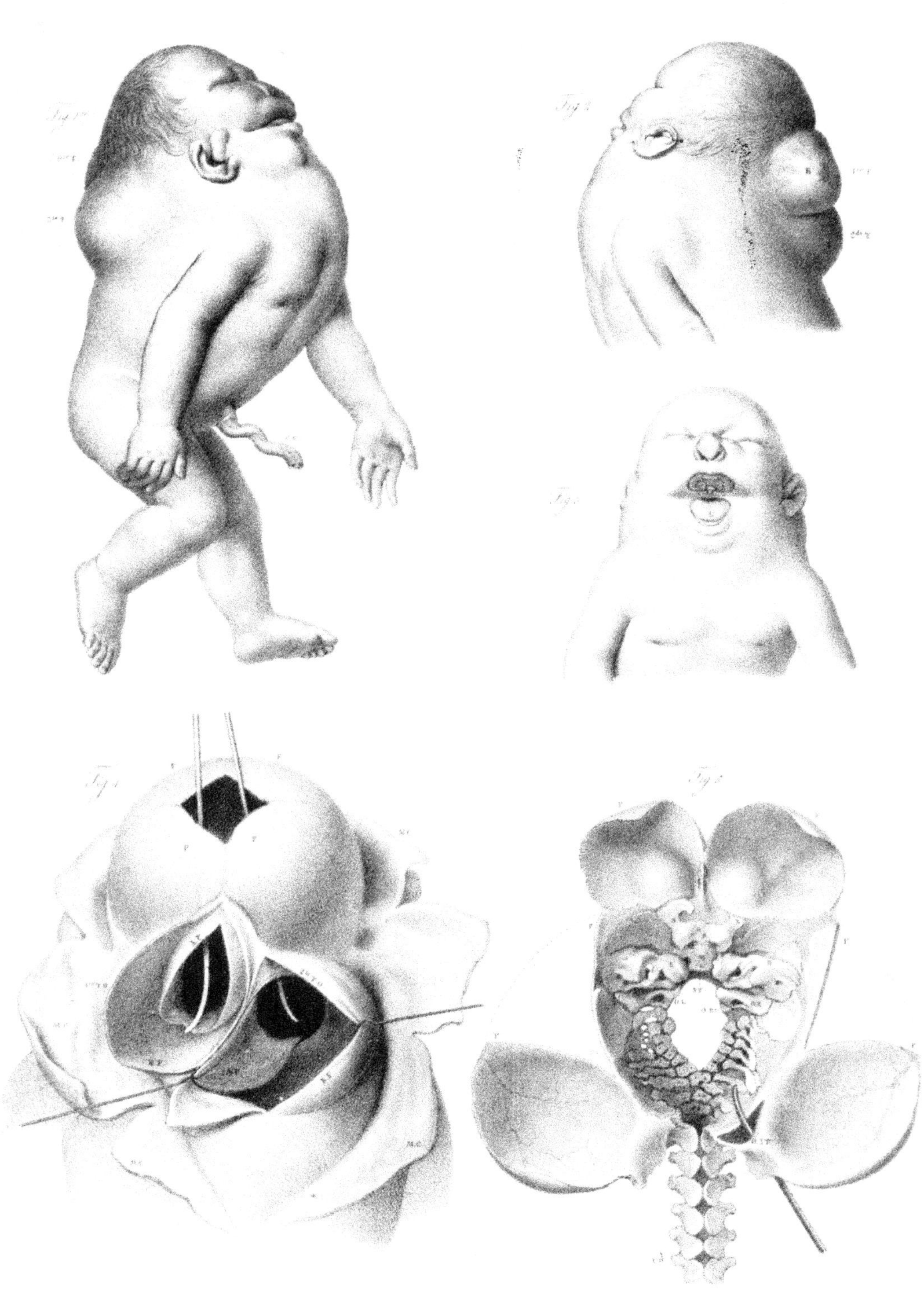

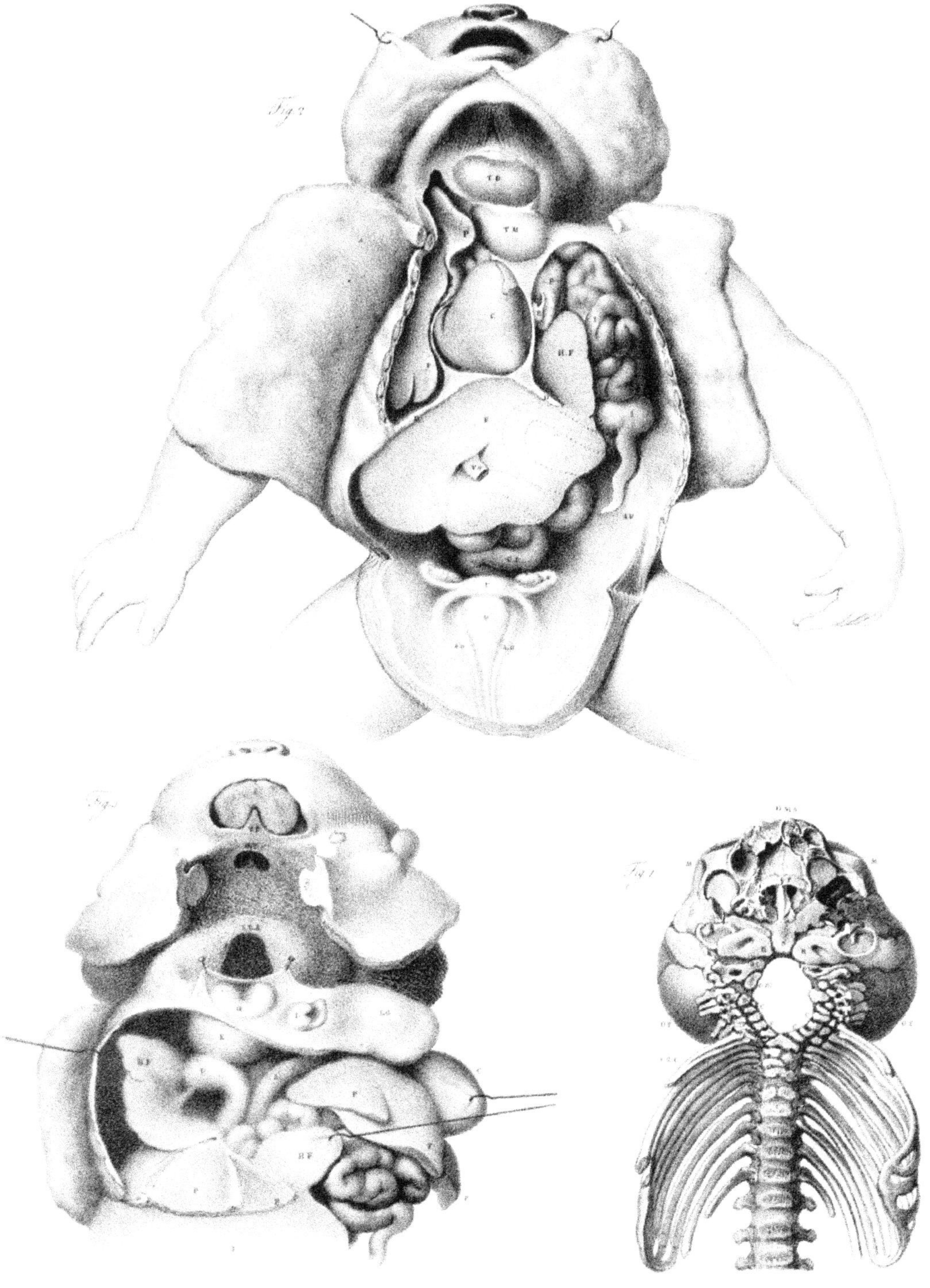

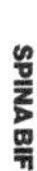

93: Spina bifida, diaphragmatic hernia.

94

94: Skeleton, abnormal; craniofacial abnormality, spina bifida.

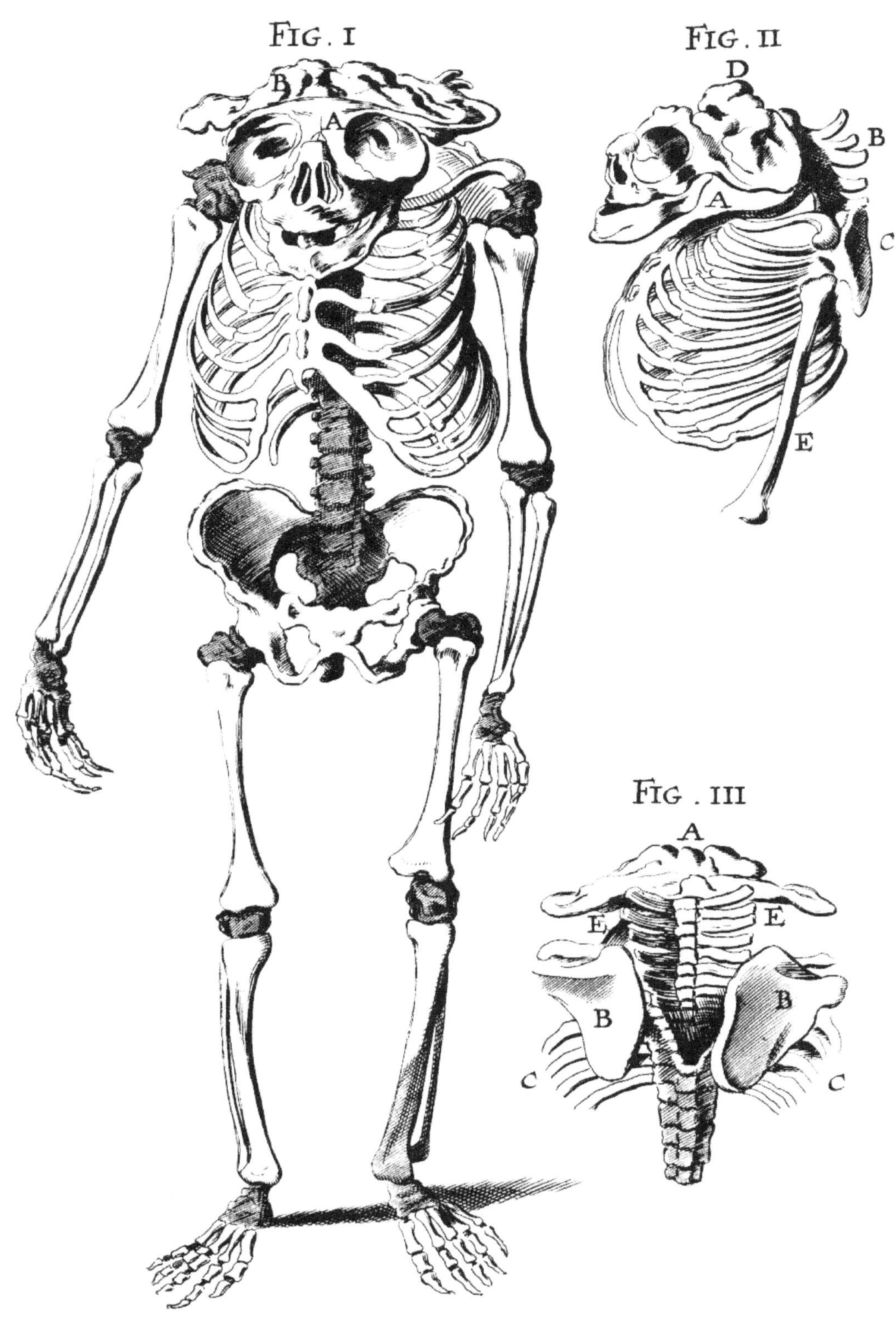

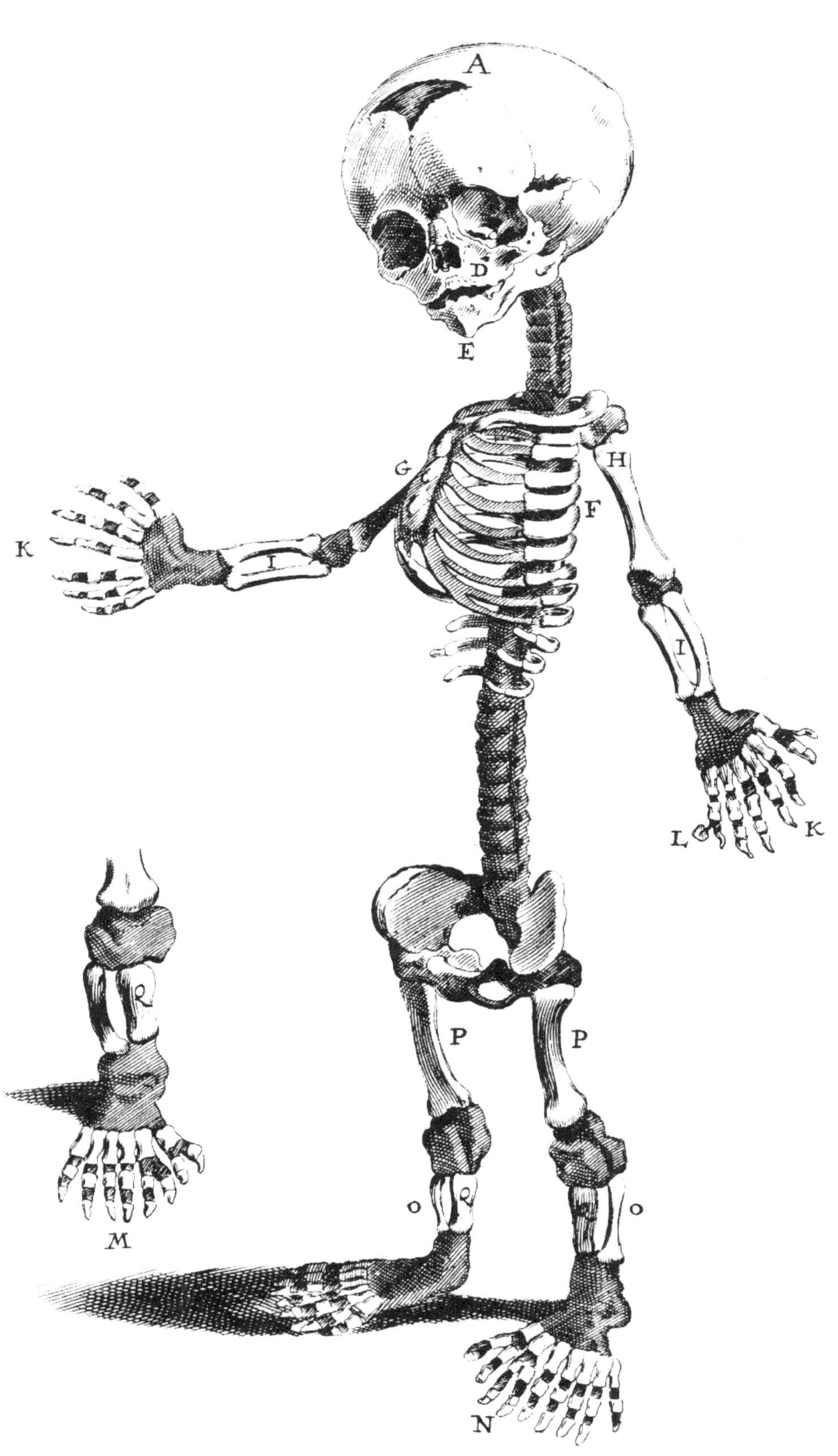

95: Infant skeleton, abnormal; polydactyly.

96

97

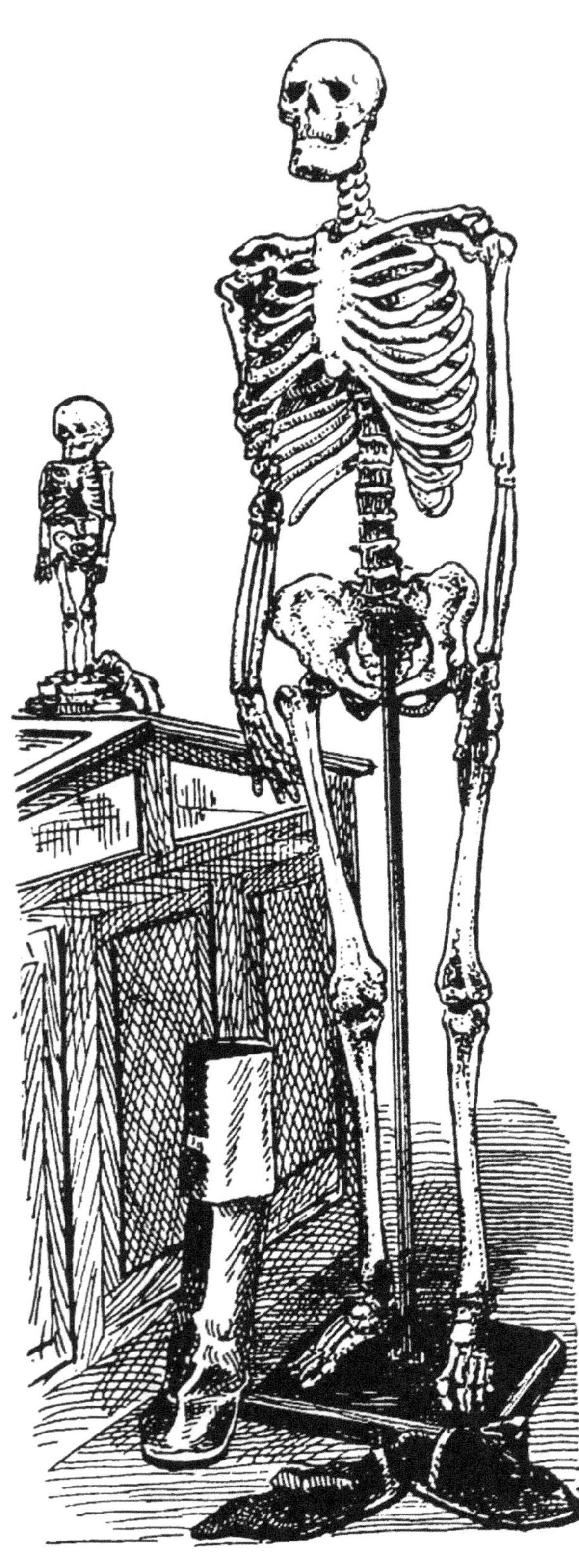

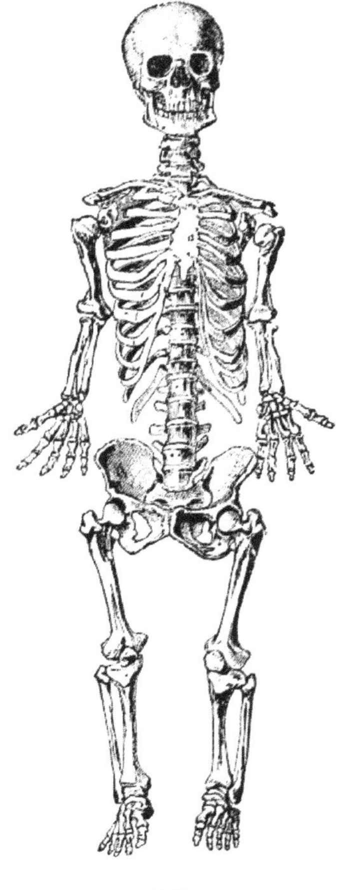

98

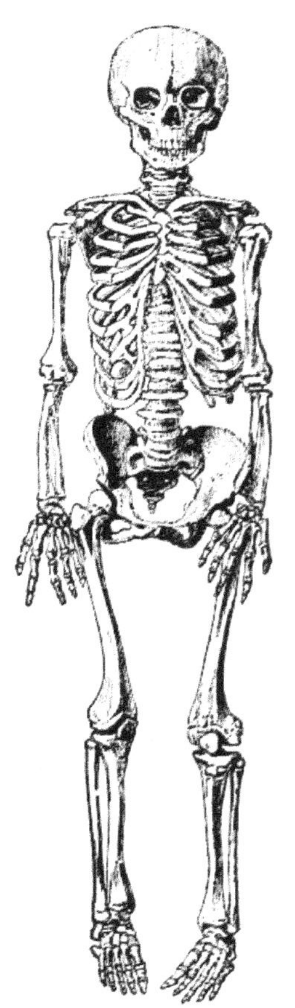

96: Skeleton of the "Irish Giant" in the Royal College of Surgeons, London.

97: Skeleton of a female dwarf, fifty—eight years of age.

98: Skeleton of a female dwarf, thirty one years of age.

99

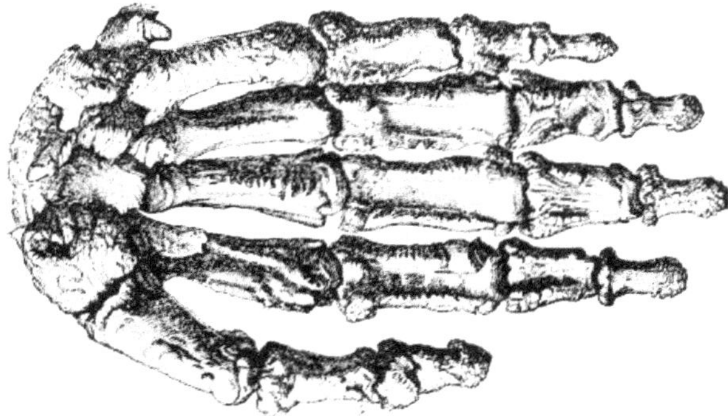

100

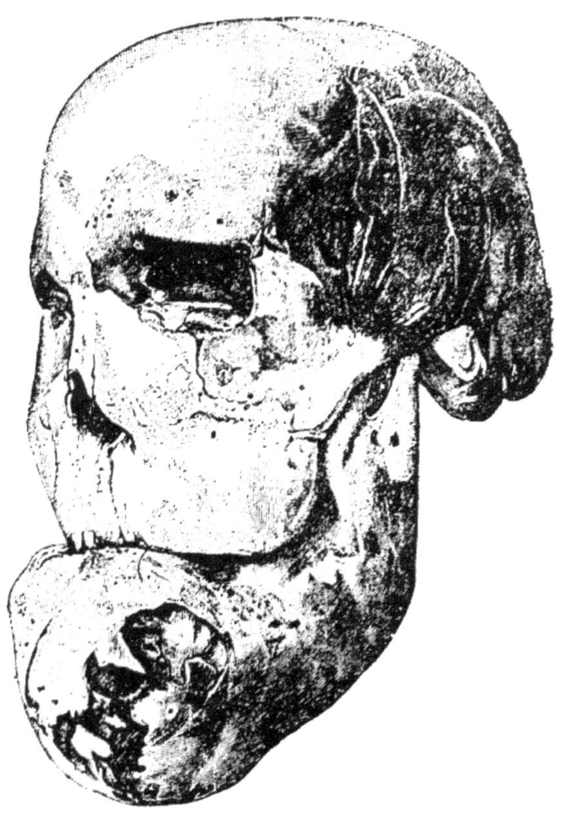

101

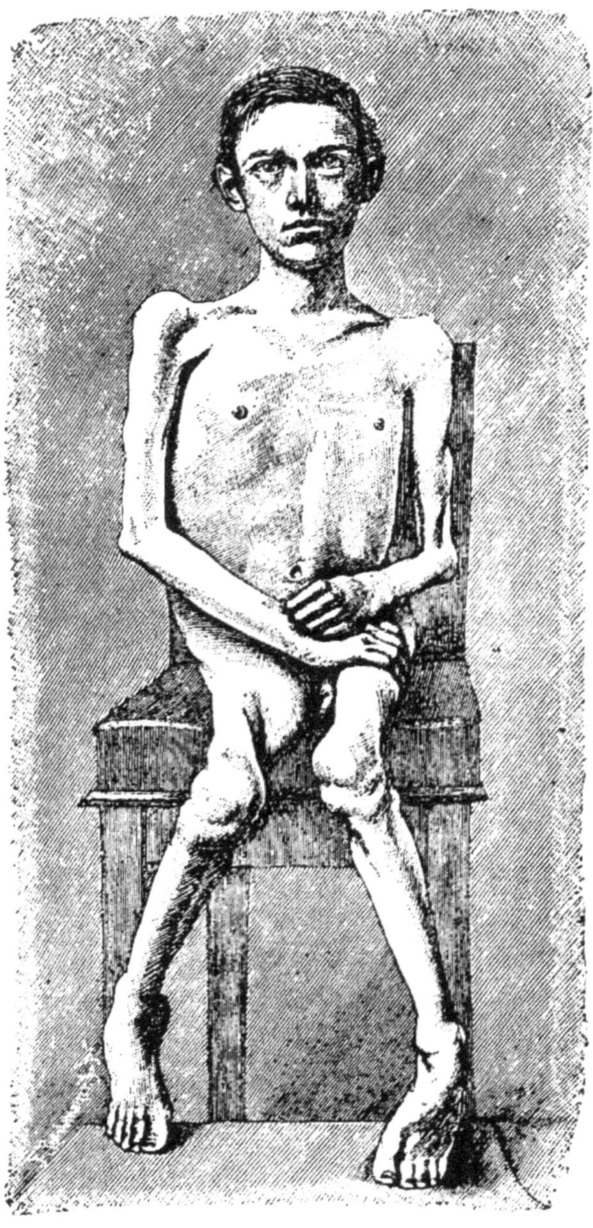

102

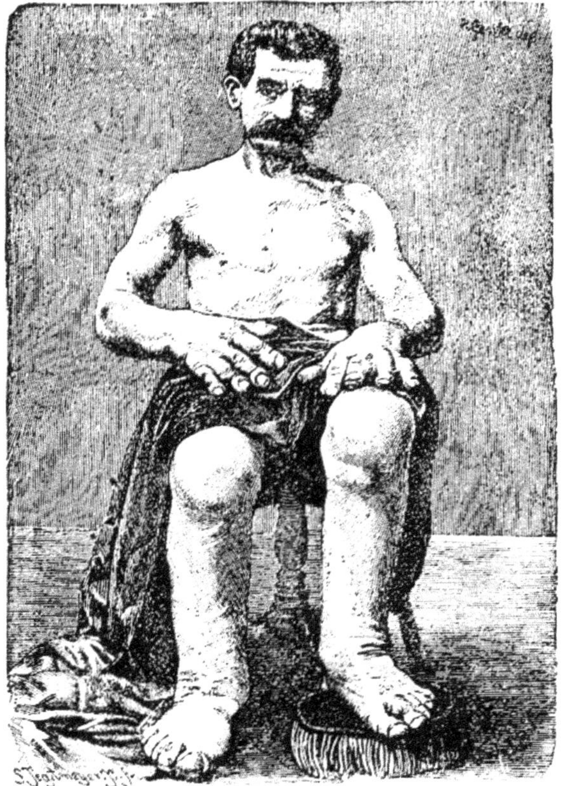

99: Skeleton of the hand with hypertrophied bones, from the case of acromegaly.

100: Leontiasis ossea, occuring in a boy of general giant growth.

101: Juvenile muscular atrophy.

102: Acromegaly.

103

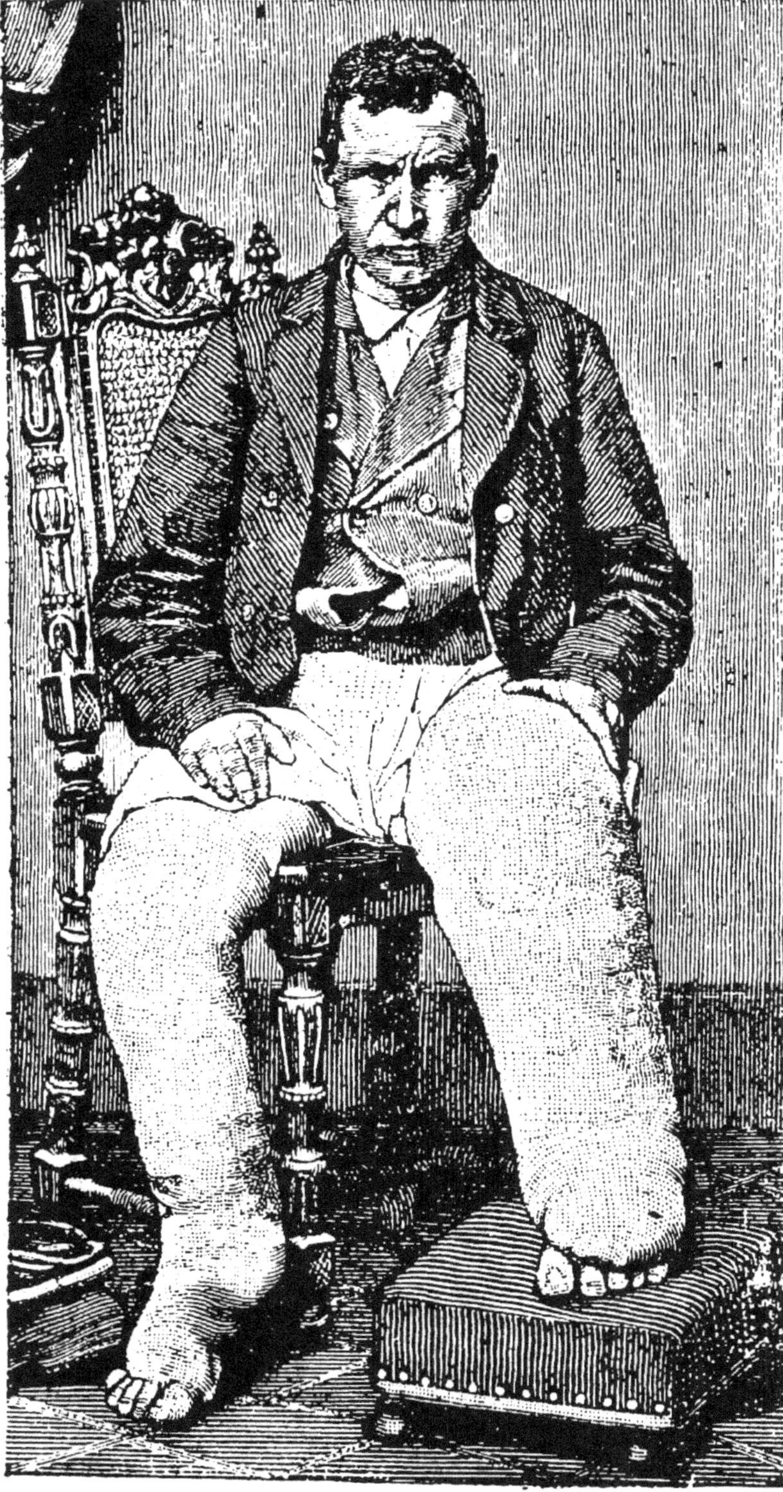

103: Elephantiasis cruris lymphagiectatica.

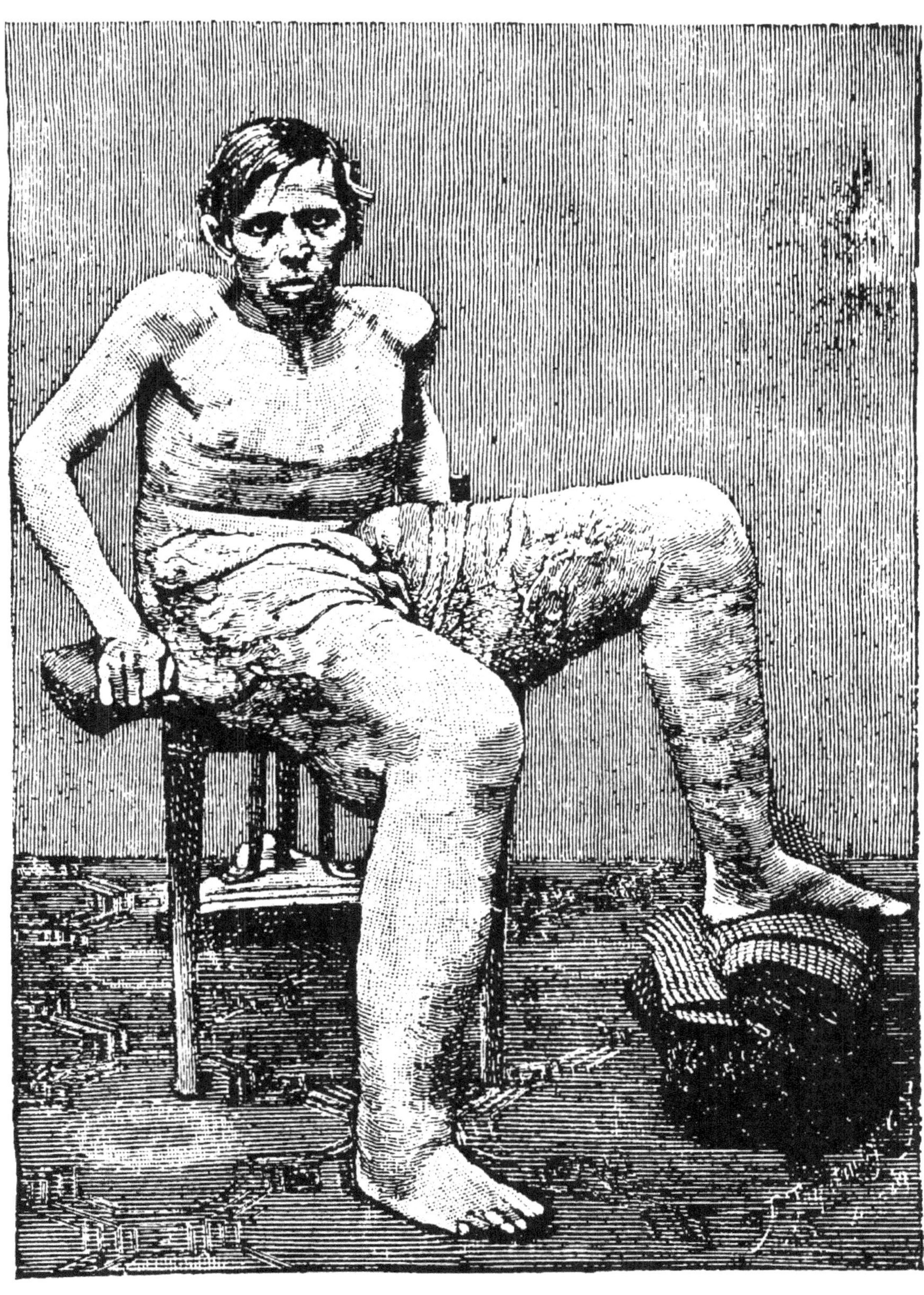

104: Elephantiasis femorum neuromatosa.

105

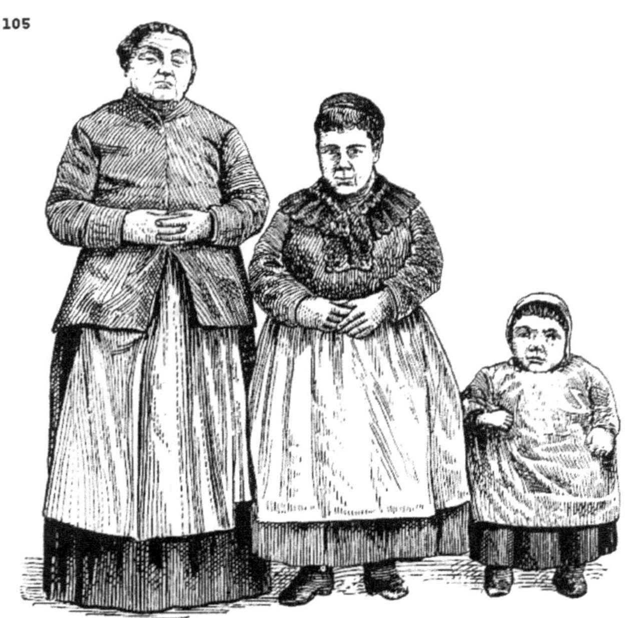

106

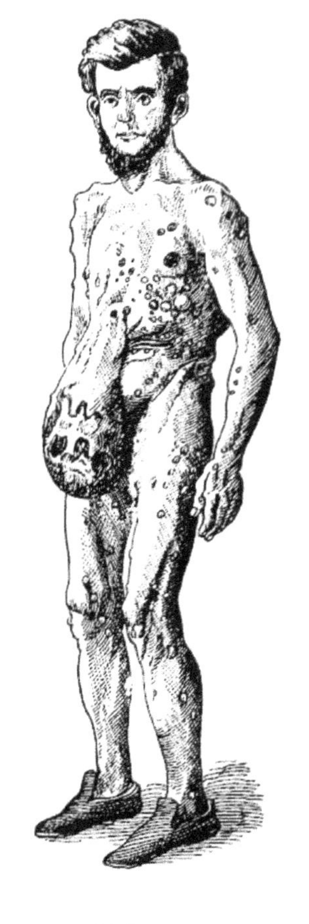

107

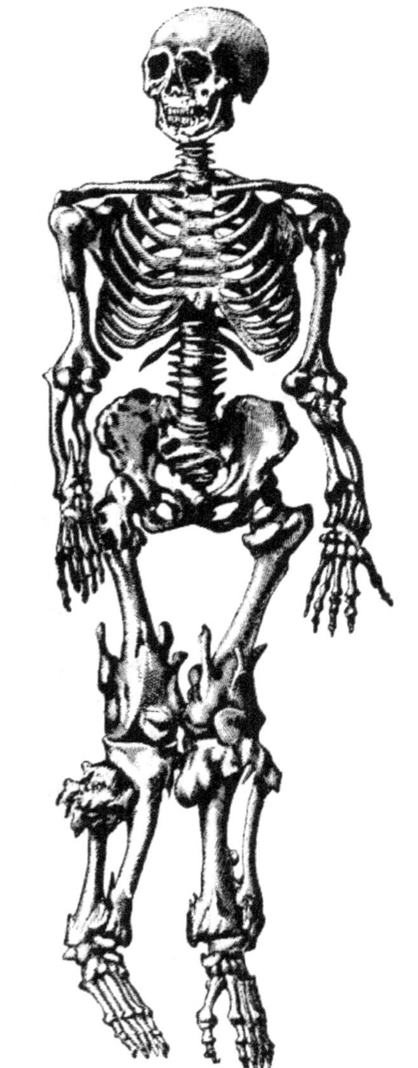

108

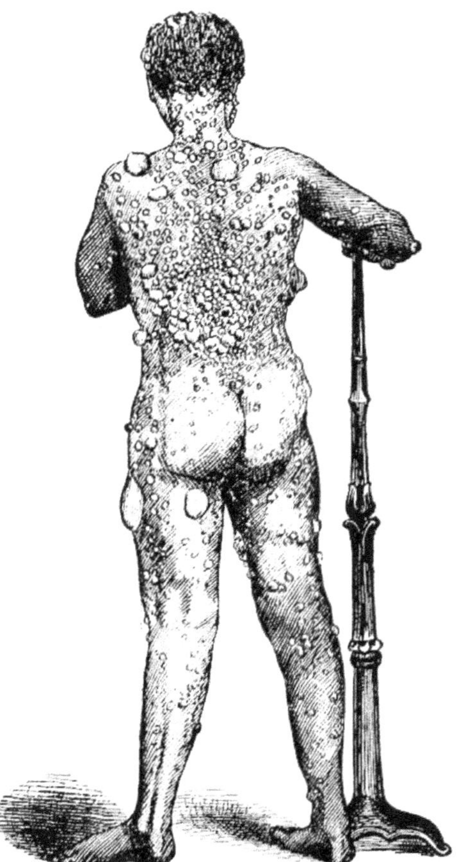

105: Cases of myxoedema and sporadic cretinism (Brissaud).

106: Fibroma molluscum (Pode).

107: Exostoses of various dimensions (Pierret).

108: Fibromata (after Octerlony).

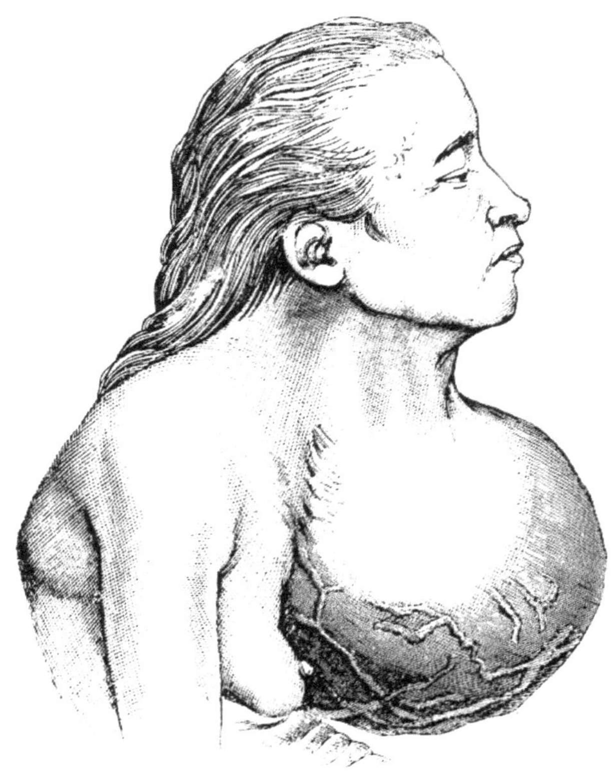

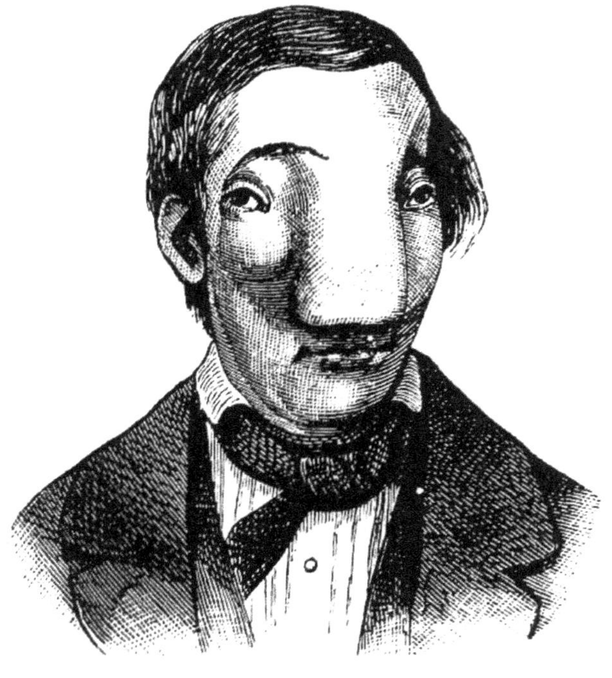

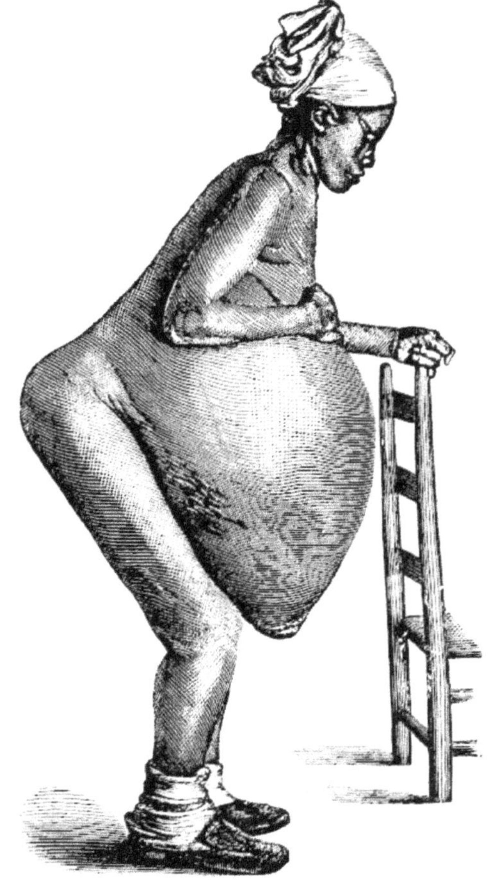

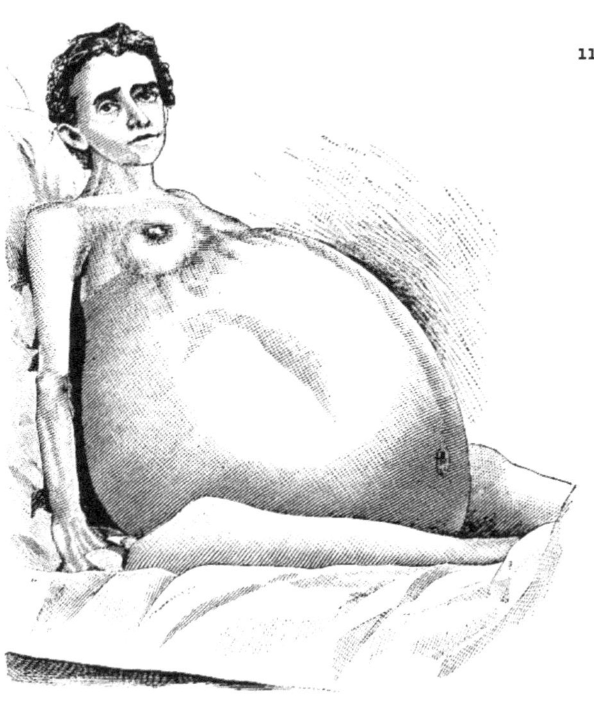

109: Enormous tutor of the thyroid gland (after Bruns).

110: Deformity produced by sarcoma of the nasal septum (after Moore).

111: Fibrocyst of the uterus, weighing 135 pounds (Stockard).

112: Large ovarian cyst, weighing 149 pounds (N.Y Med Journal).

113

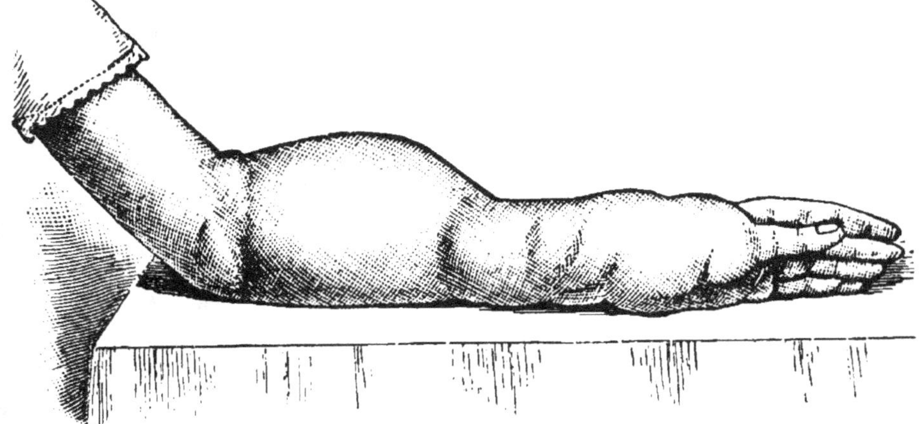

114

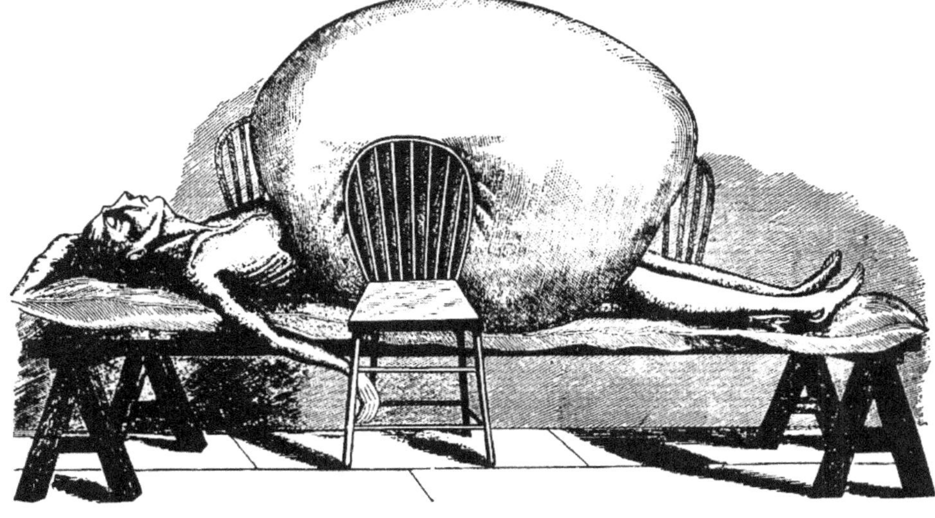

115

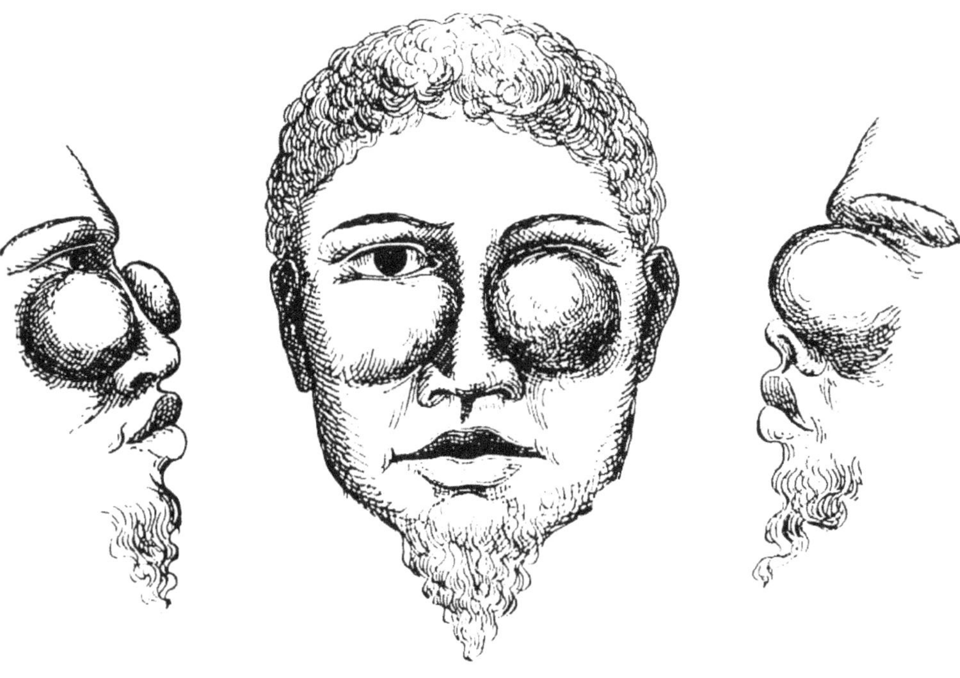

113: Arm in which the musculo—spiral nerve was neuromatous (after Campbell de Morgan).

114: Enormous glandular ovarian cystoma (Rodenstein).

115: Gros—nez (Macland).

116

117

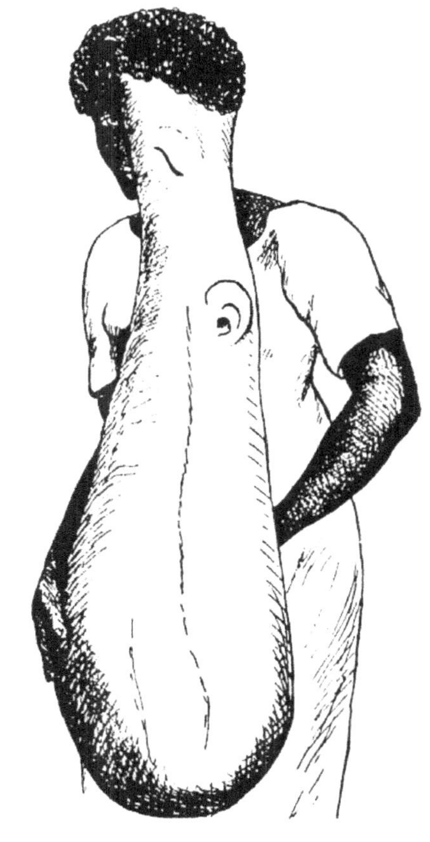

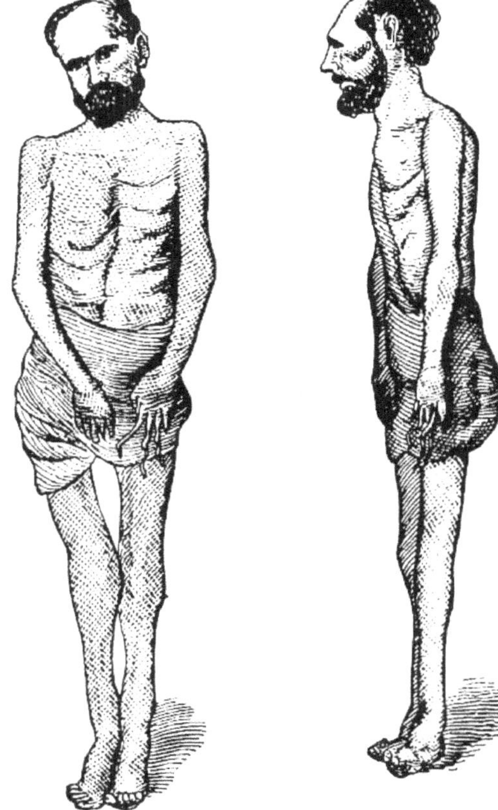

118

119

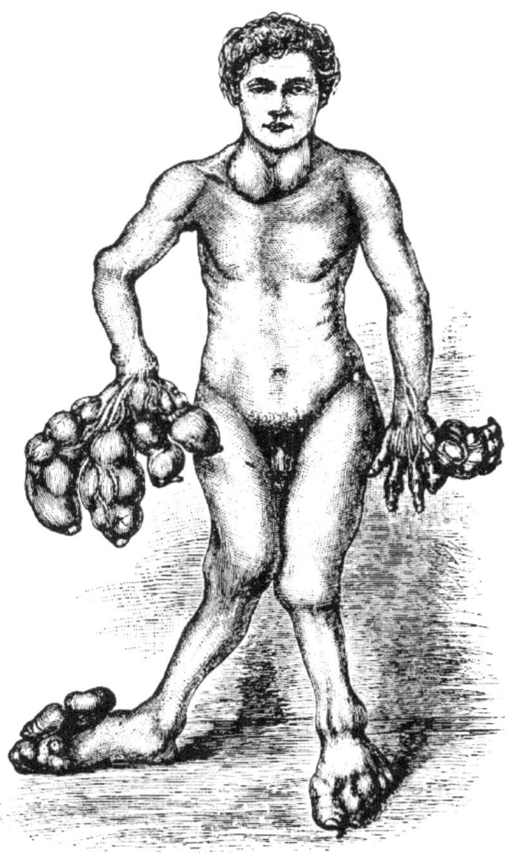

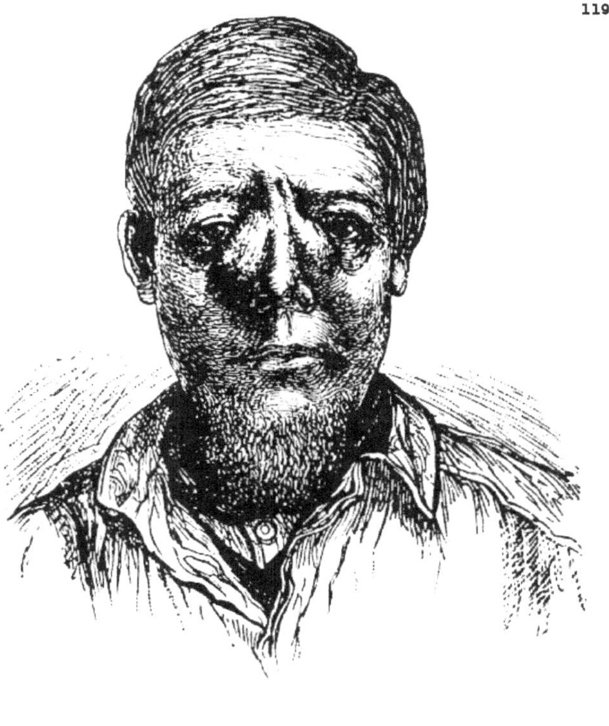

116: Enormous lipoma of the parietal region.   117: Ossified man.   118: Lady twenty years of age with multiple chondromata (after Steudel).   119: Symmetric osteopath of the nasal processes of the superior maxilla (after Hutchinson).

120

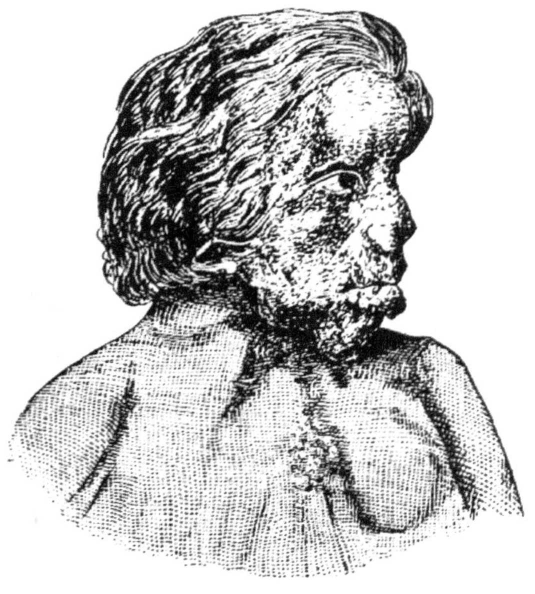

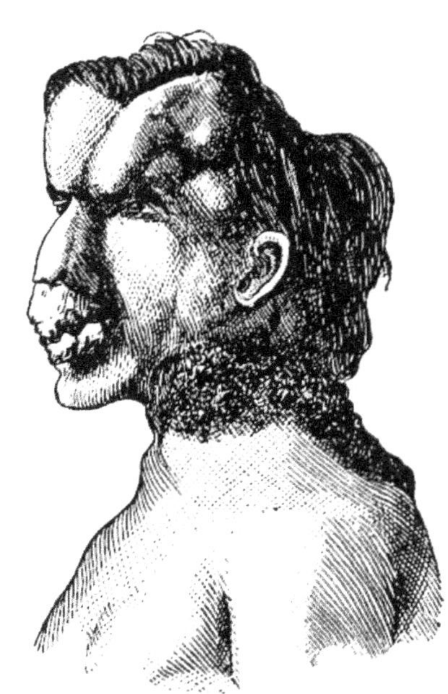

121

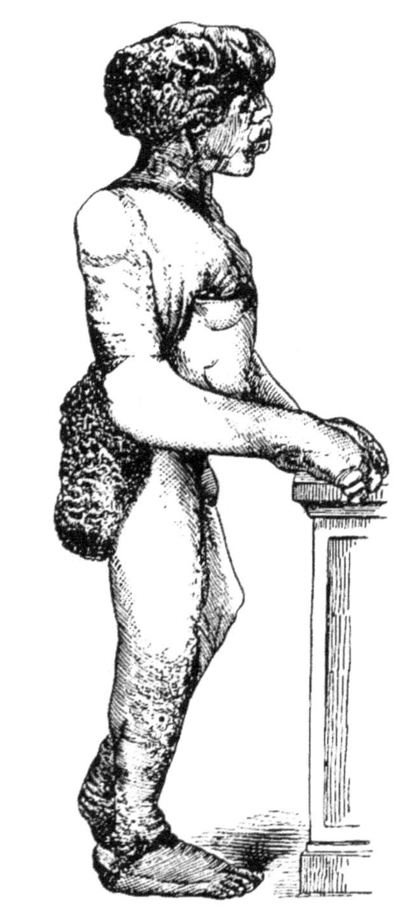

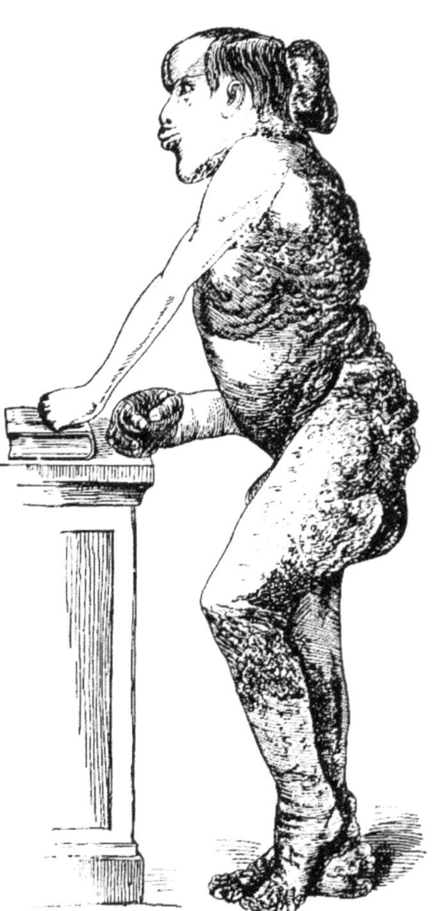

120: Head of the 'Elephant-man'.

121: The 'Elephant-man' (Treves).

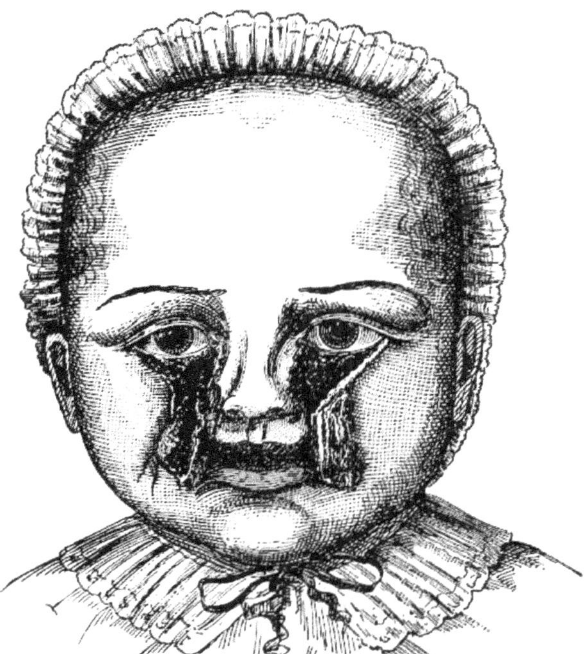

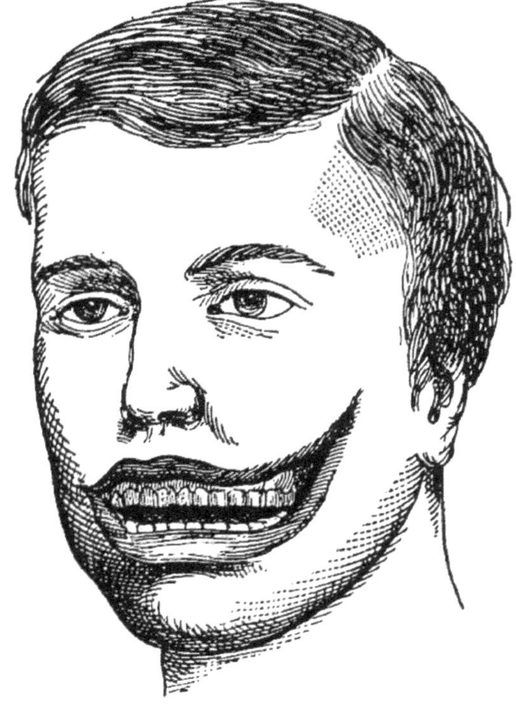

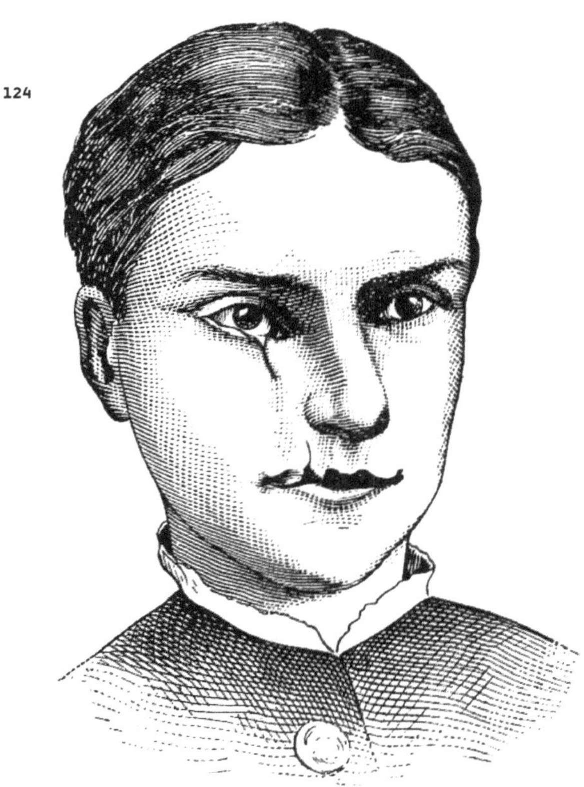

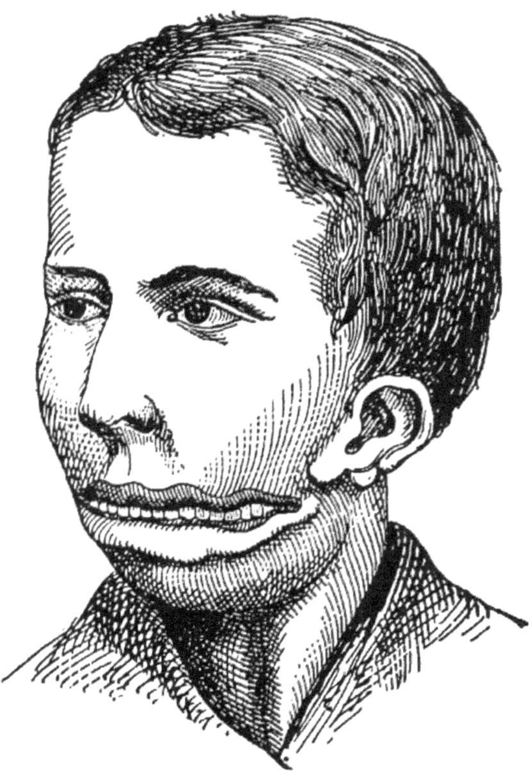

122: Double hare–lip.

123: Macrostoma by ascending lateral fissure.

124: Slight hare–lip, with fissure of the lower eyelid (Kraske).

125: Macrostoma by lateral fissure.

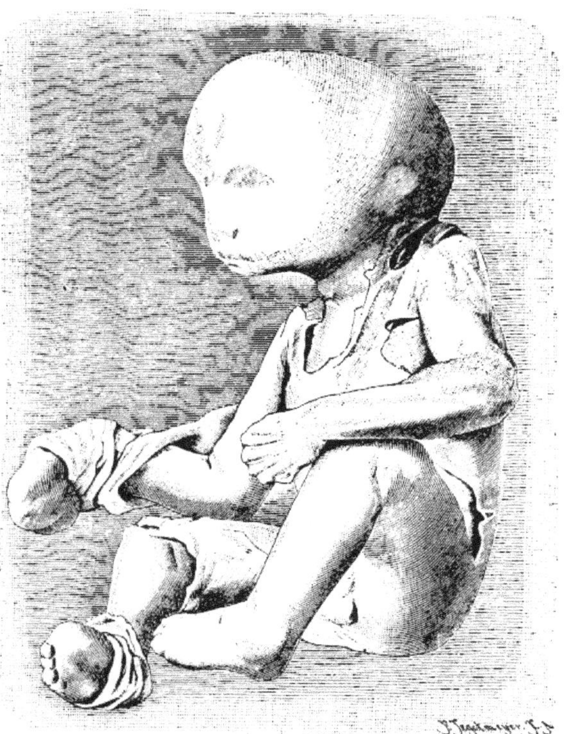

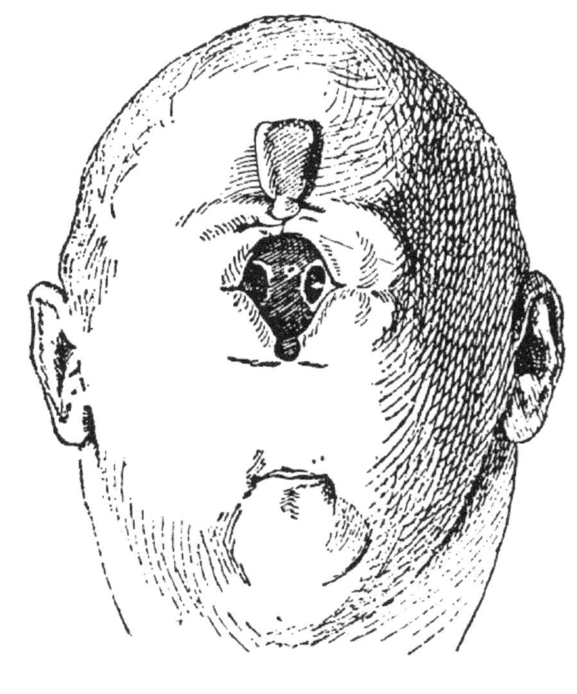

128

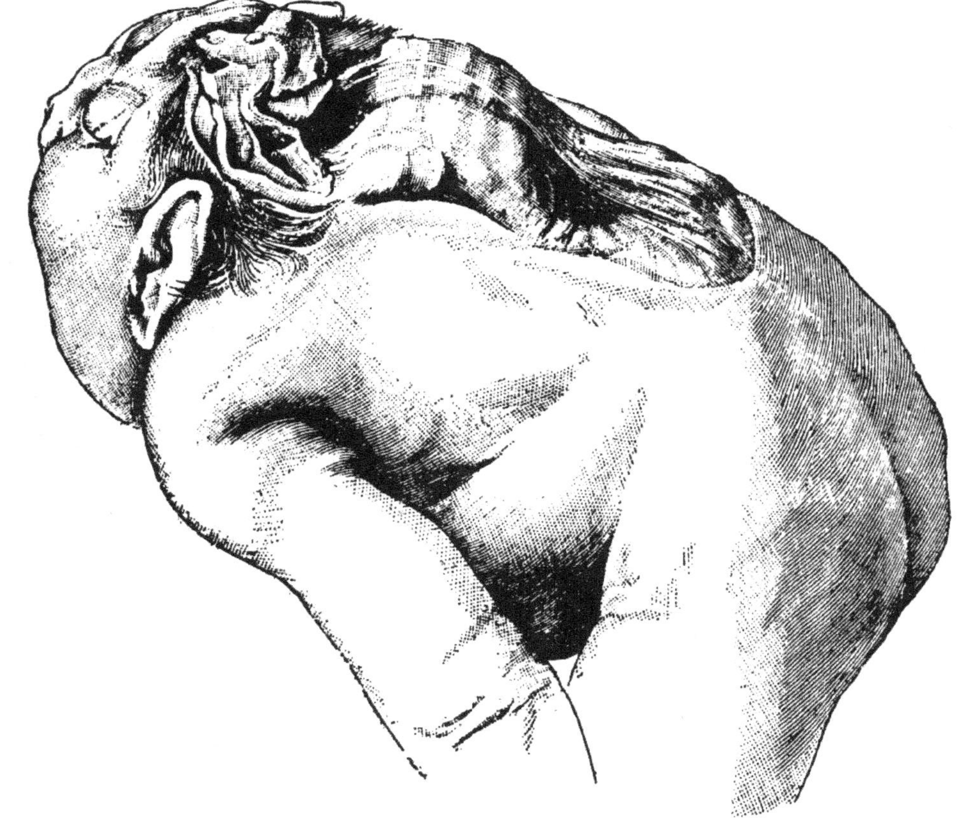

126: Foetus entirely inclosed in fibrous membranes.

127: Cyclopia or synophthalmia.

128: Craniorachischisis, with total absence of the brain and spinal cord.

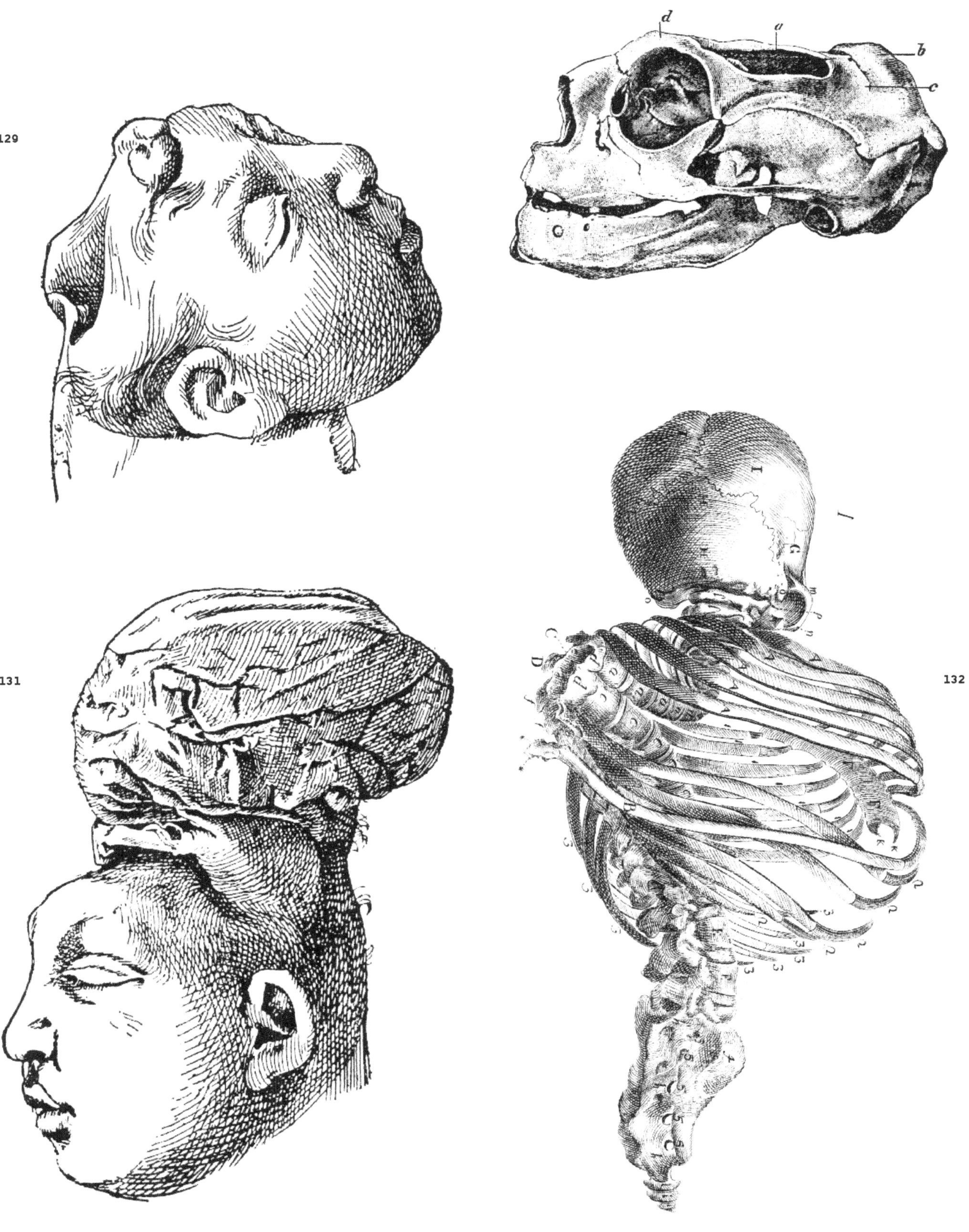

129: Acrania anencephaly.

130: Partial agenesia of the bones of the cranium in anencephalia.

131: Cranioschisis with encephalomeningocele.

132: Severe deformity of the spine.

133

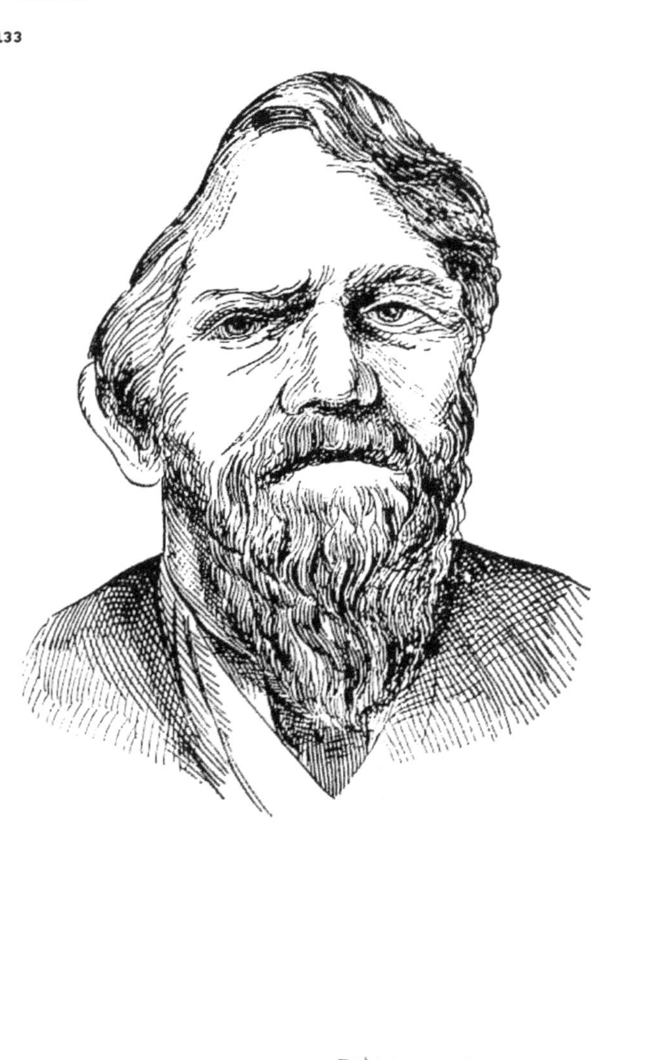

134

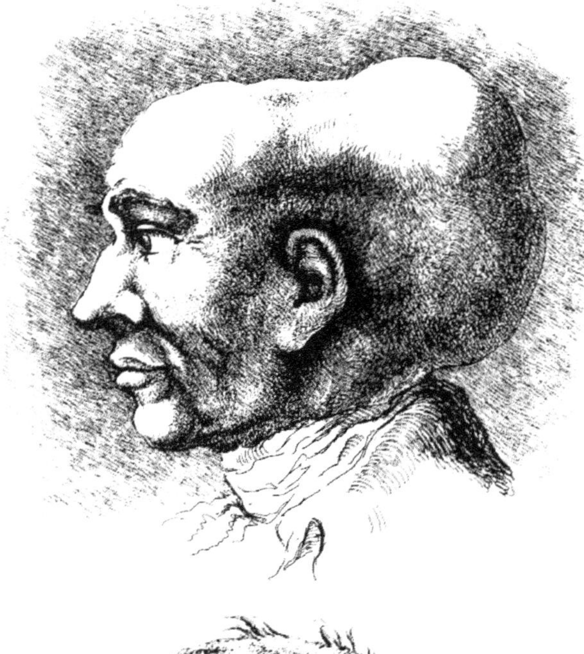

135

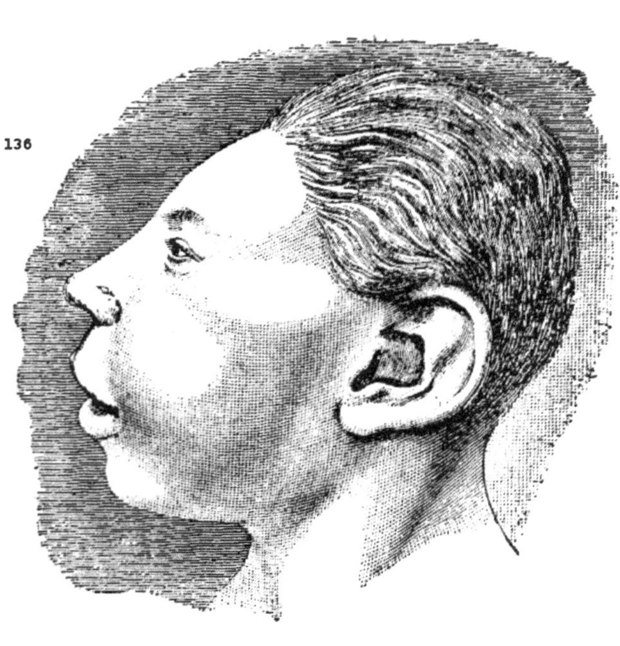

136

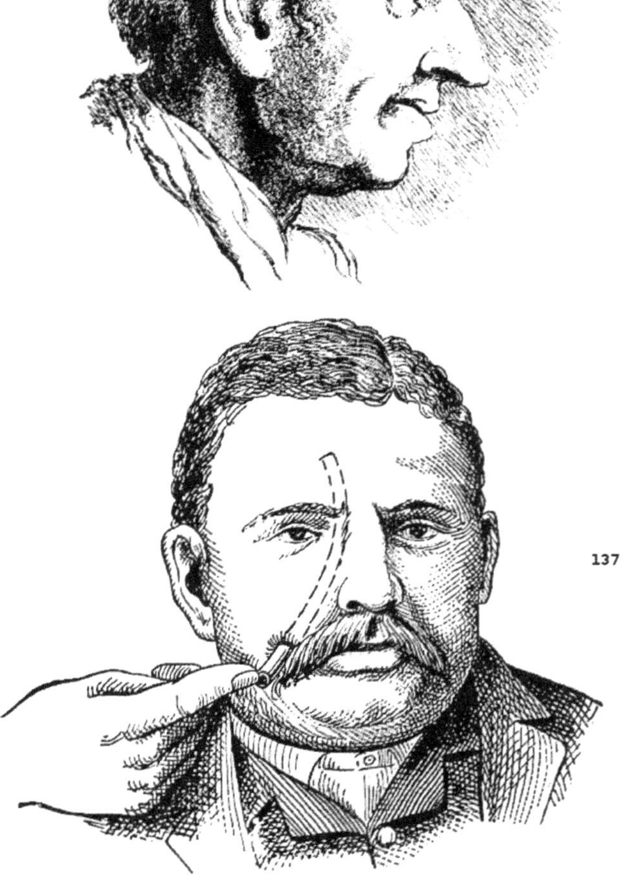

137

133: Skull injury with extensive loss of cranial and cerebral substance.

134: deformity of the skull.

135: Depression in the formation of the skull.

136: Microcephaly.

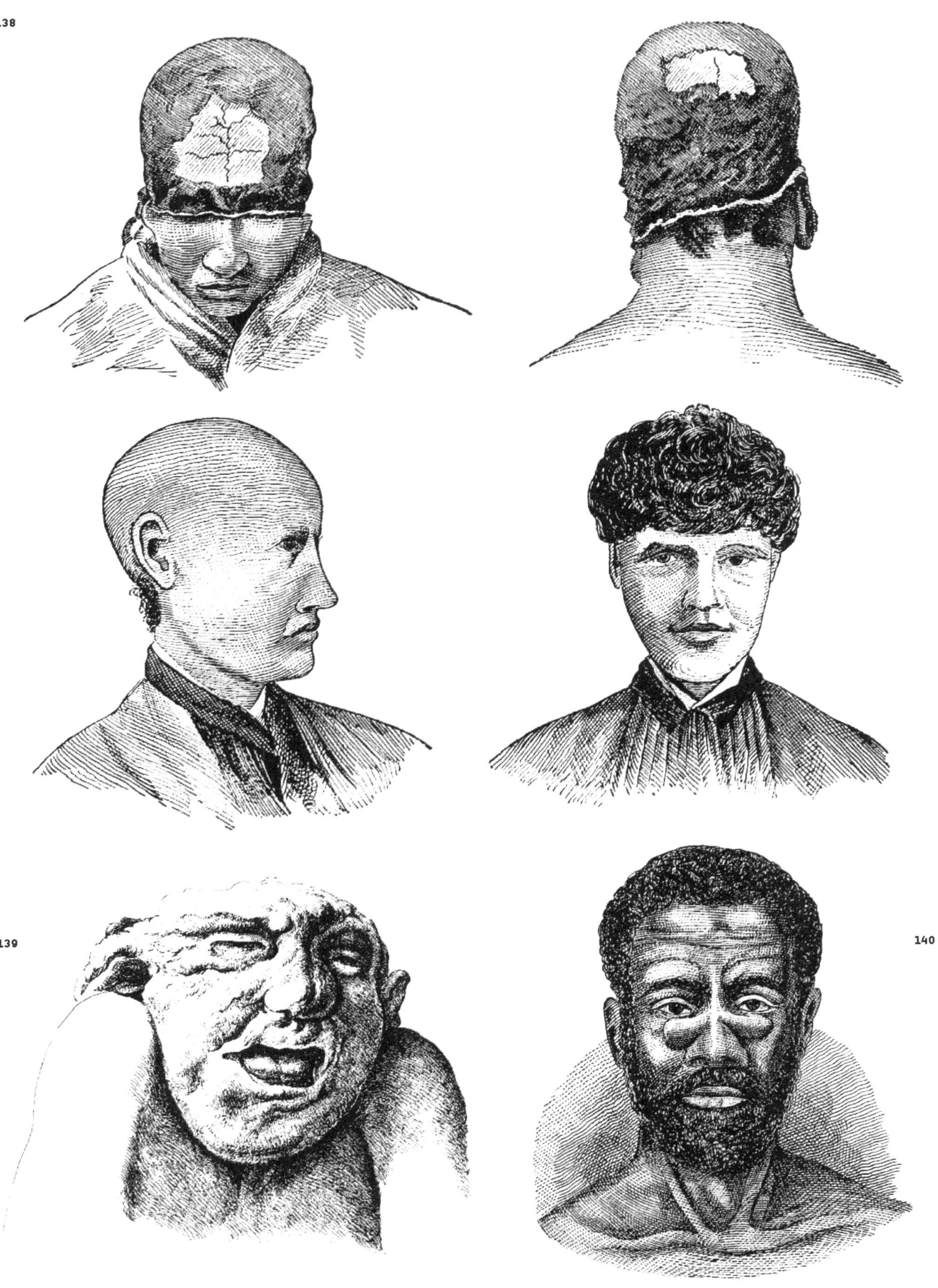

138

139

140

137: Diagram showing the trajectory of an oil spout which had punctured the cheek and penetrated the brain (Abel and Colman).

138: Scalp injury and skin graft (schaeffer).

139: Severe deformity of the skull and face.

140: 'African horned man' (Lamprey).

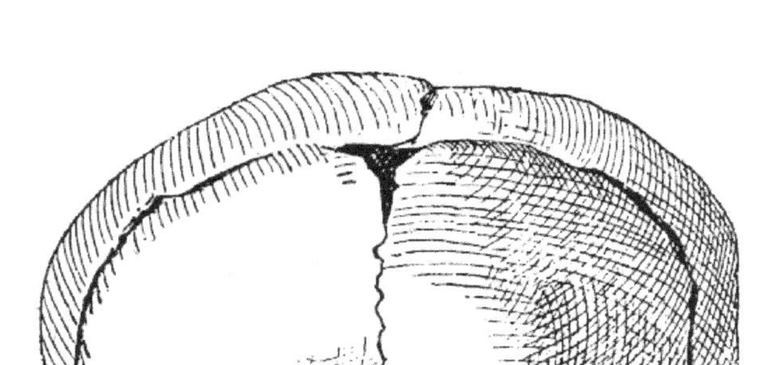

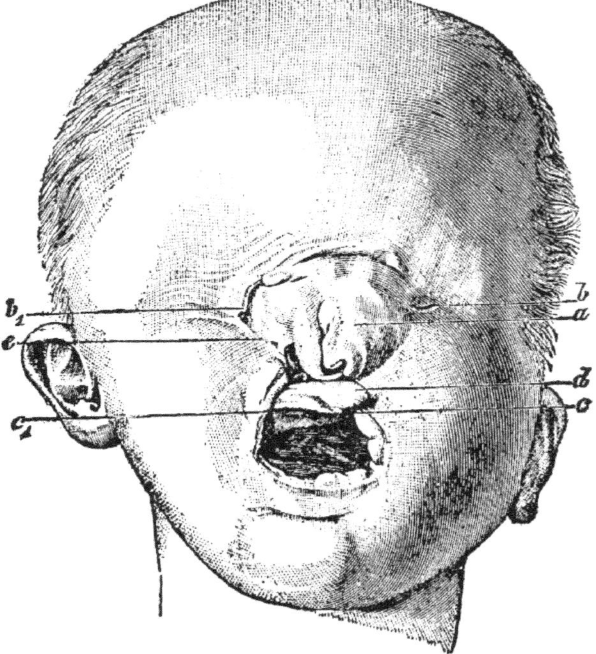

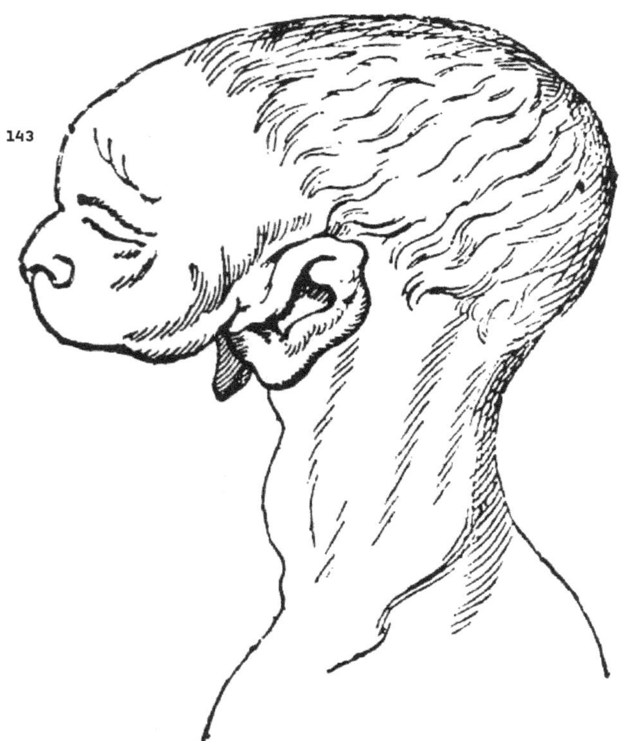

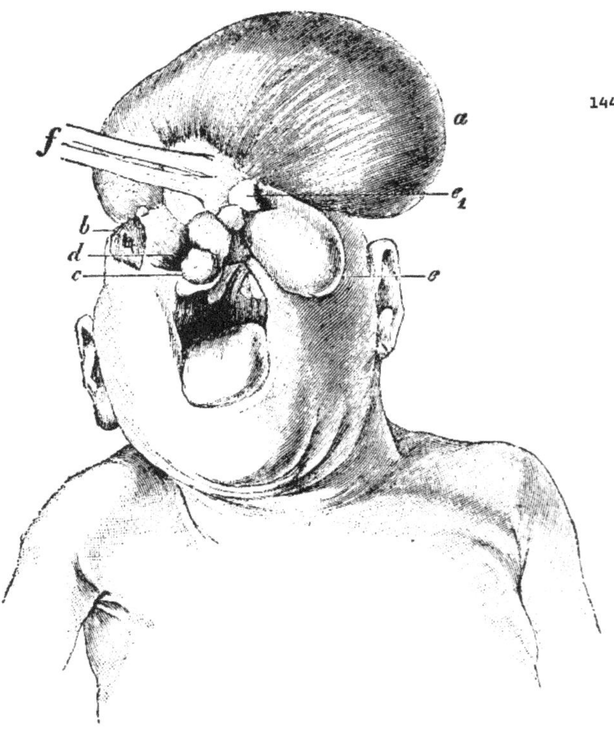

141: Double cheilognatho-palatoschisis.

142: Malformation of the face caused by amniotic adhesions and pressure.

143: Agnathia and synotia (Guardan).

144: Malformation of the head, due to adhesions of the membranes to the frontal region.

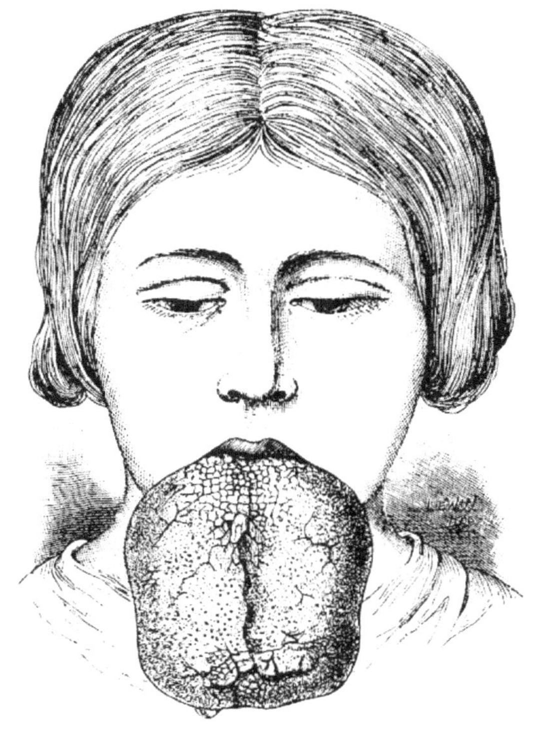

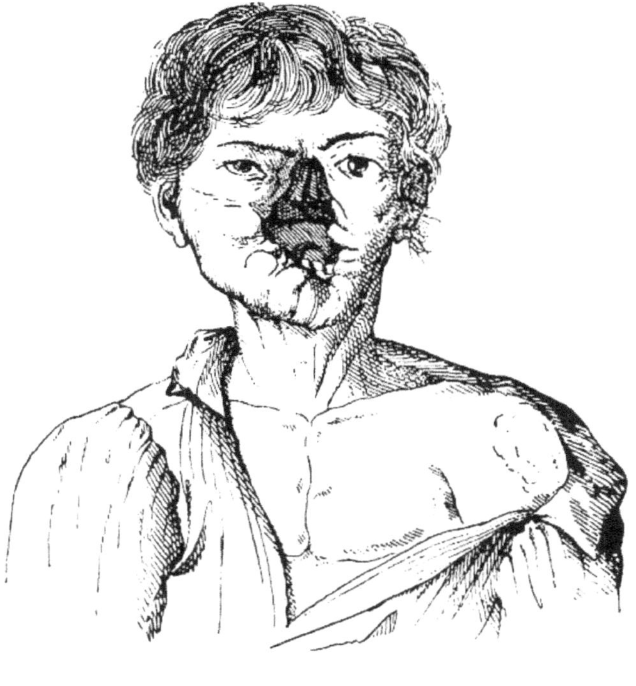

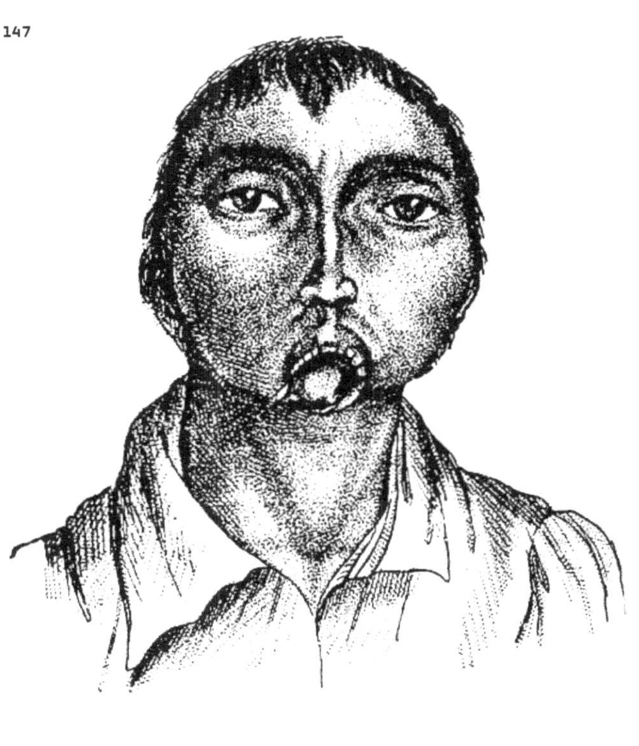

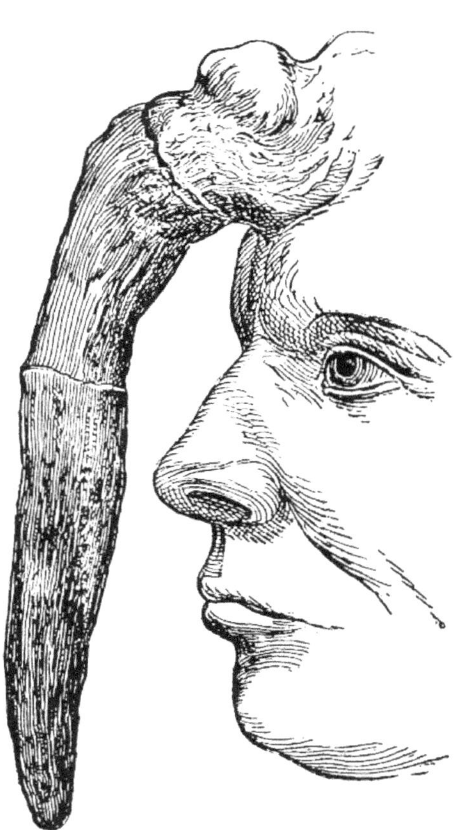

145: Marcoglossia in a girl eleven years old (after Murphy).

146: Gunshot injury of the face.

147: Gun shot injury to the lower jaw.

148: Wax model of a large frontal horn.

149

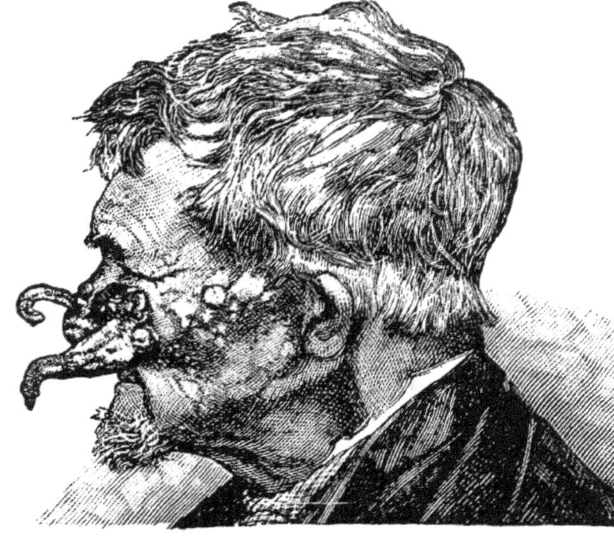

150

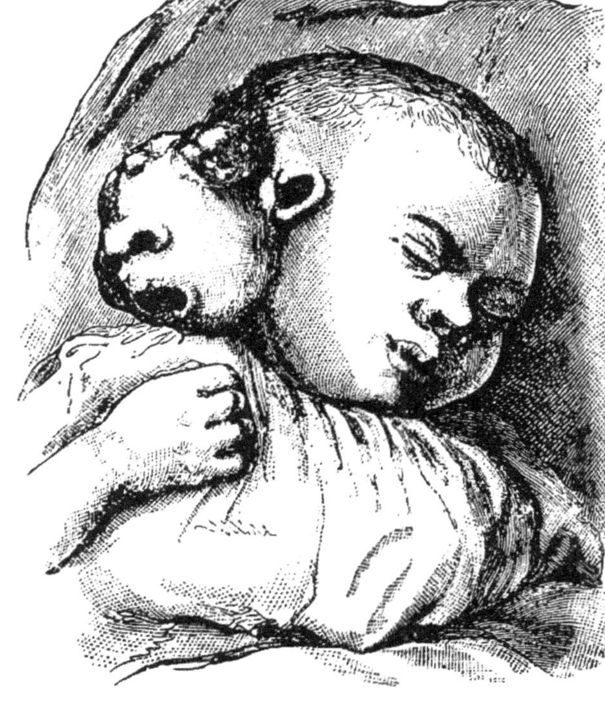

151

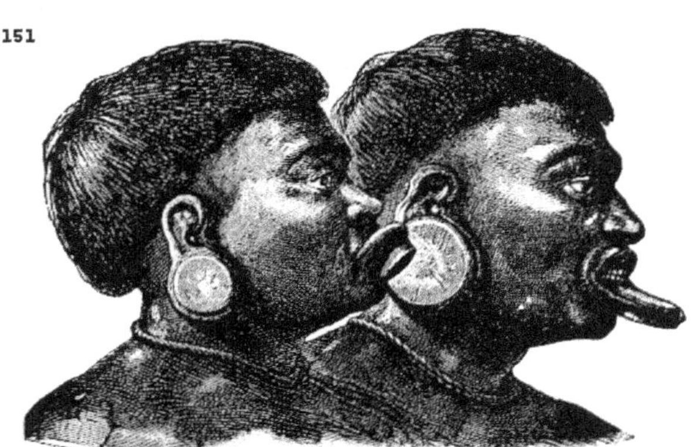

152

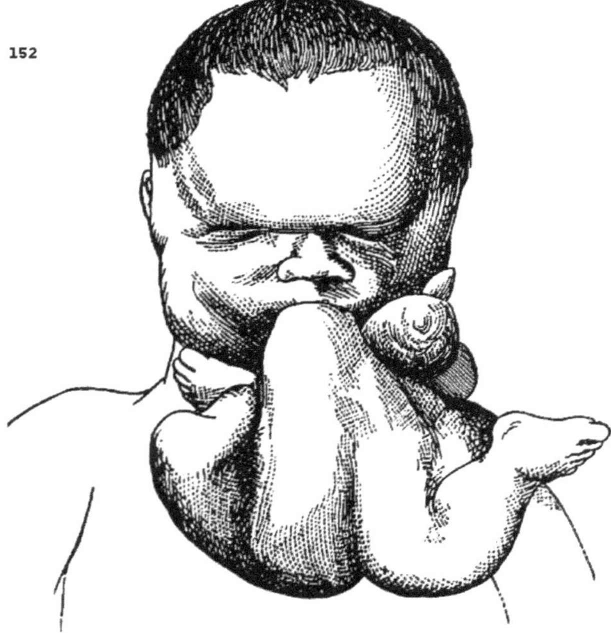

153

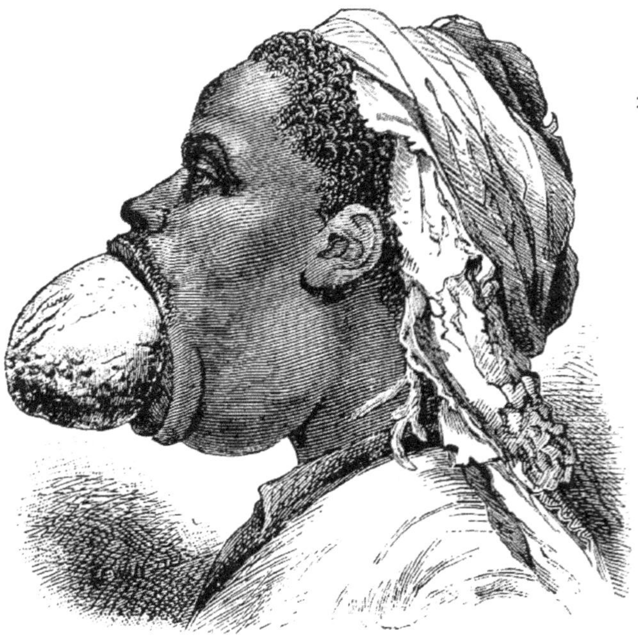

149: Cutaneous horns. Showing beginning epitheliomatous degeneration of the base (after Panocast).

150: Infant with supernumerary head (after Sutton).

151: Perforation of the ears and lip practised by the Botocudos.

152: Epignathus.

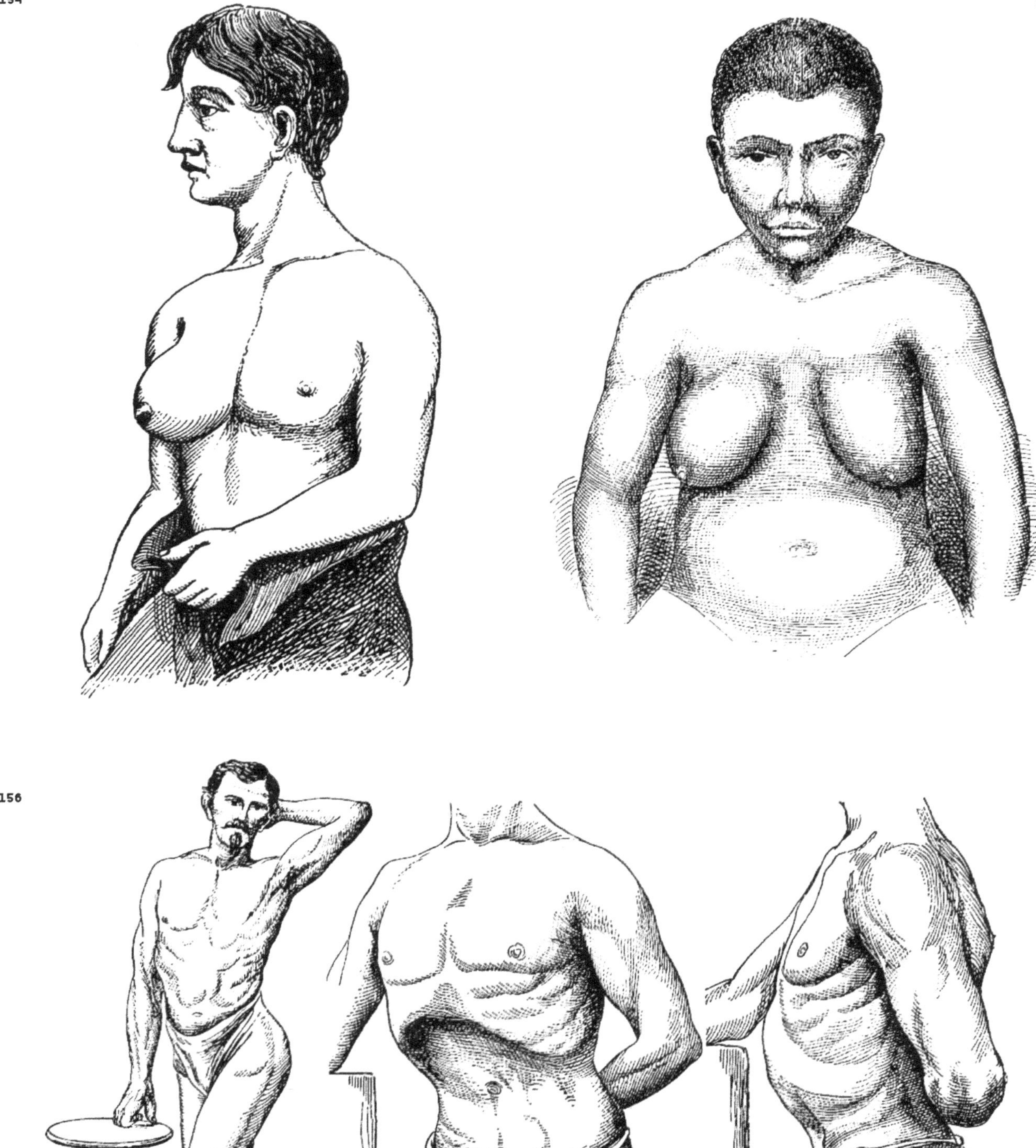

153: Large lingual dermoid protruding from the mouth (after Gray).

154: Abnormal development of right breast in a young man.

155: Man with fully developed mammary (Laurent).

156: Charles Warren, the celebrated dislocationist.

157

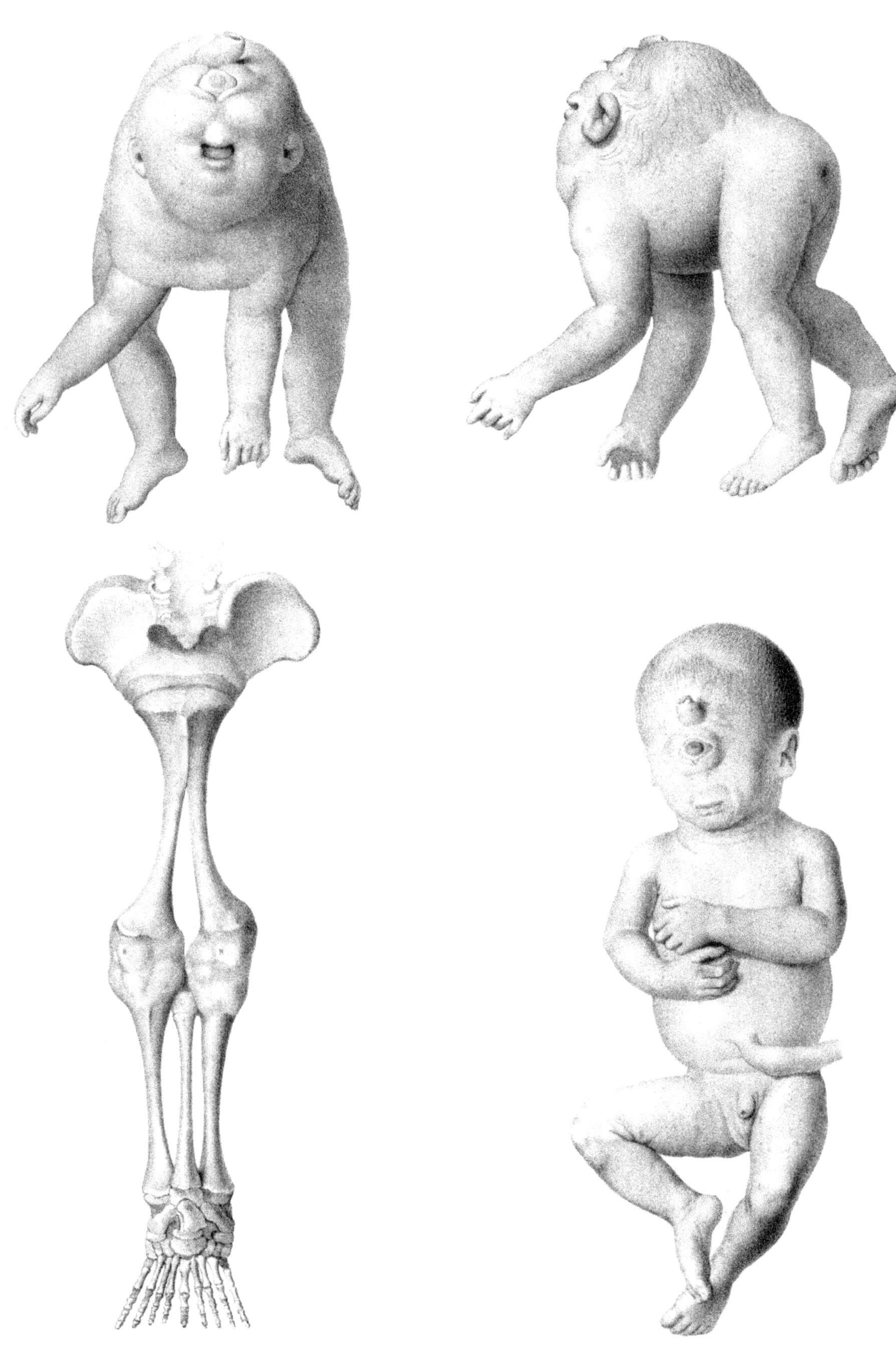

157: Malformed fetus, holoprosencephaly.

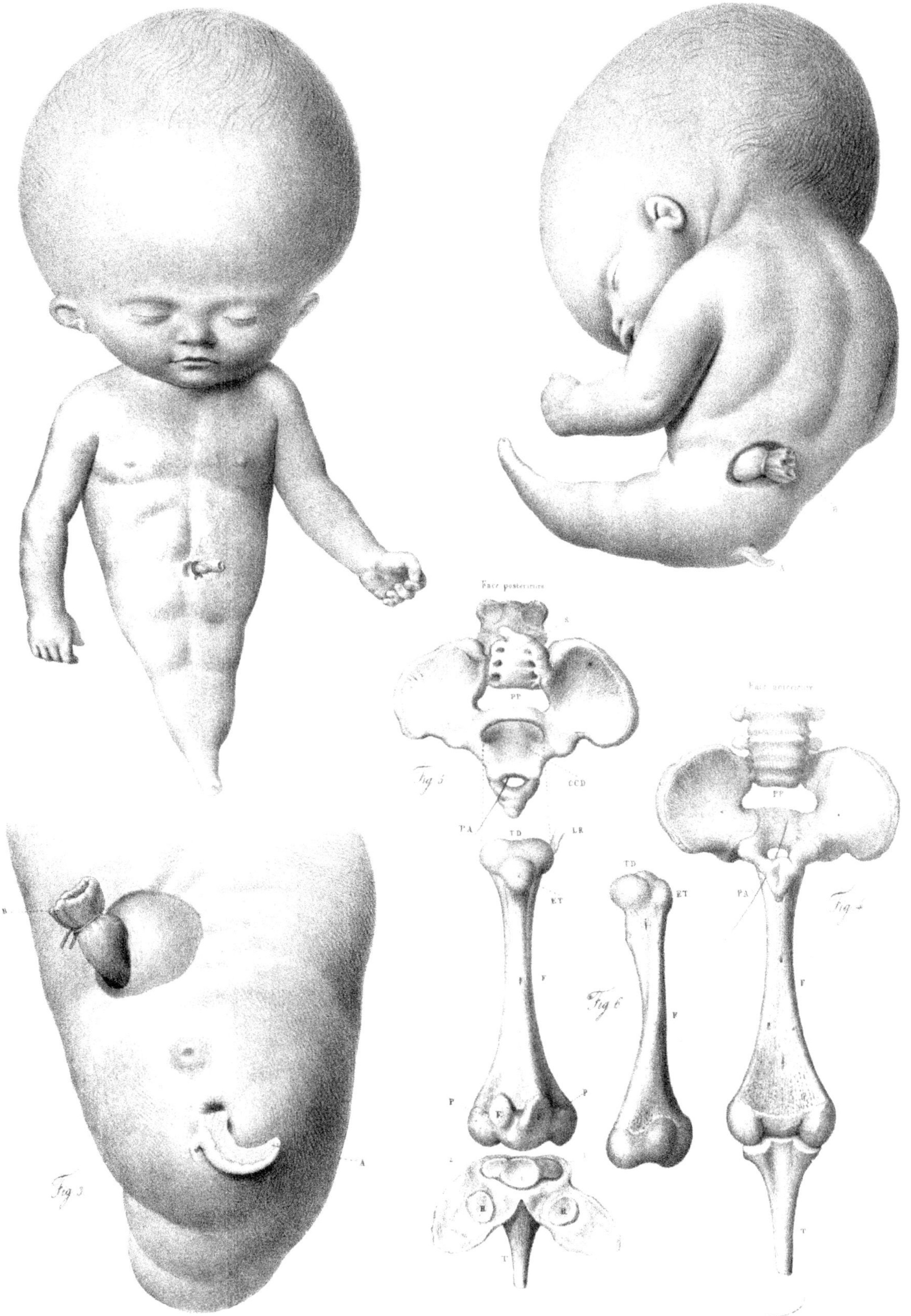

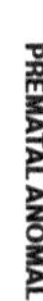

158: Malformed fetus; sirenomelia.

159

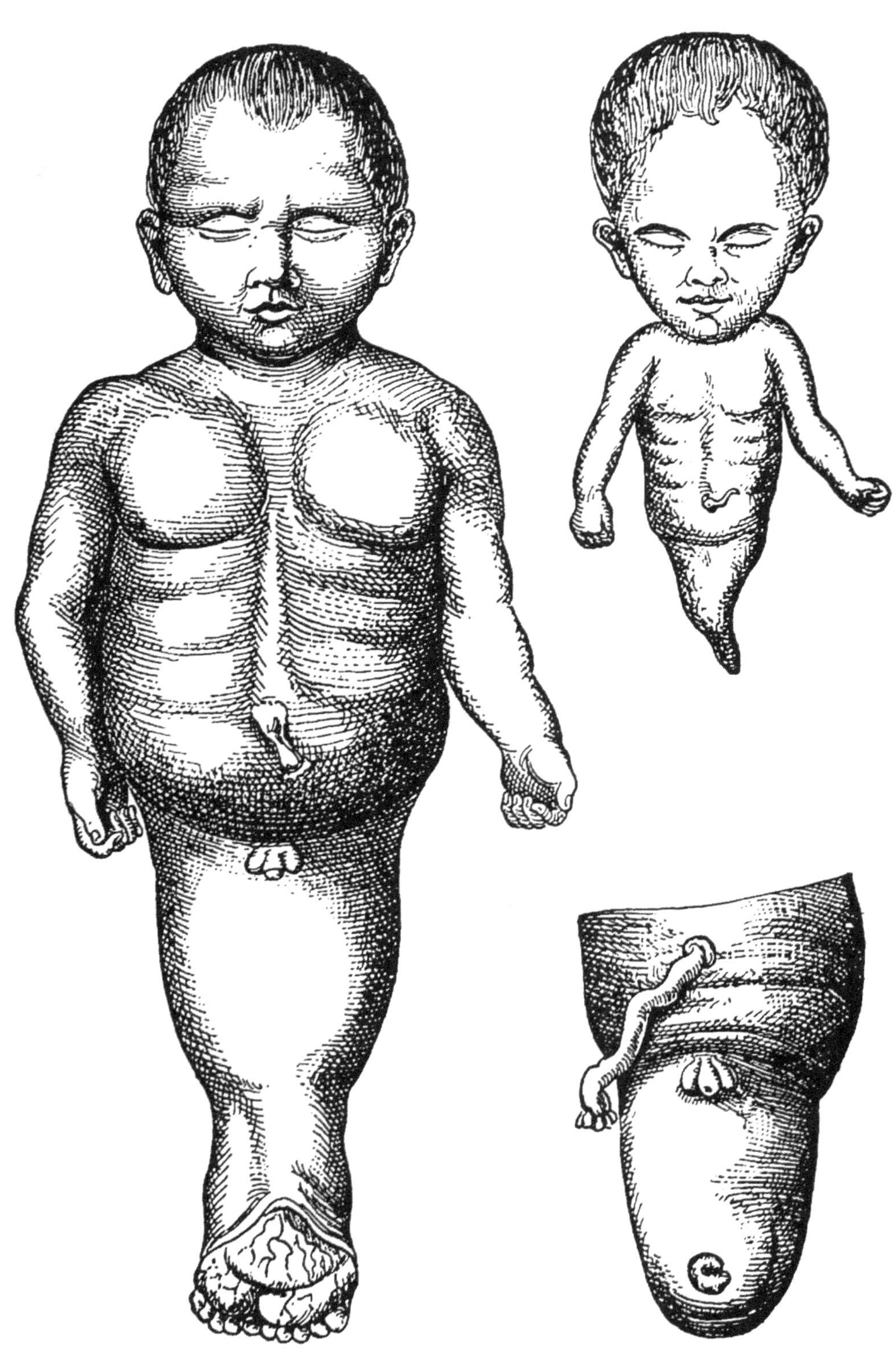

159: Examples of 'Sirens' showing fusion of the
lower extremities.

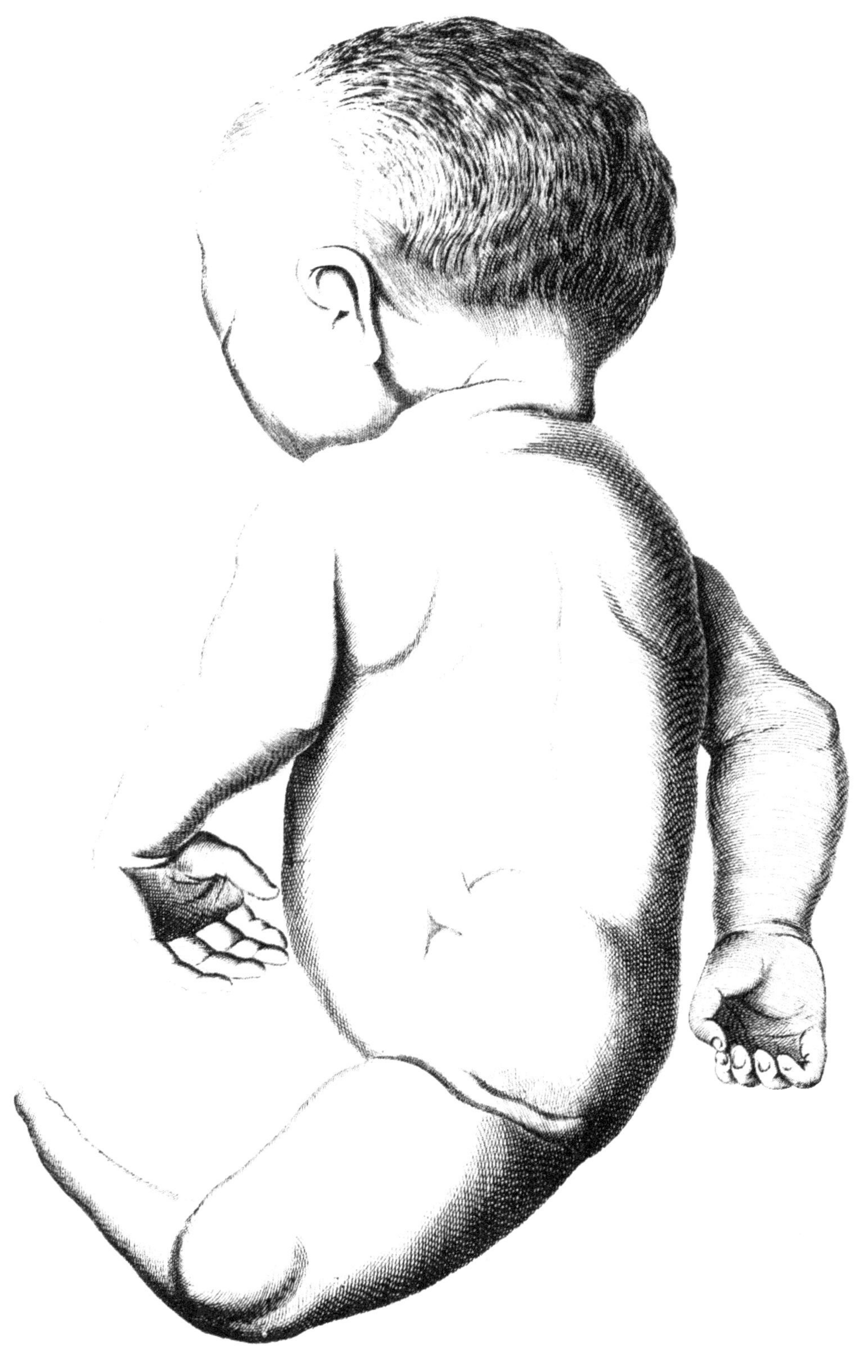

160: Fusion of the lower extremities.

161

162

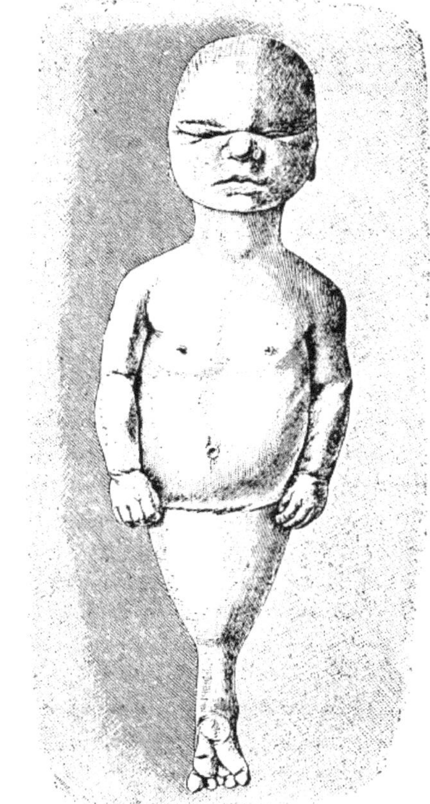

163

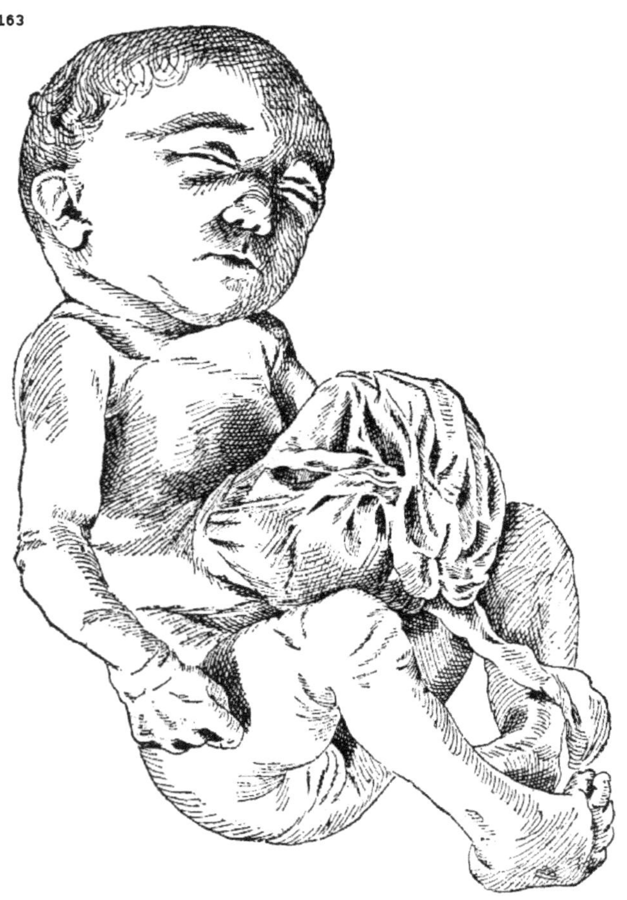

164

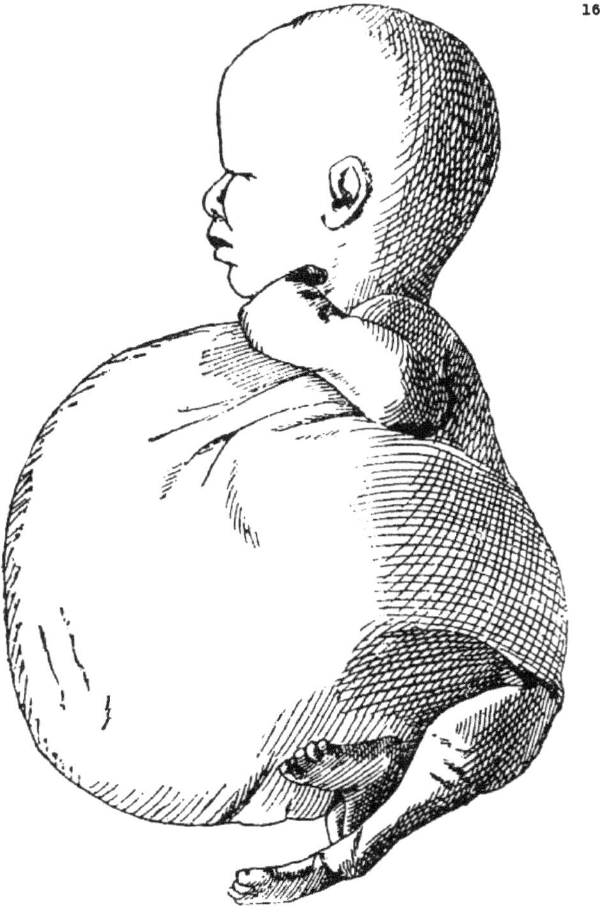

161: Sympus apus.

162: Sympus dipus.

163: Hernia funiculi umbilicalis.

164: Urethral atresia causing extreme dilation of the bladder.

165

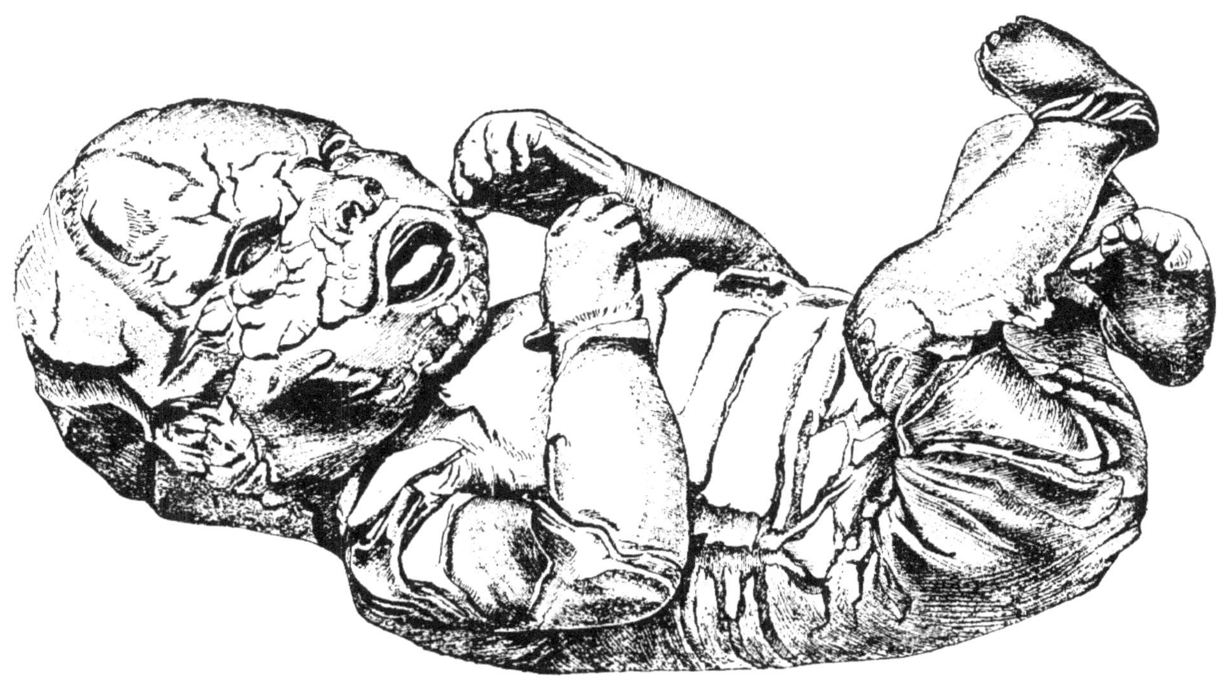

166

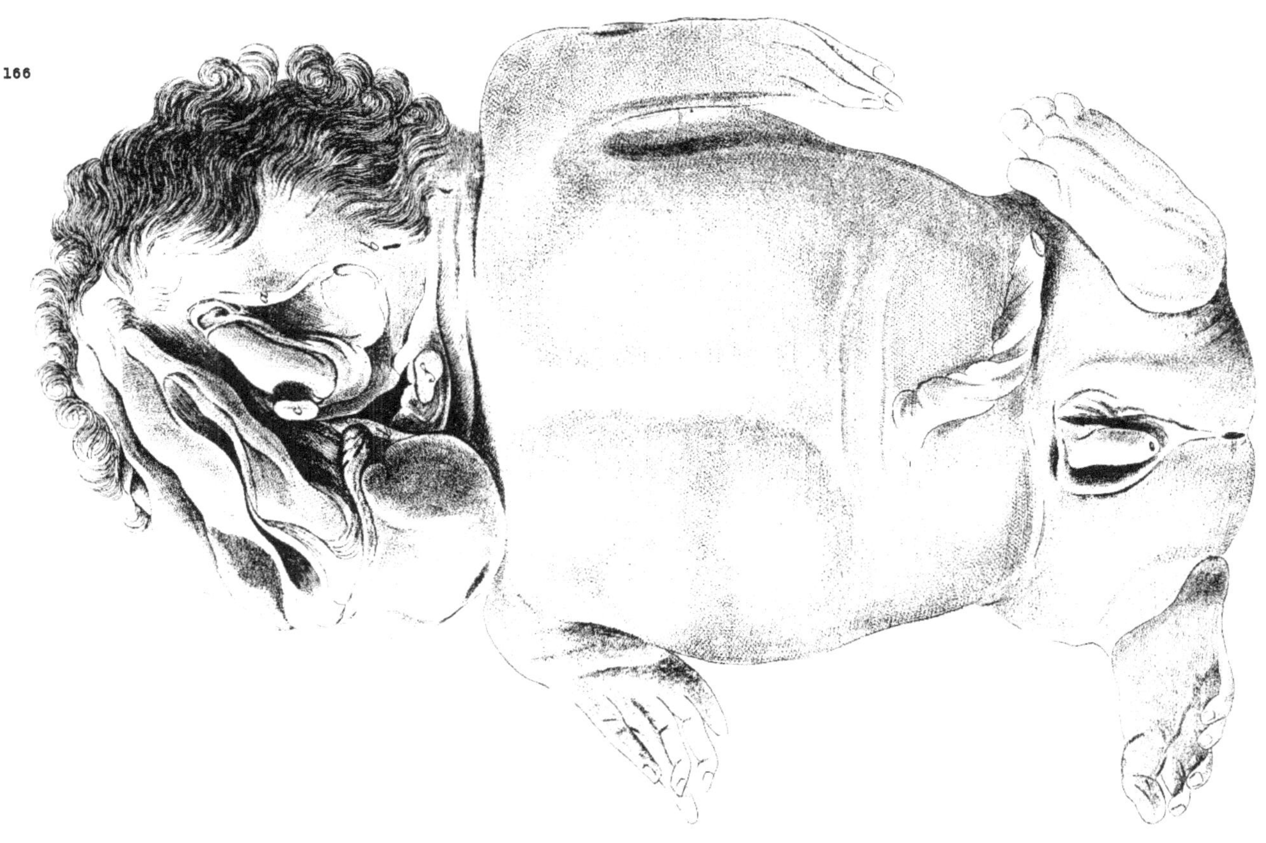

165: Ichthyosis congenita.

166: Infant with severe deformity of the limbs
and face with the lower jaw completely missing.

167

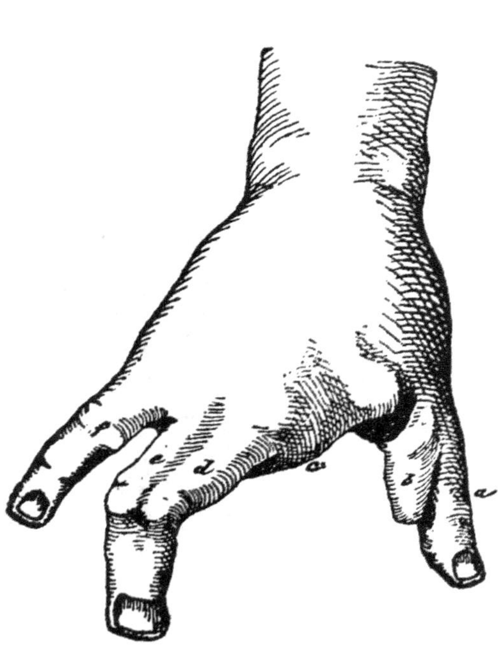

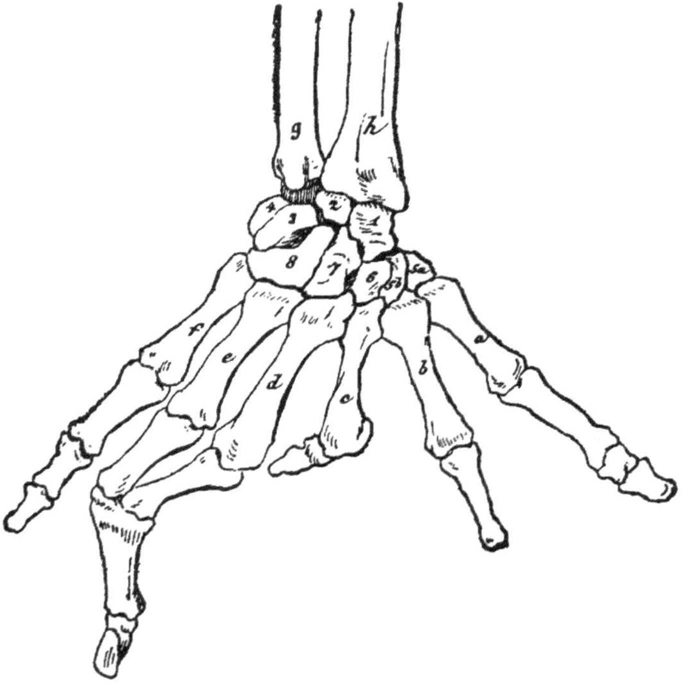

168

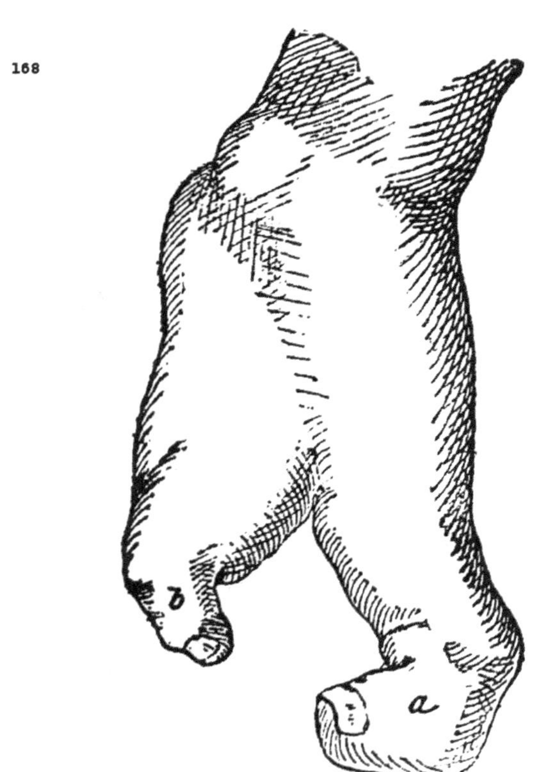

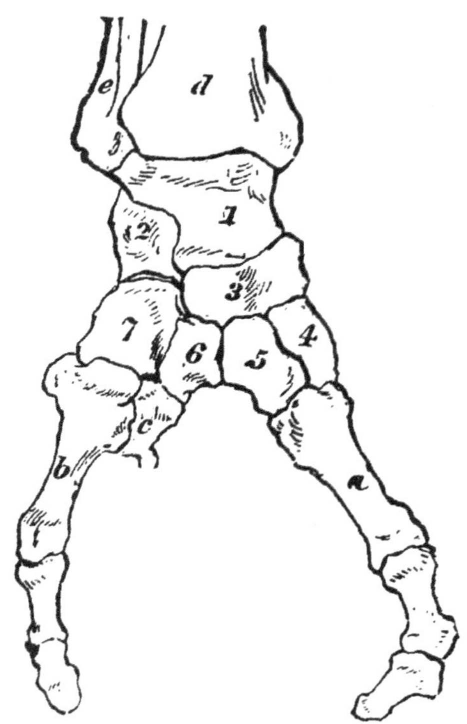

167: Malformation of the right hand (perochirus) with coalescence of the fingers (After Otto).

168: Peropus dexter.

169

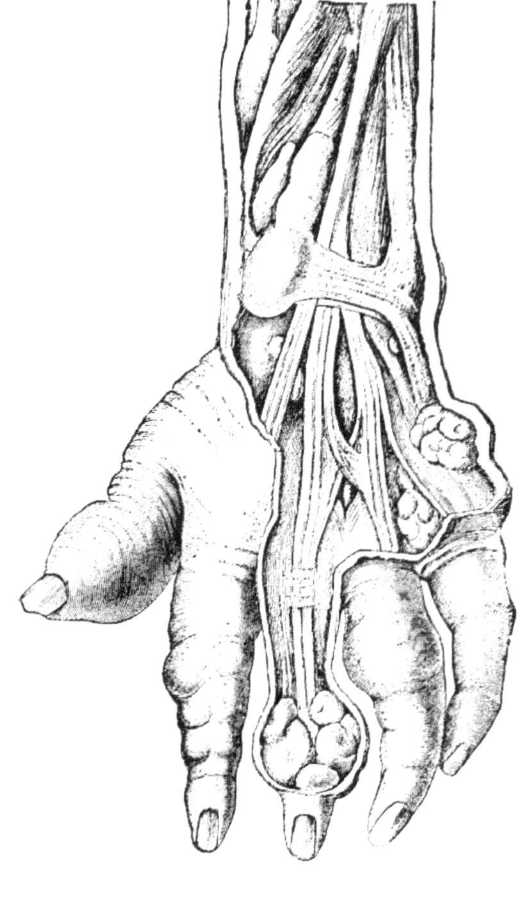

170

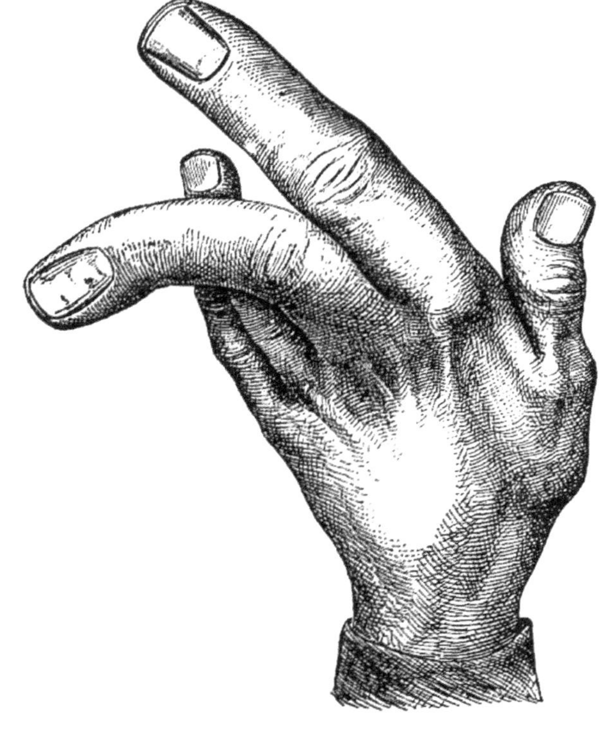

171

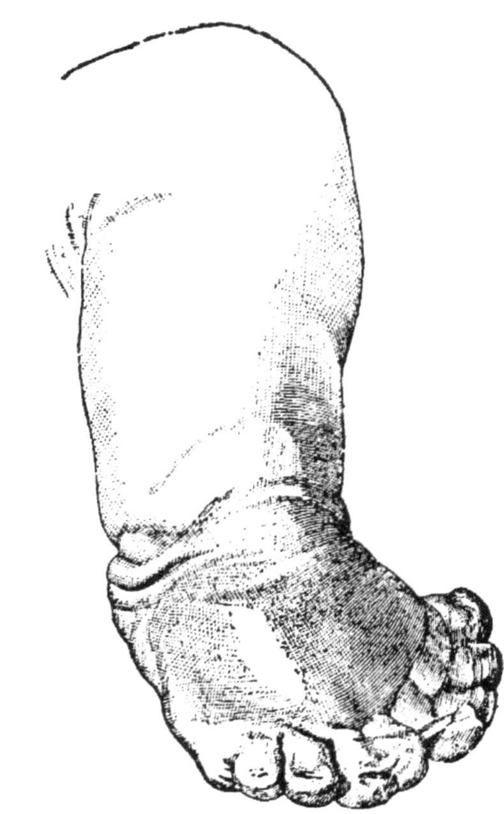

172

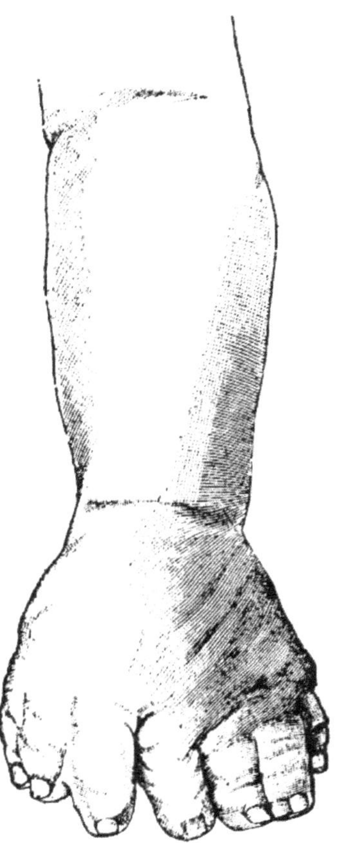

169: Gouty nodes of the hand (After lancereaux).   170: Hypertrophied fingers.   171: Polydatylism and syndactylism of the right foot.   172: Polydatylism and syndactylism of the left hand.

173

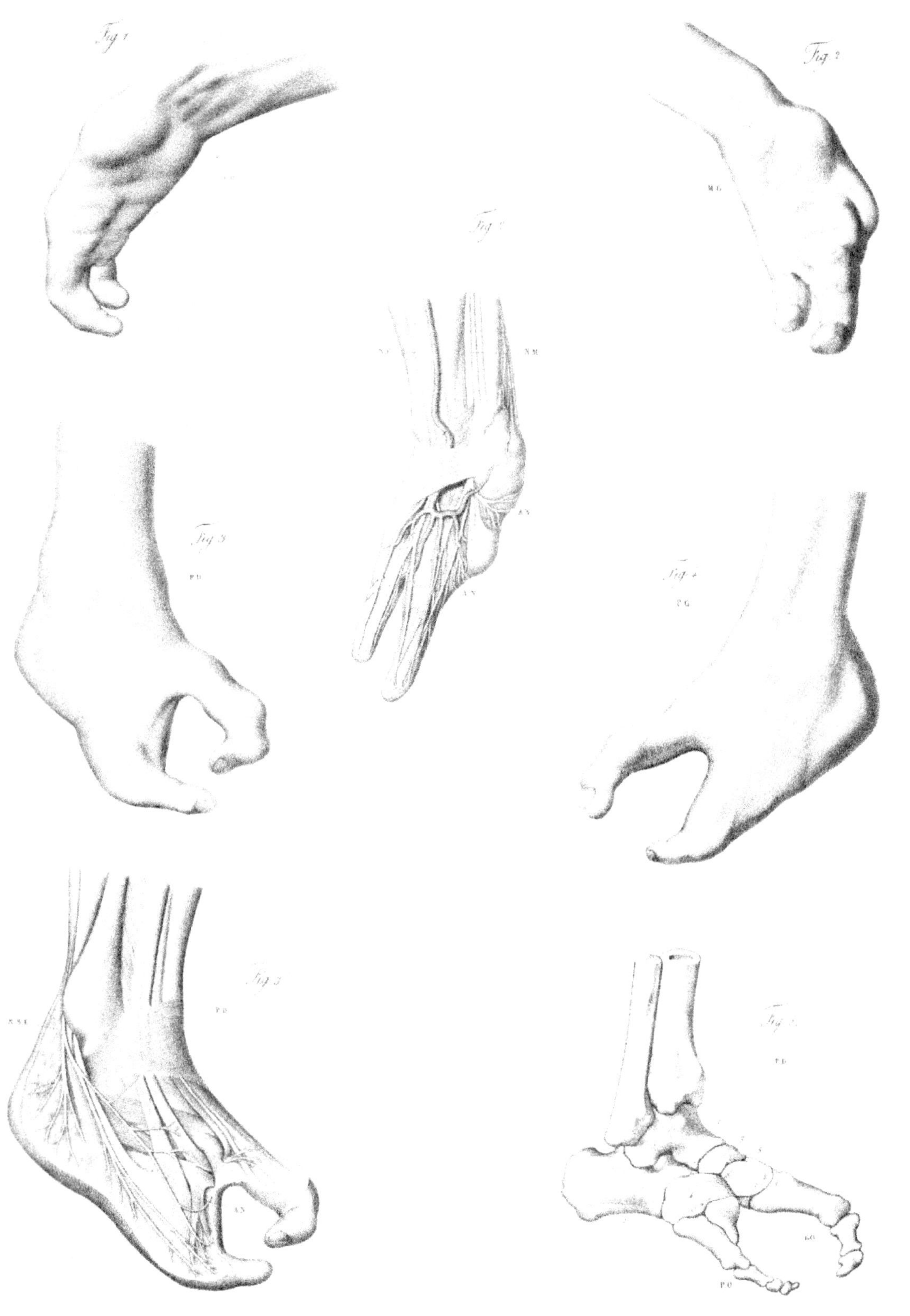

173: Hand and foot deformities; lobster claw or
split hand/split foot deformity.

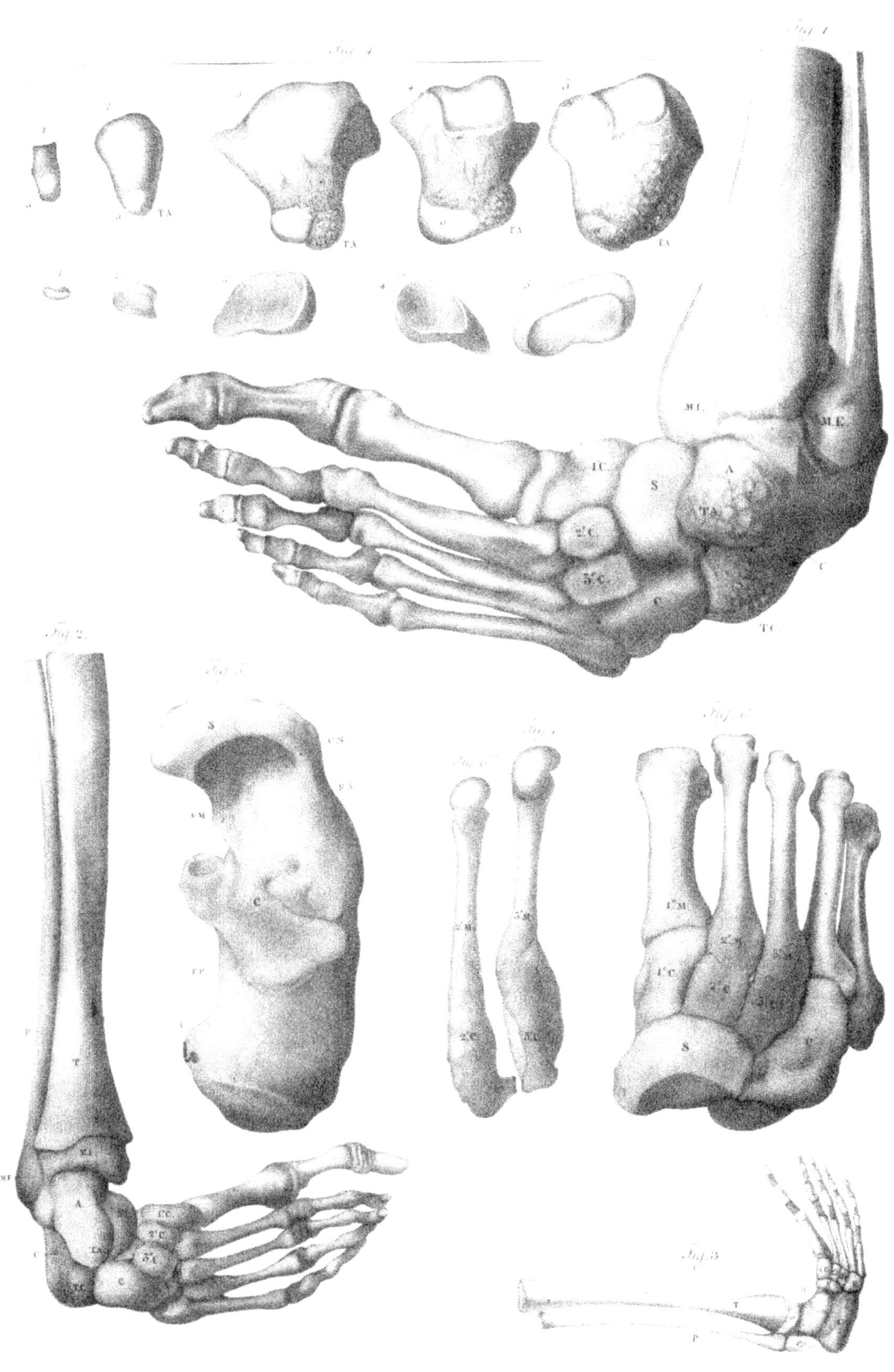

174: Leg and foot bones, clubfoot.

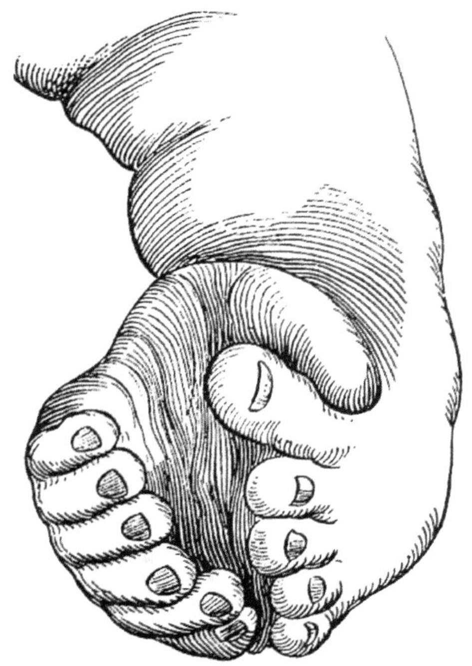

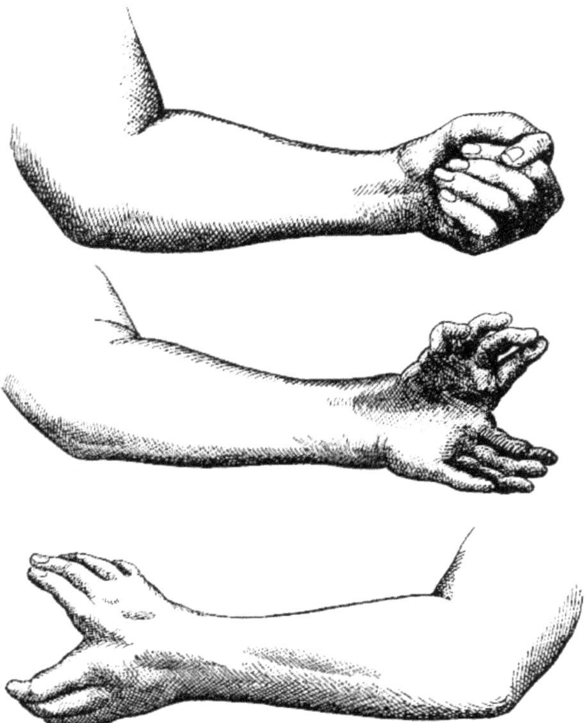

MALFORMATION & ANOMALIES OF THE LIMBS AND EXTREMITIES

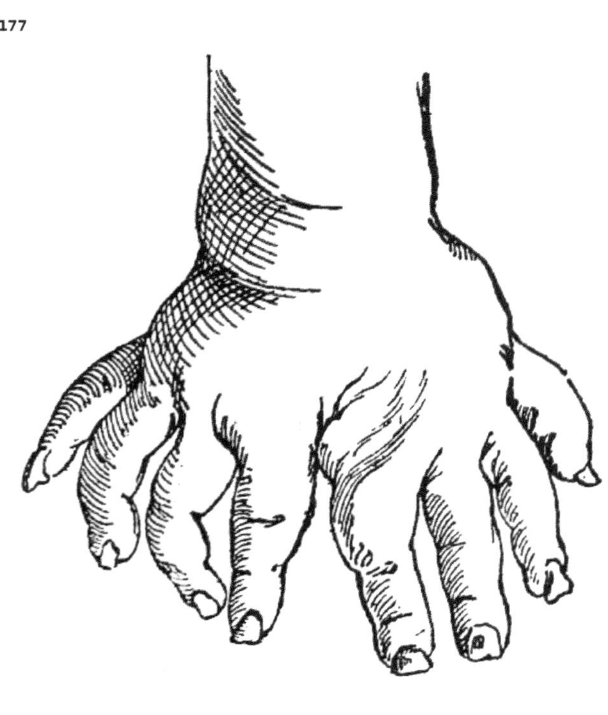

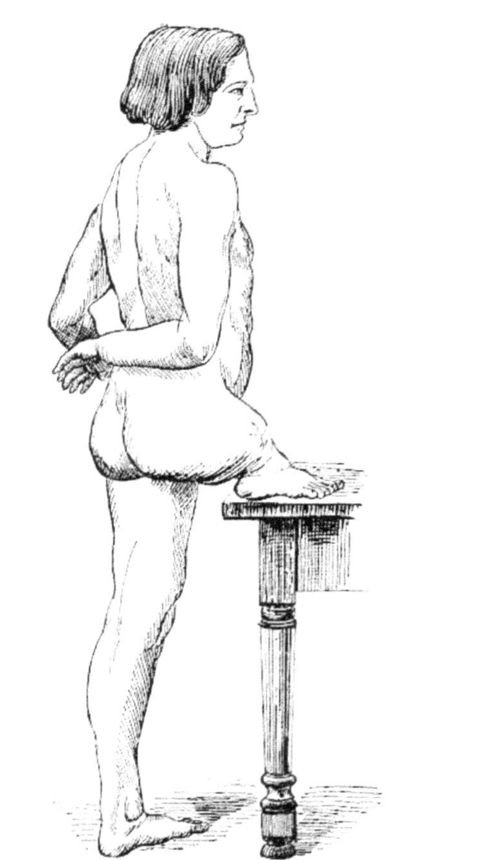

175: Double foot (Bull).   176: Double hand (Murray).   177: Supernumerary fingers.   178: Defective development of the right leg.

179

180

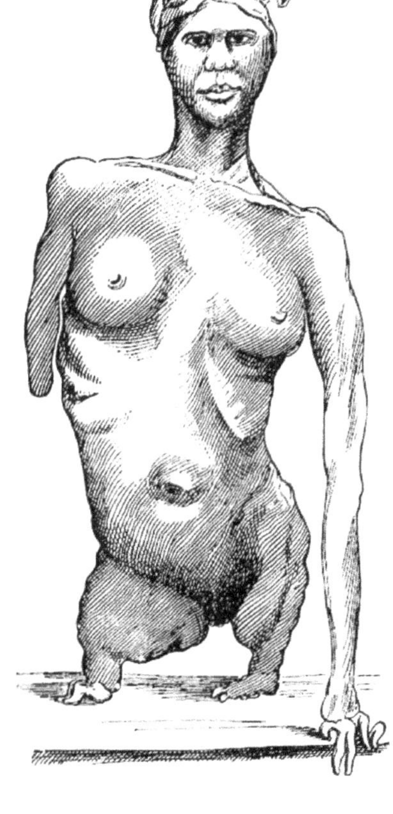

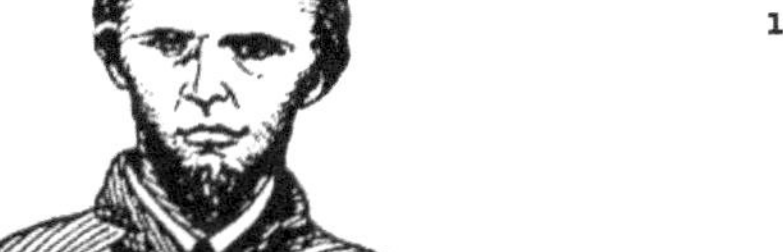

181

182

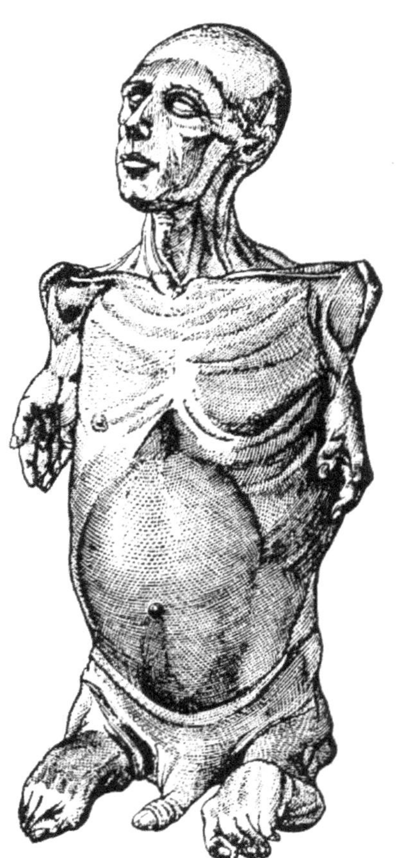

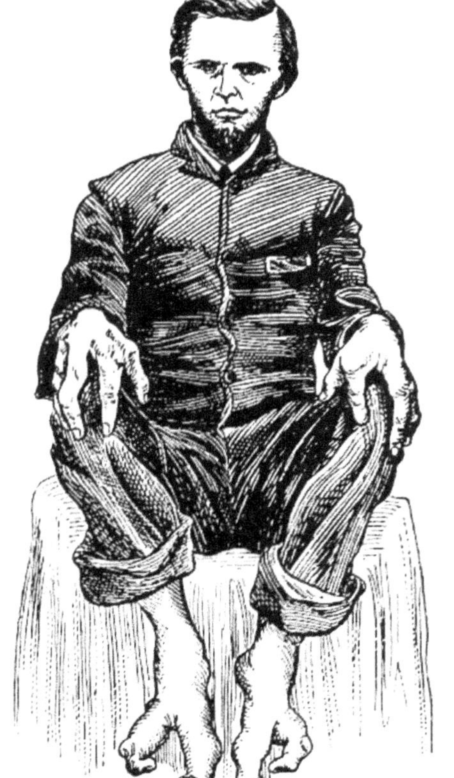

179: Legs represented by cellular tissue and fat covered by skin.

180: Defective development of the upper and lower limbs.

181: Male with deformed upper and lower limbs.

182: Suppression and deformity of digits (Köher).

183

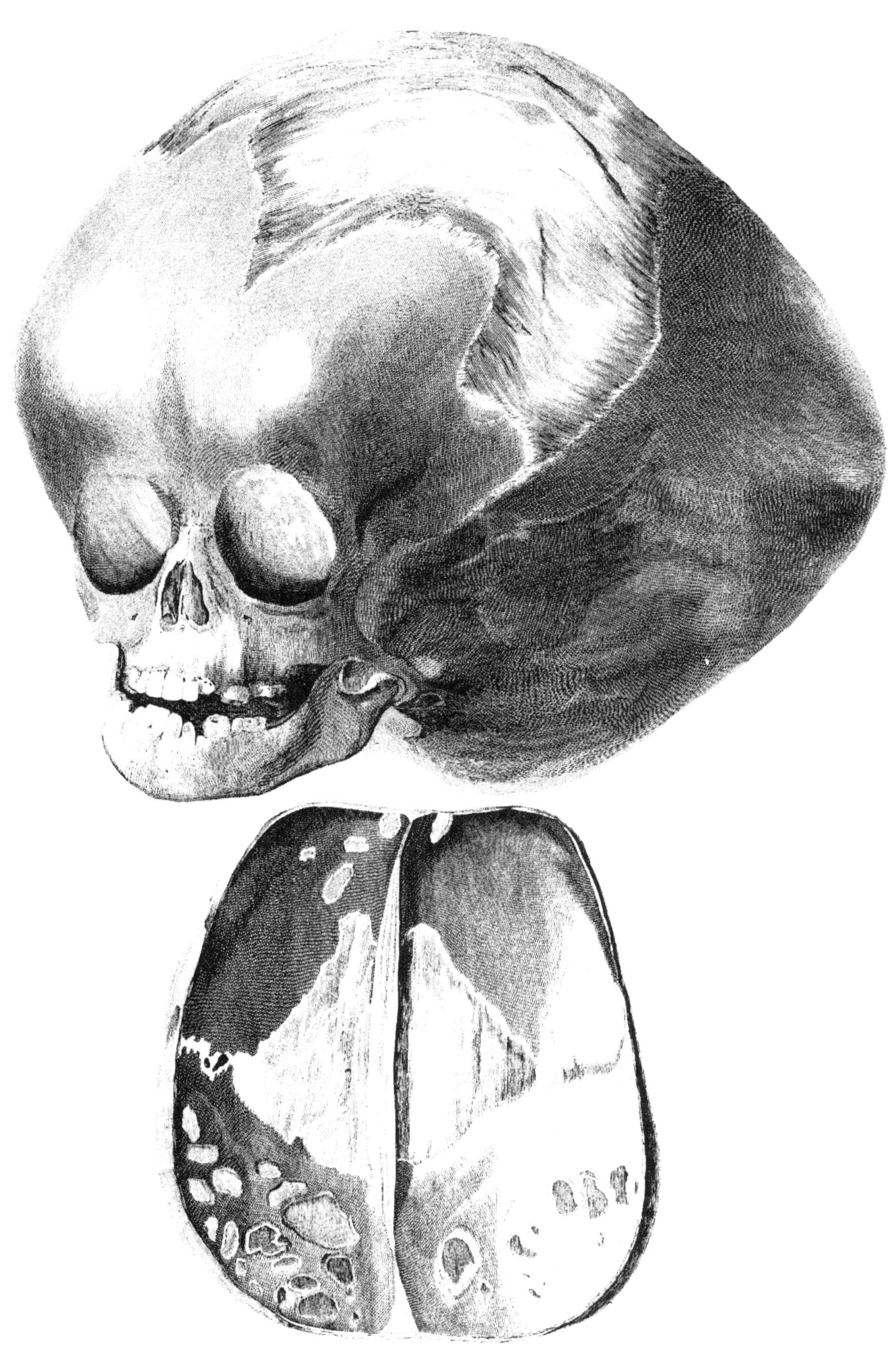

183: Skull of a child with hydrocephalus.

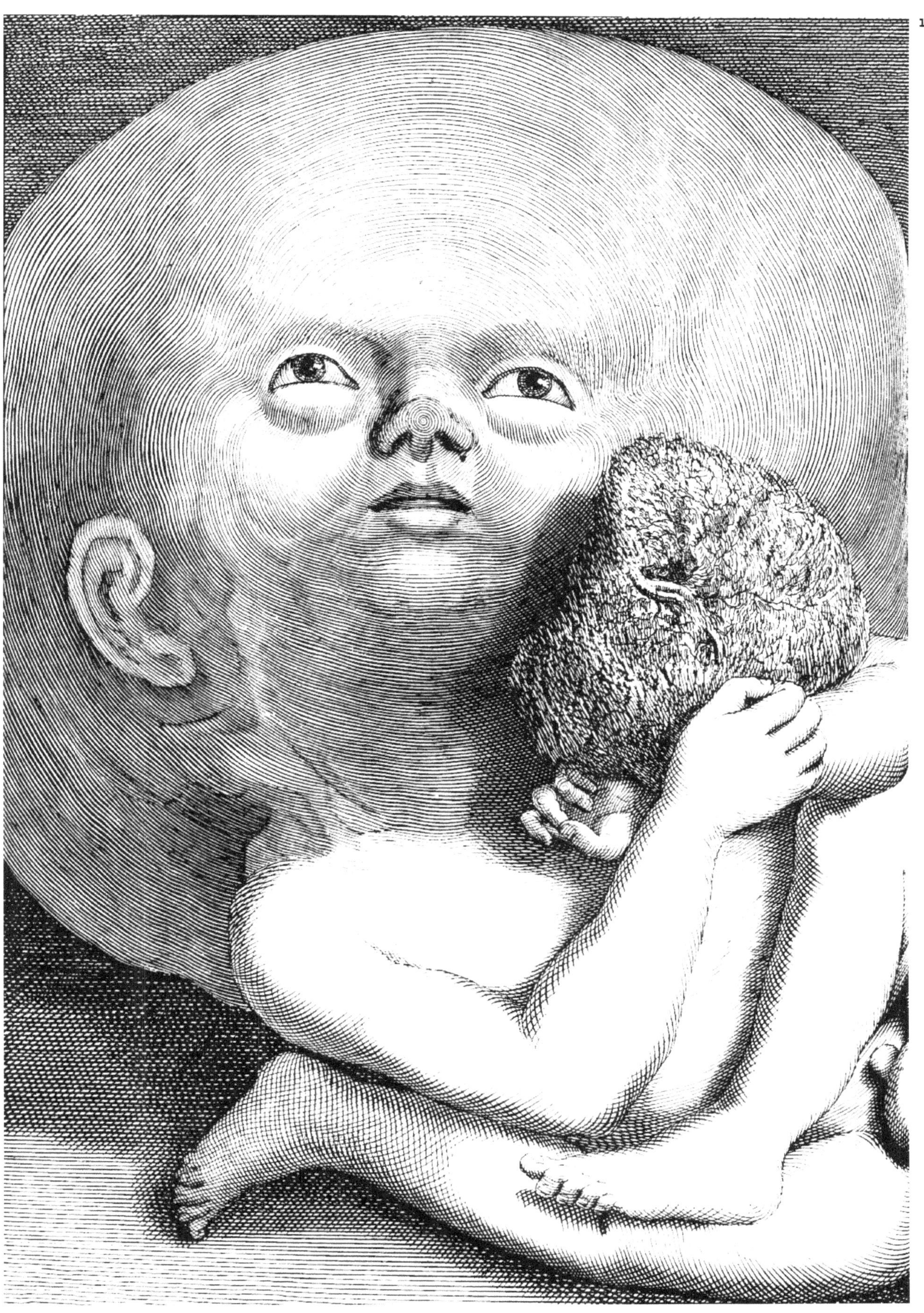

184: Infant with hydrocephalus.

185

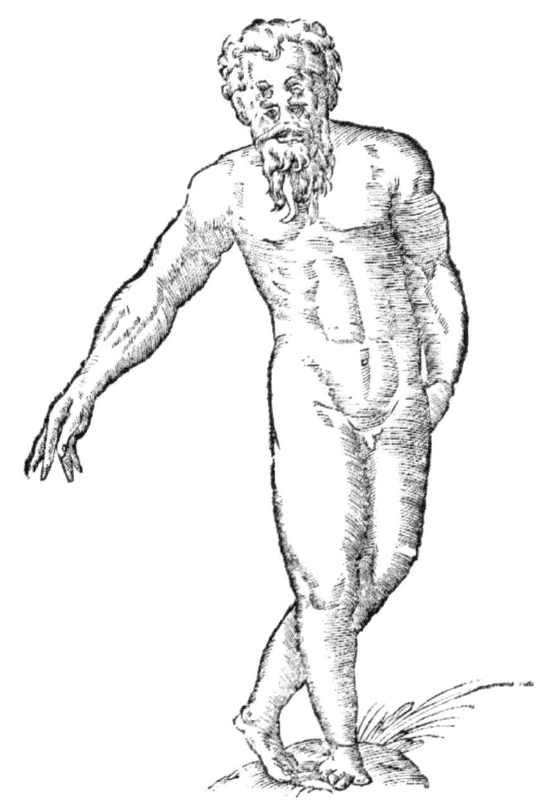

186

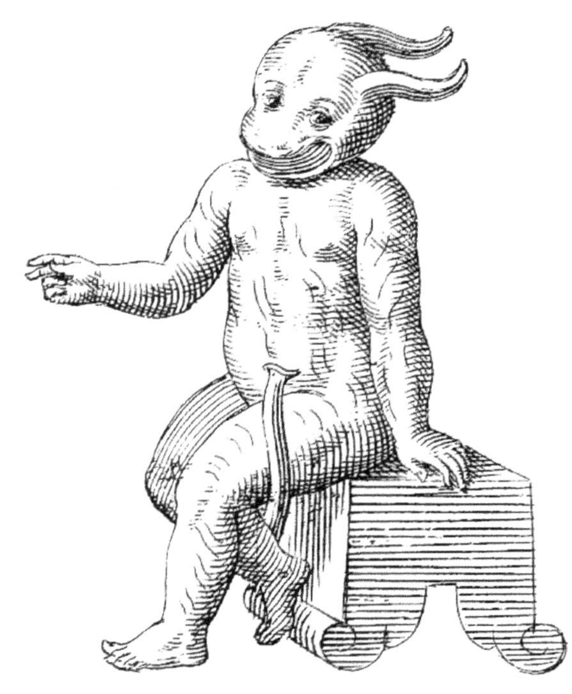

187

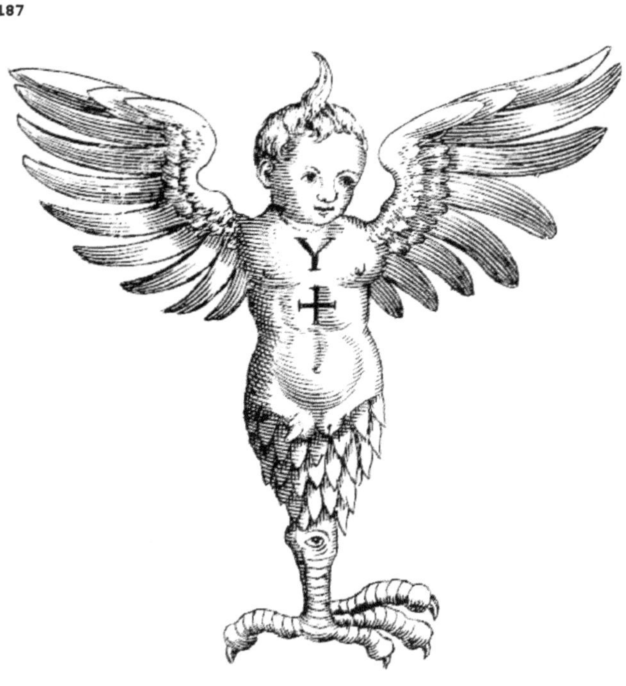

188

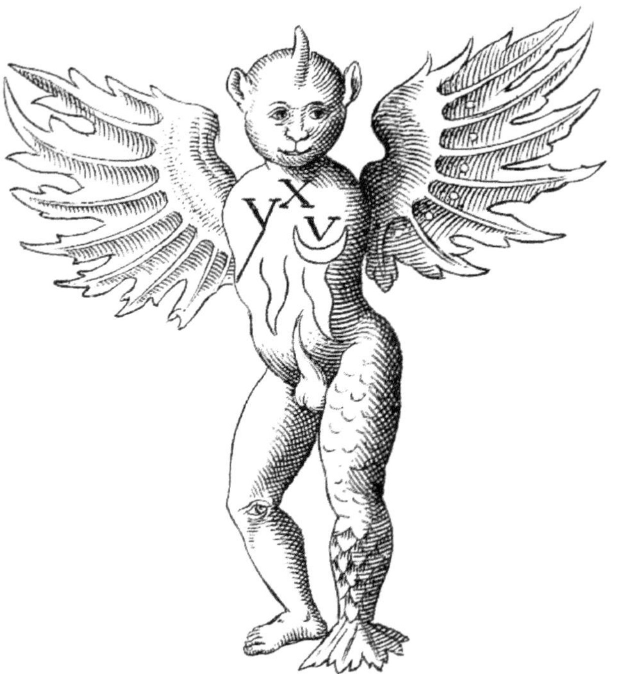

185: A man with four eyes.

186: A horned-headed infant.

187: A monstrous infant with wings and a tallon with an eye in place of its legs.

188: A monstrous infant with wings, a single horn on its head, webbed foot, scaled leg and and an additional eye on its leg.

189

190

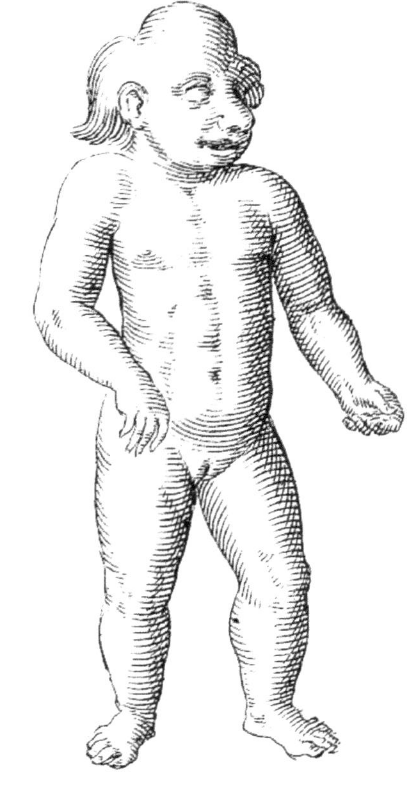

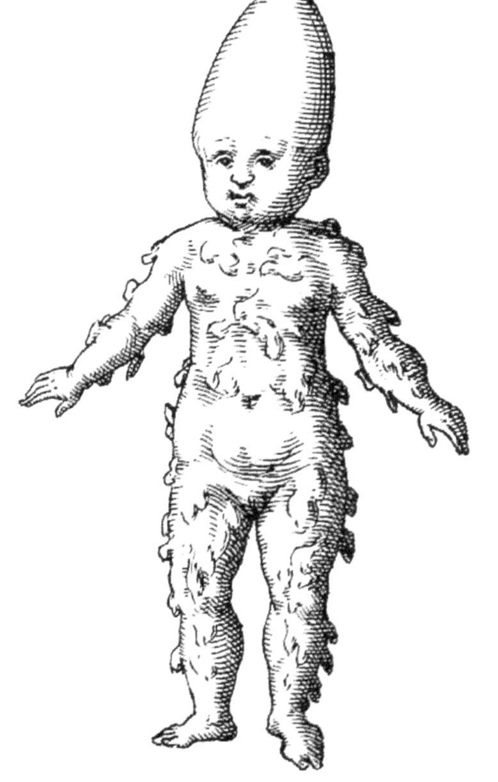

191

192

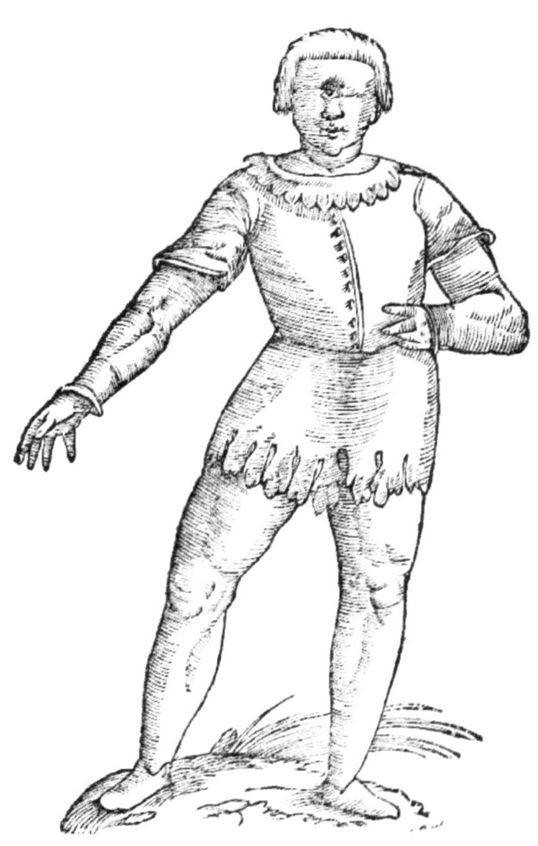

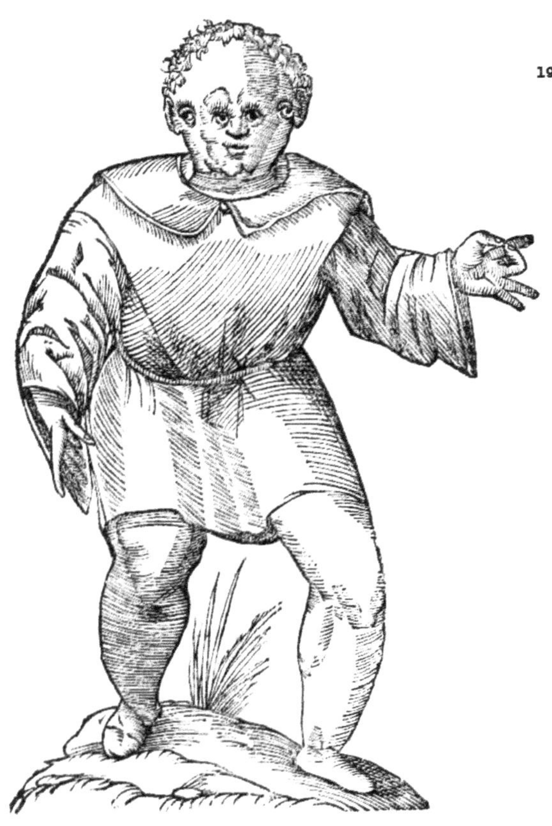

189: 'Monstrous birth of a child with a horrendous head'.

190: 'A monstrous infant with a hideous appearance and a misshapen head'.

191: A man born with one eye.

192: A man born with four eyes.

193

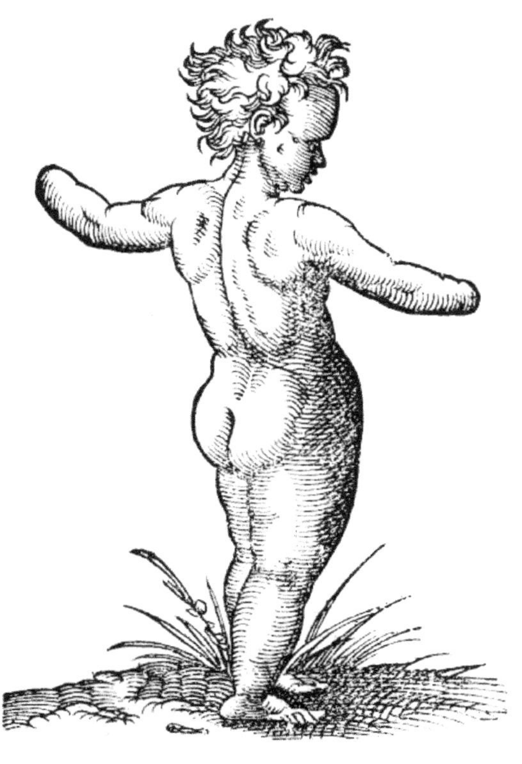

194

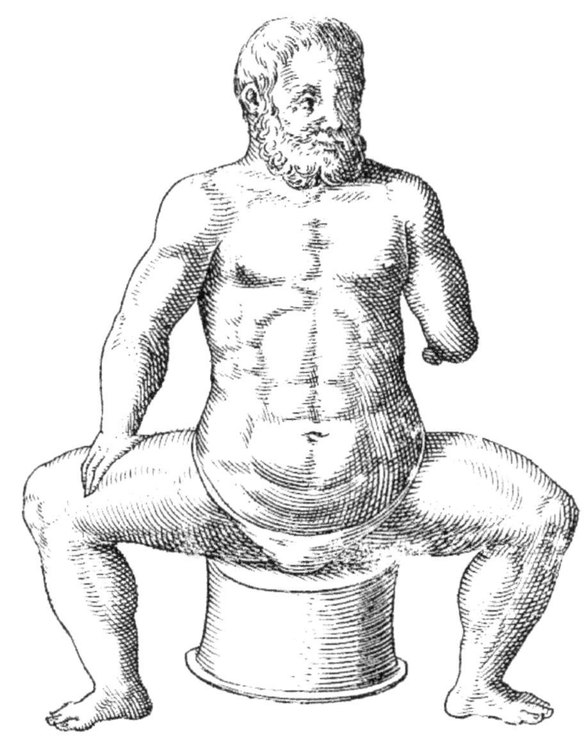

195

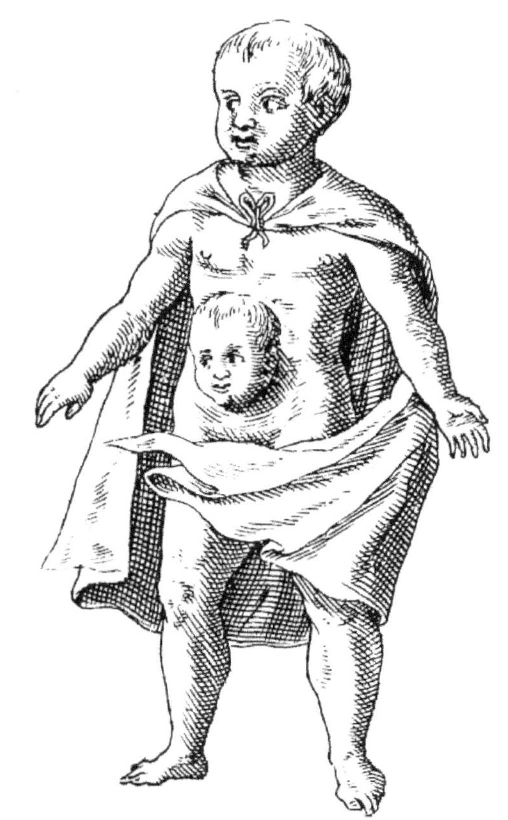

196

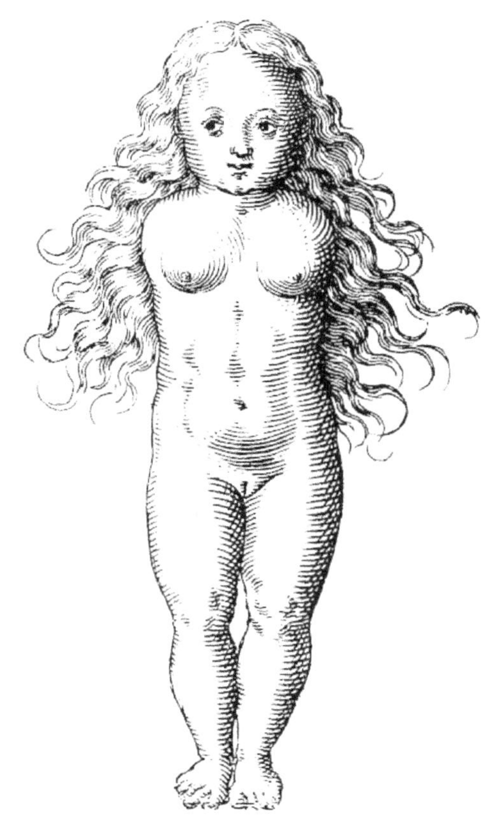

193: An infant birn without hands.

194: Severe deformity of the left limb and extremitites.

195: A child with a second head petruding from the abdomen.

196: A female infant born without upper limbs.

197

198

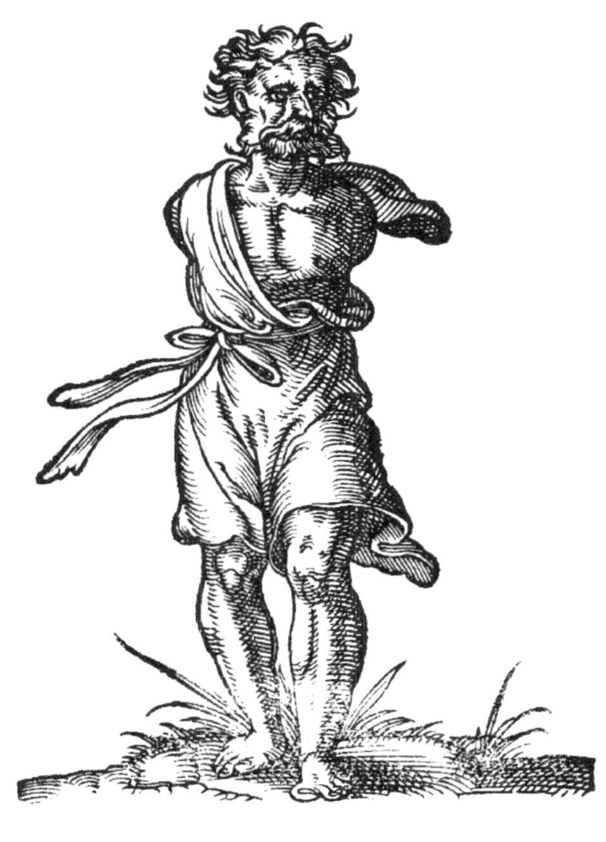

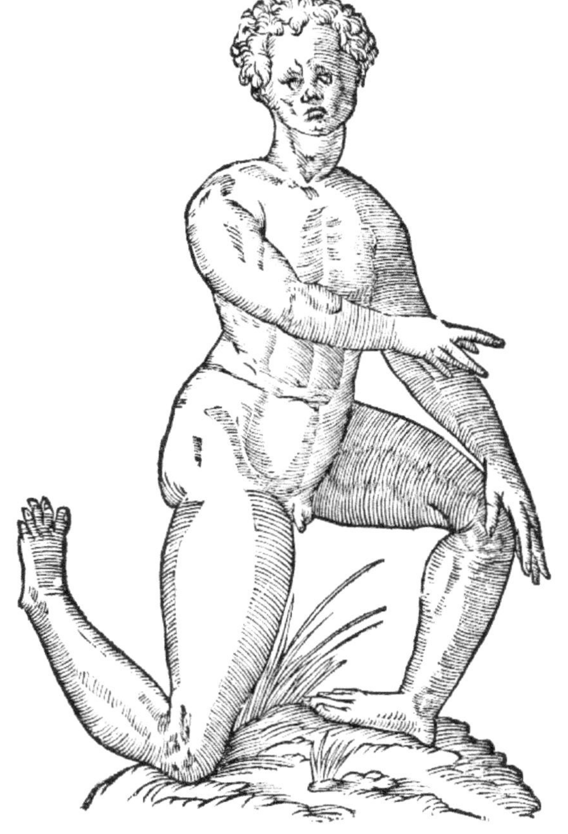

199

200

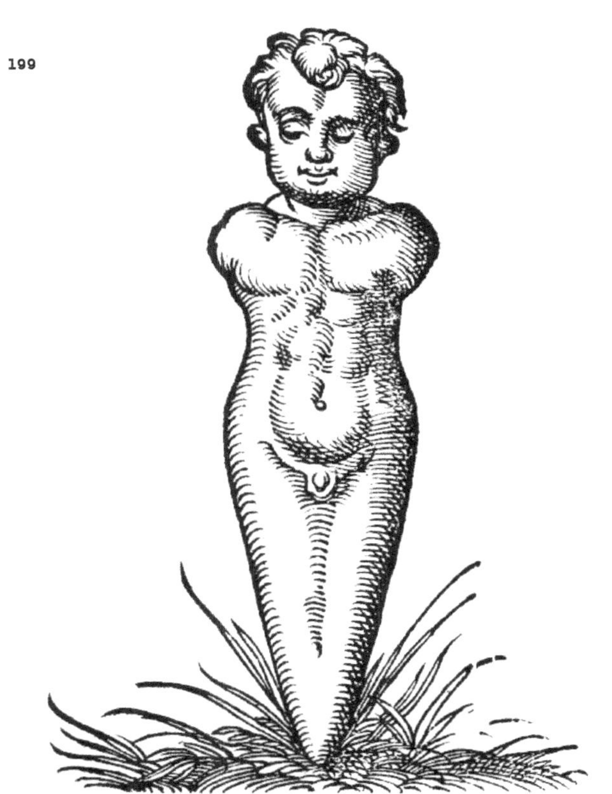

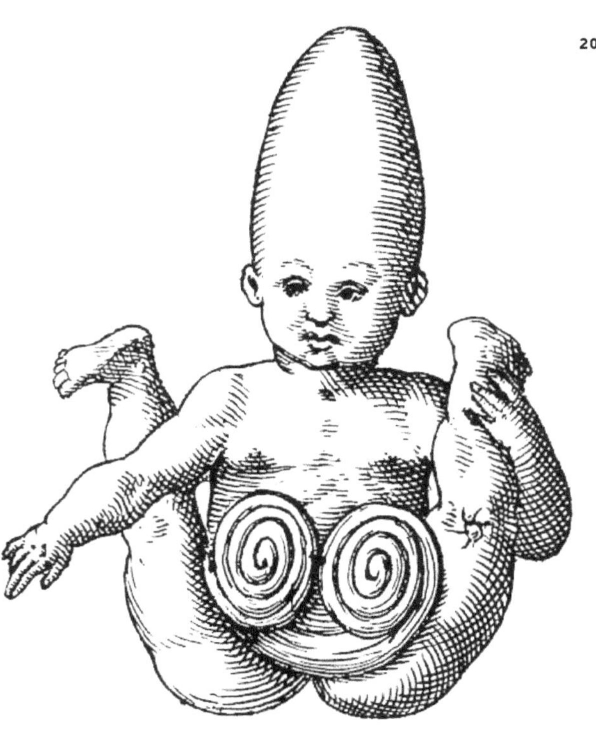

197: A man withour upper limbs.

198: A man with inverted feet.

199: An infant born with no arms and fused lower limbs.

200: An infant born with no spine and an exposed intestine.

201

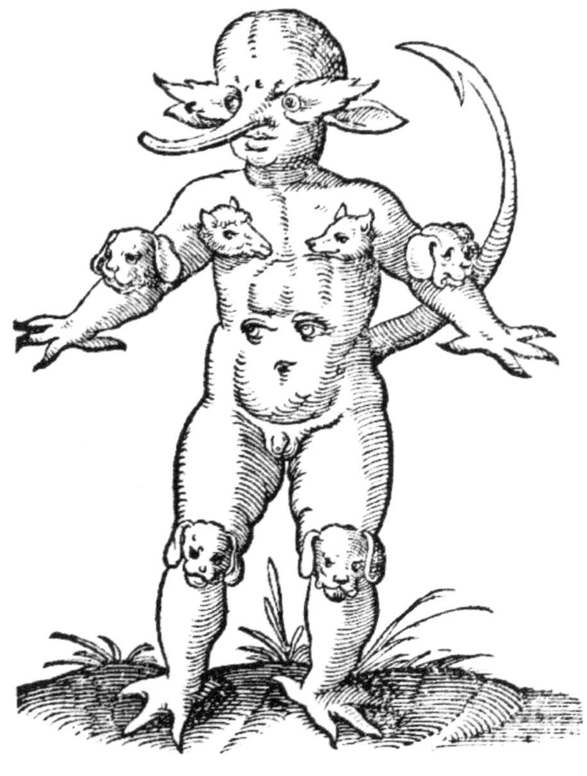

202

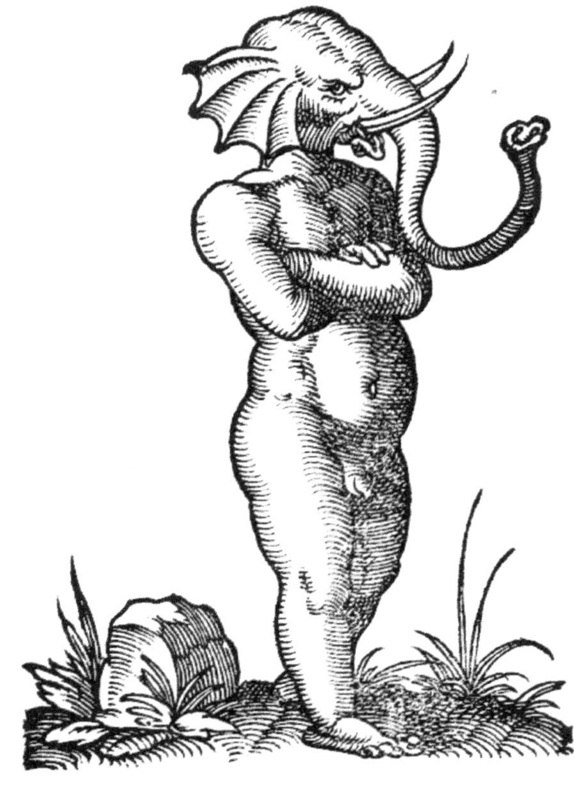

203

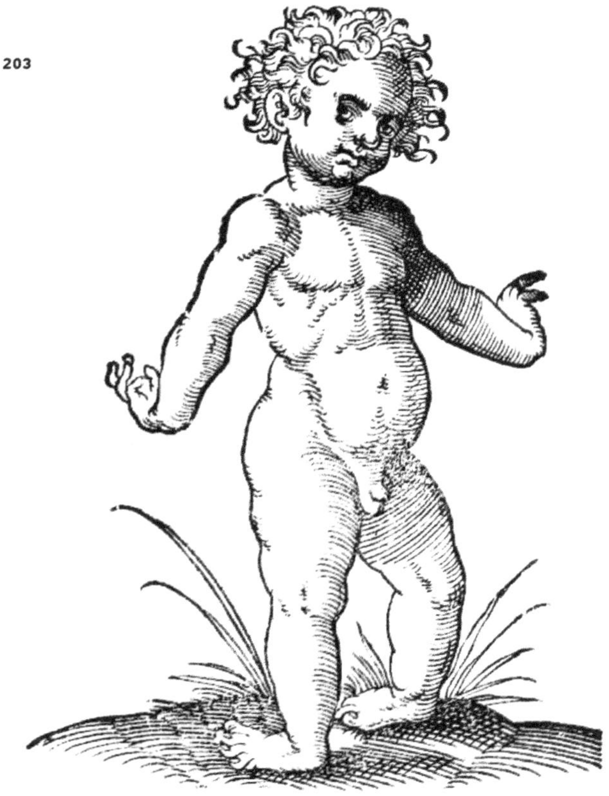

204

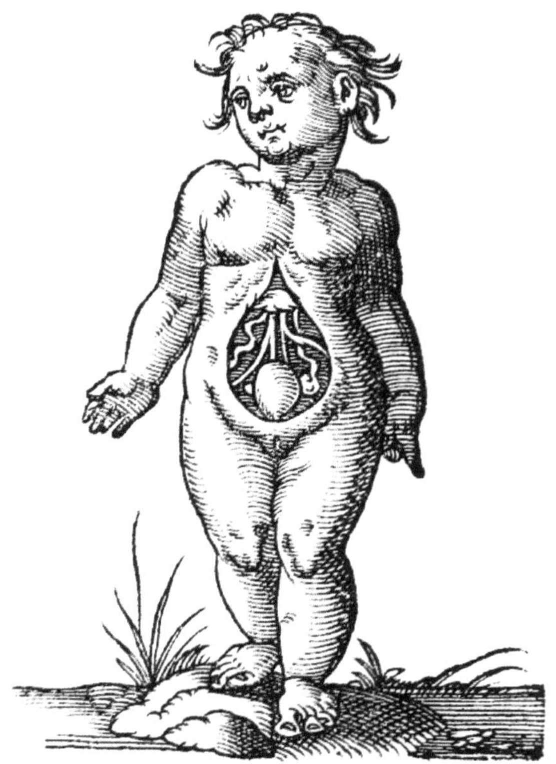

201: A monstrous infant with animal heads protruding from it's body and eyes in its abdomen.

202: An infant born with the head of an elephant.

203: An infant with inverted hands and feet.

204: An infant born with exposed internal organs.

205

206

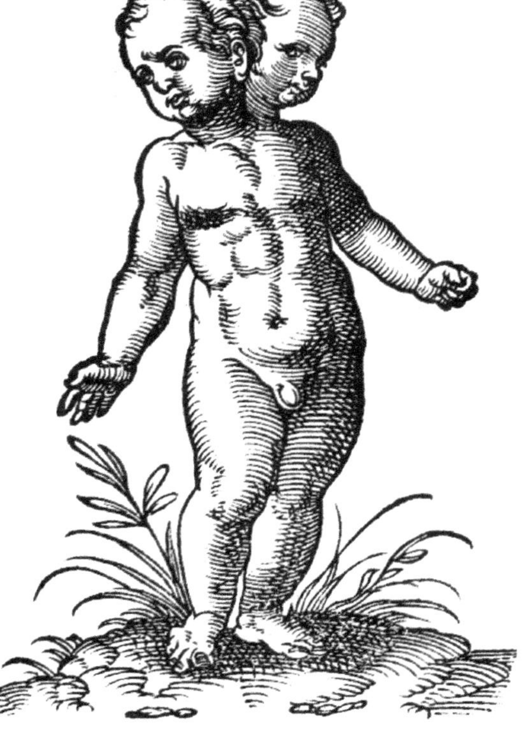

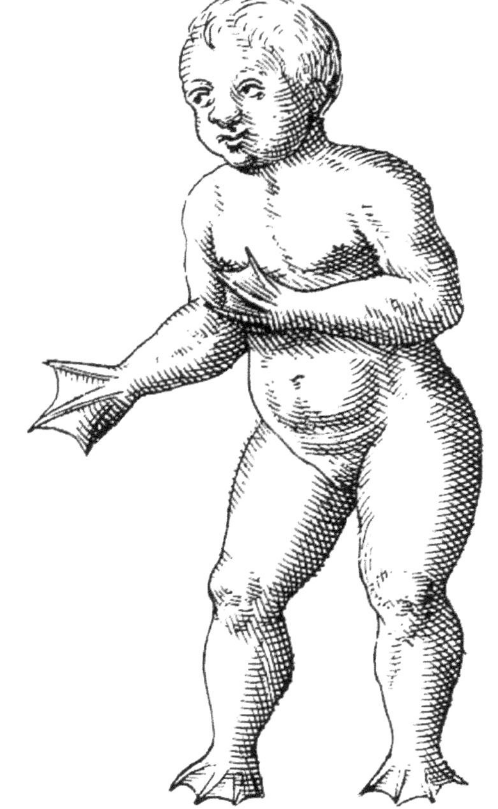

207

208

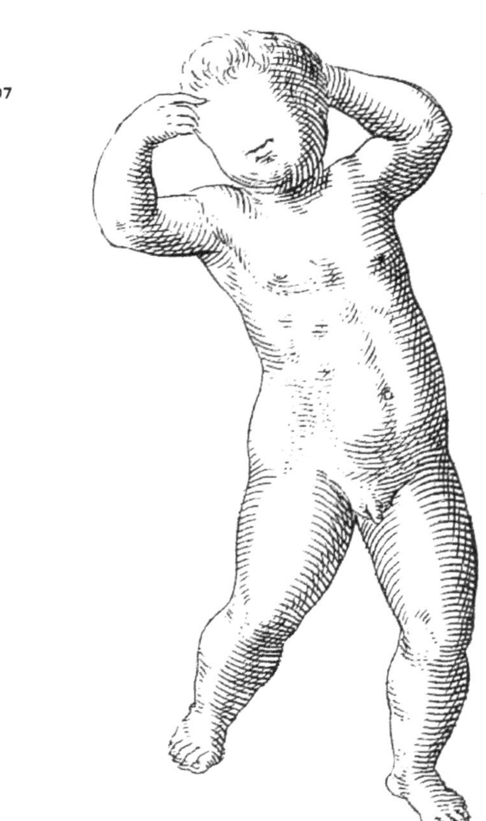

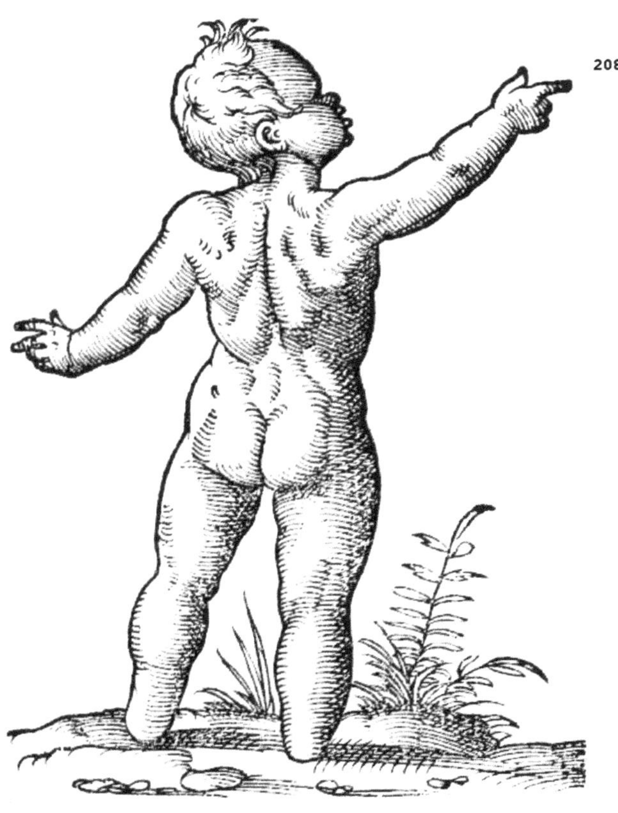

205: An infant born with two heads.   206: An infant born with webbed hands and feet.   207: An infant born without eyes.   208: An infant born without feet.

209

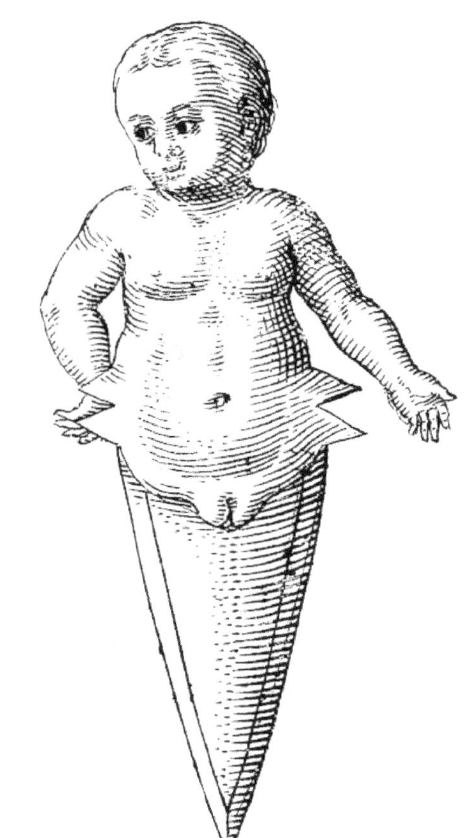

210

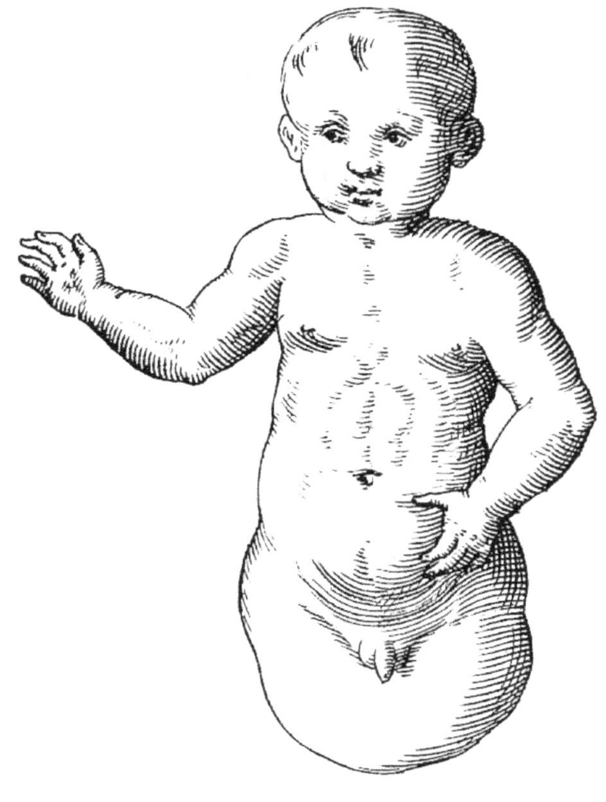

211

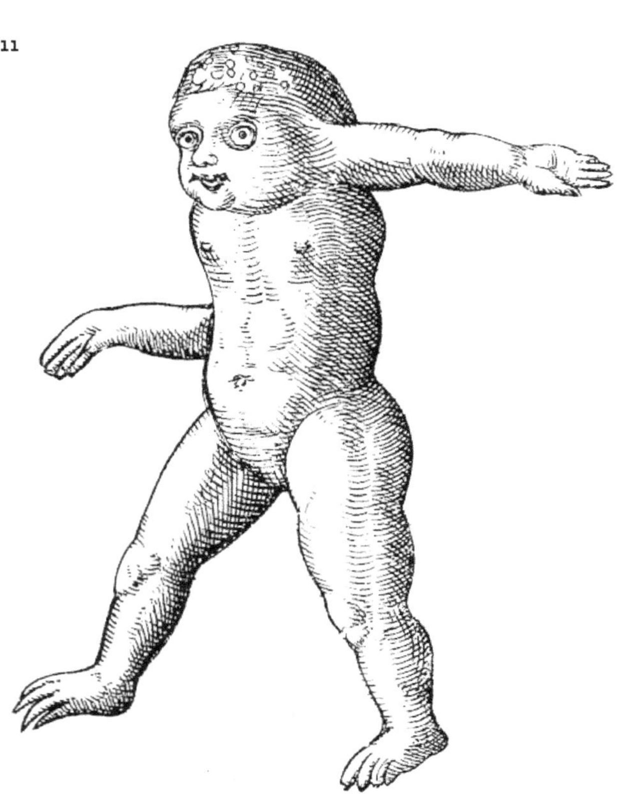

212

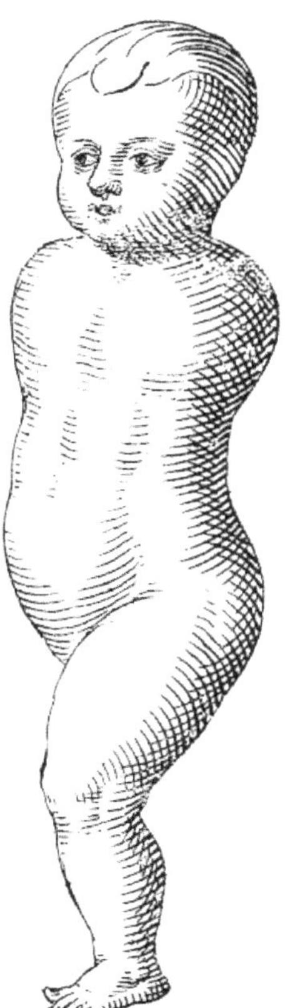

209: An infant born without human feet with claws projecting from its sides.

210: An infant born without lower limbs.

211: An infants with an arm in place of the ear.

212: An infant born without upper limbs and only one leg.

213

214

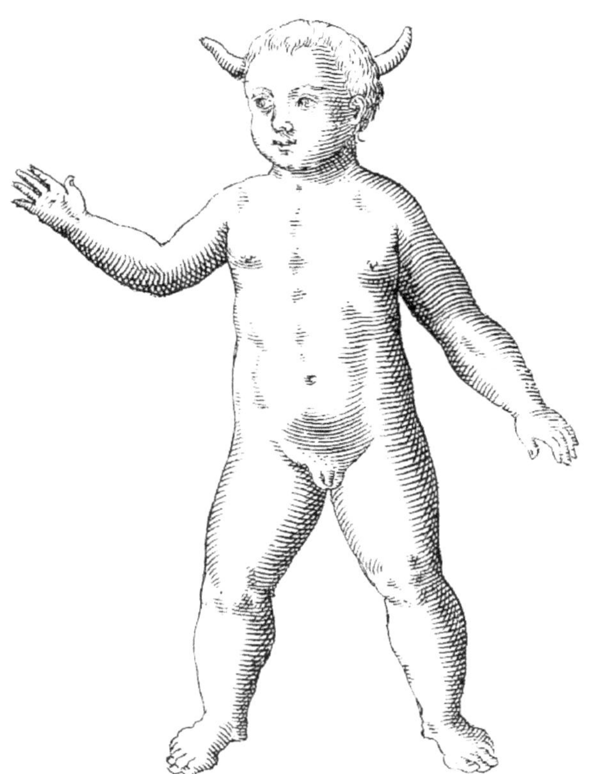

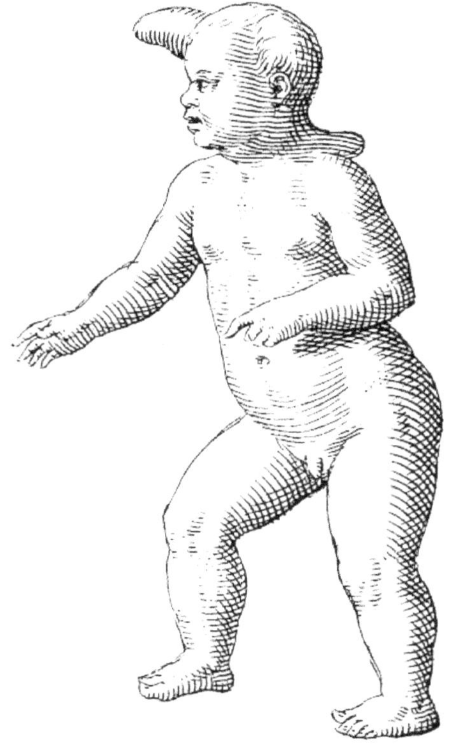

215

216

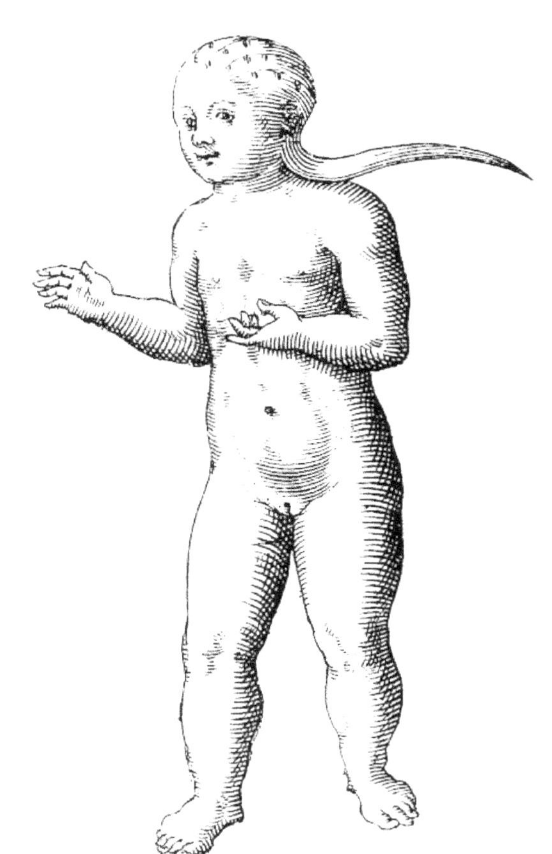

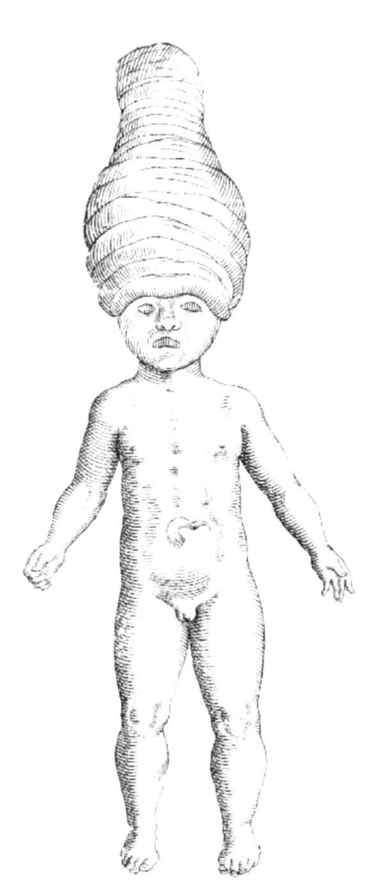

213: An infant with two horns growing from its head.

214: Infant with large growth at the front and back of its head.

215: An infant with a horn growing from the rear of its head.

216: Male infant whose head and face is covered with excess flesh.

217

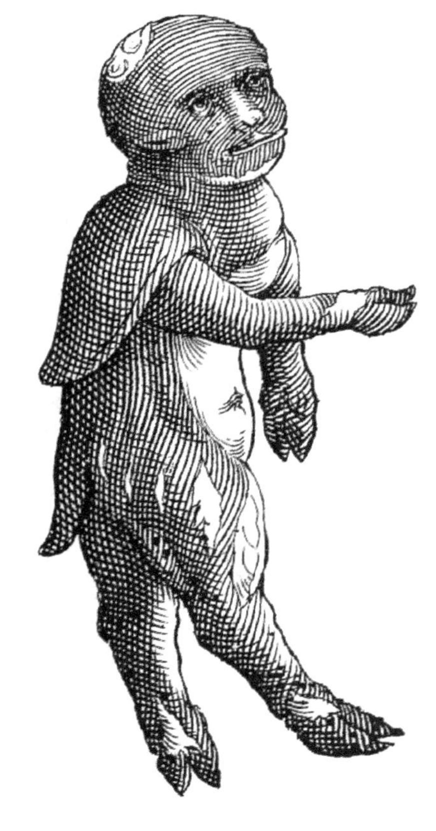

218

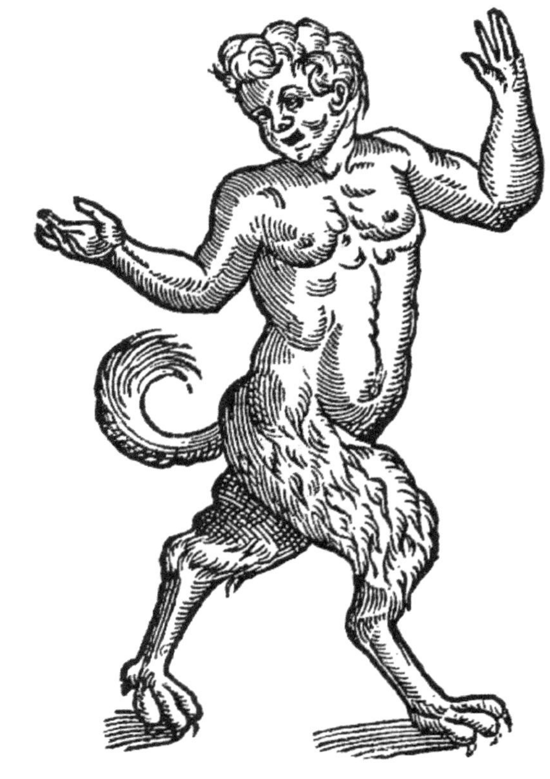

219

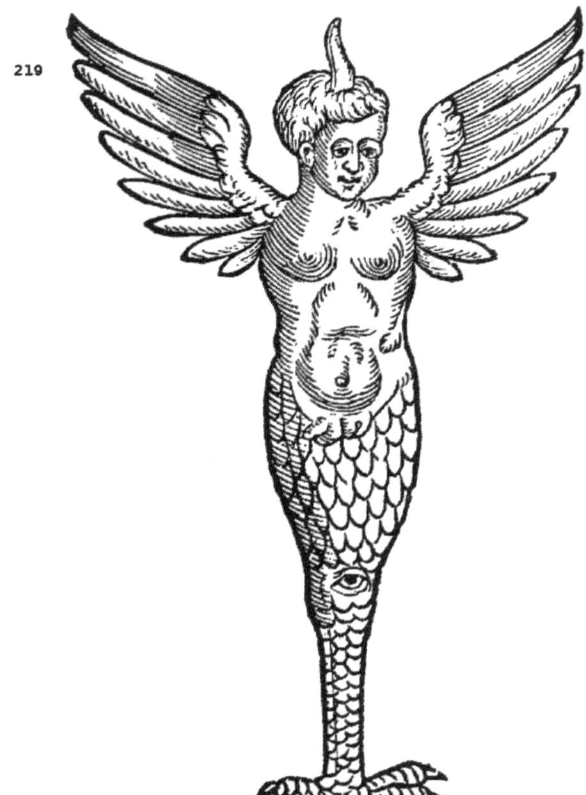

220

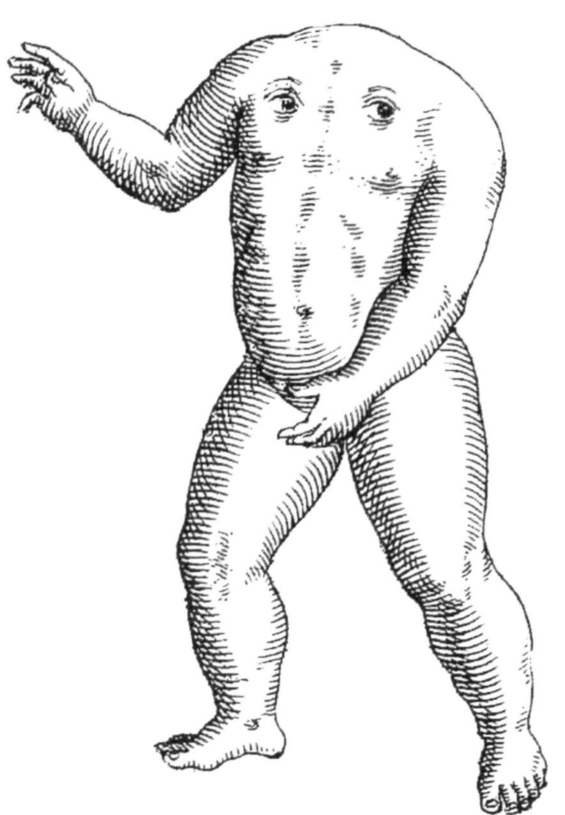

217: Monstrous being with the hood of a monk and the belly and feet of a calf.

218: "Dog-boy" (after Paré.

219: Bird-boy (after Paré).

220: Man born with eyes in his chest.

221

222

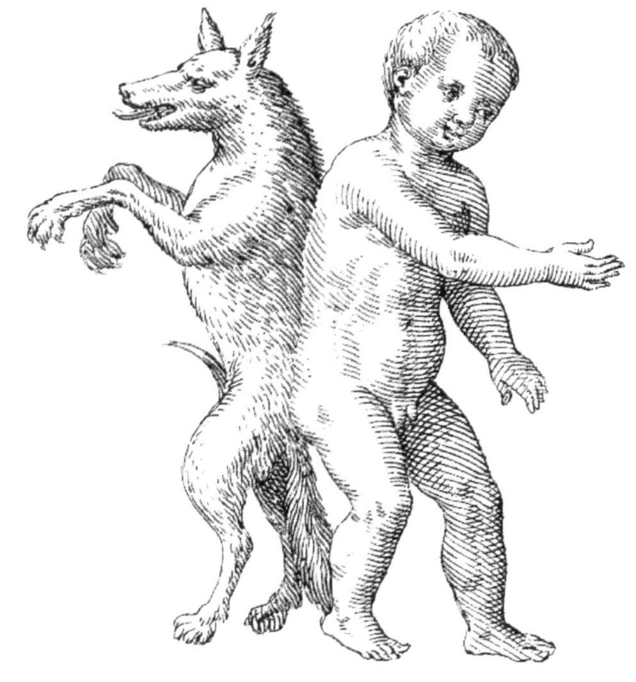

223

224

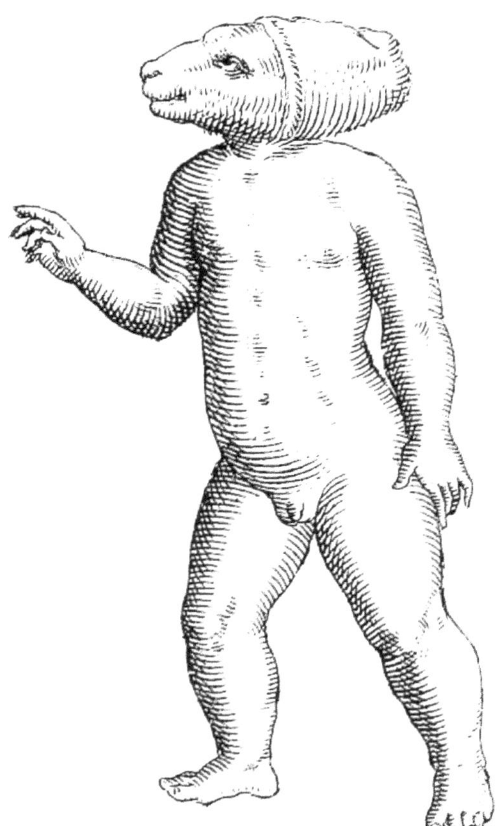

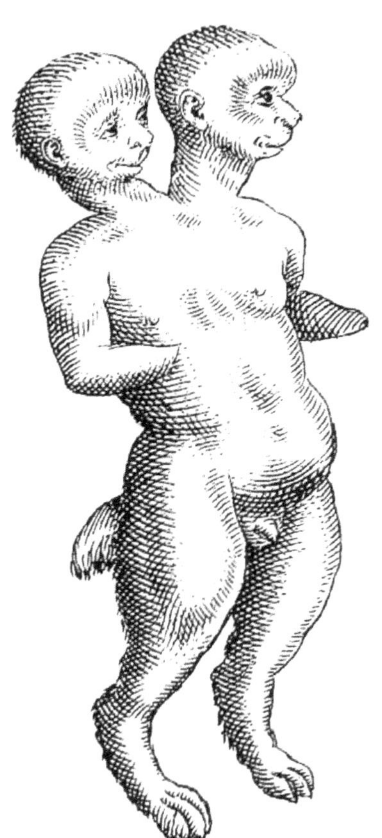

221: An infant with the ears of a hare.

222: An infant fused at the back with a wolf.

223: Male infant with a face that resembles that of a dog.

224: Human monster with two heads, mutilated arms and a fox's tail.

225

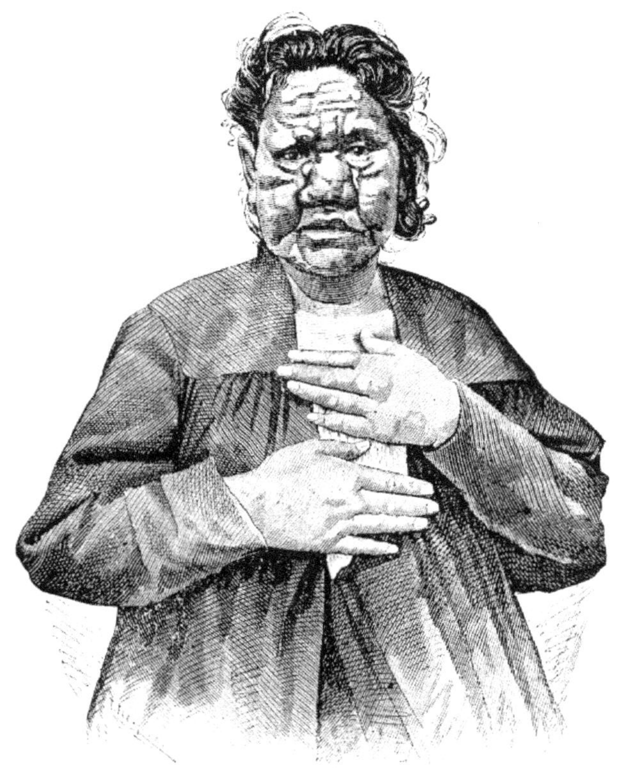

226

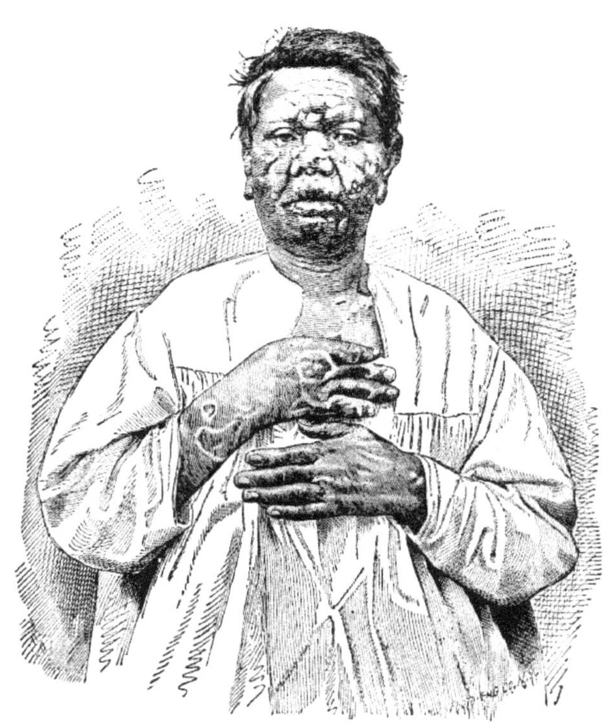

227

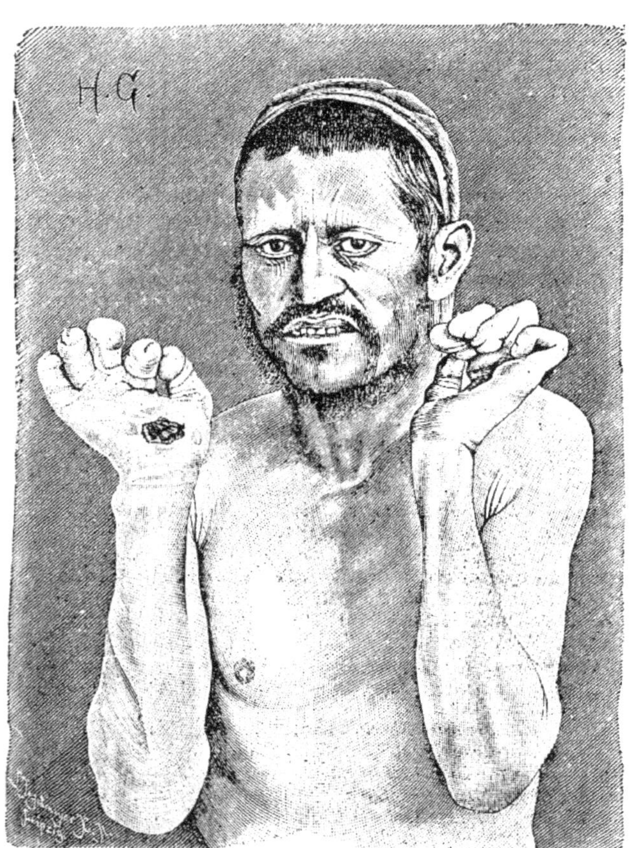

228

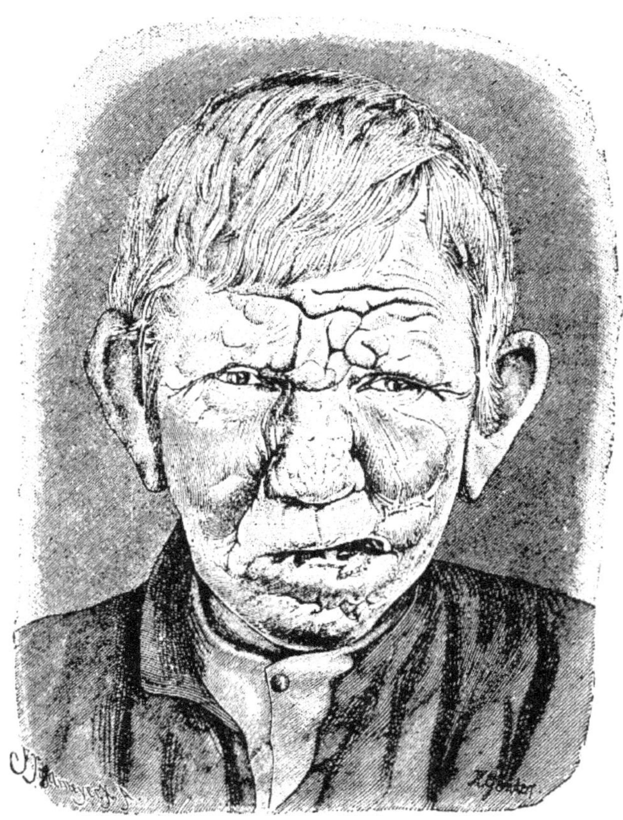

225: Leprosy.

226: Leprosy.

227: Lepra anaesthetica mutilans (After G. Münch).

228: Leontiasis leprosa.

229

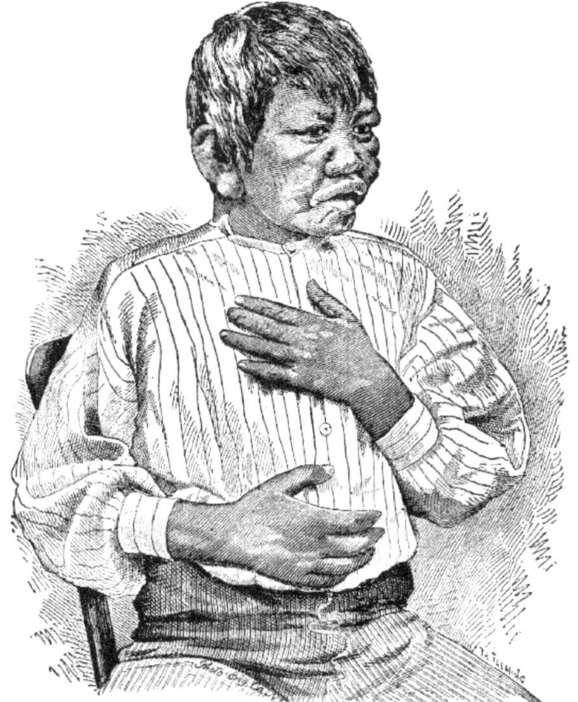

230

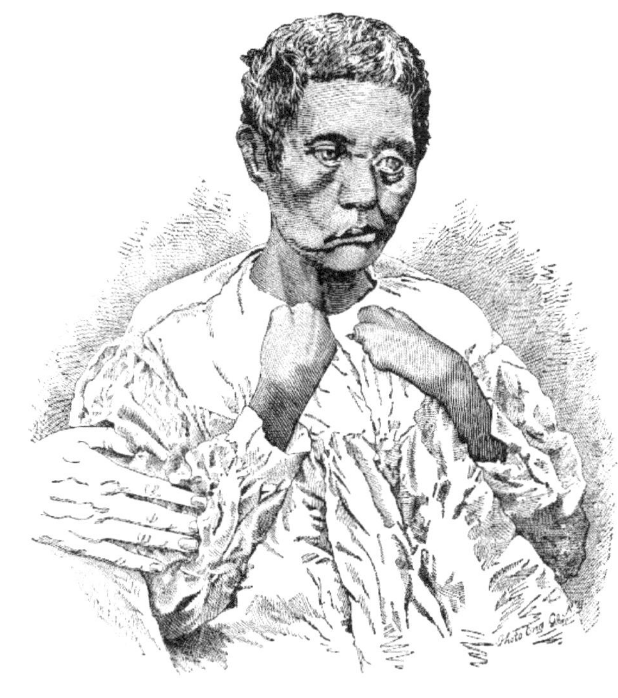

231

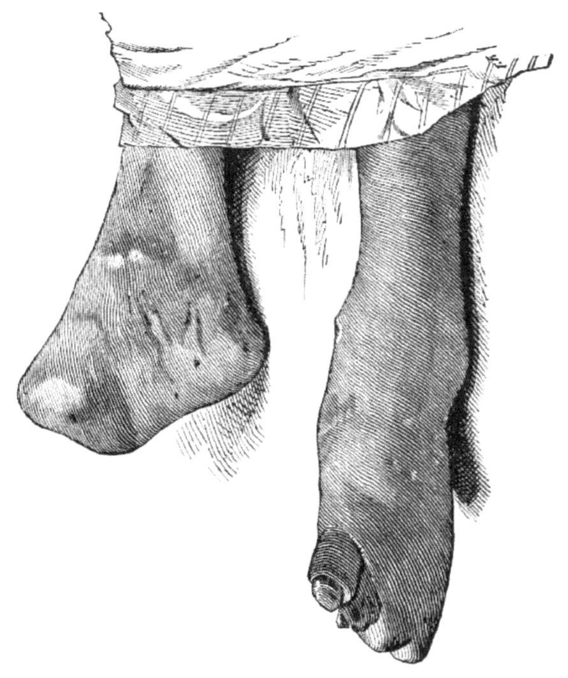

232

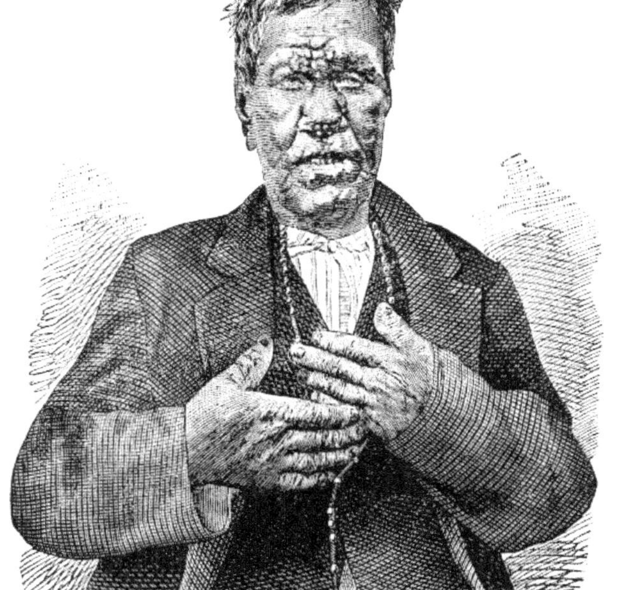

229: Leprosy.　　　230: Leprosy.　　　231: Leprosy.　　　232: Leprosy.

233

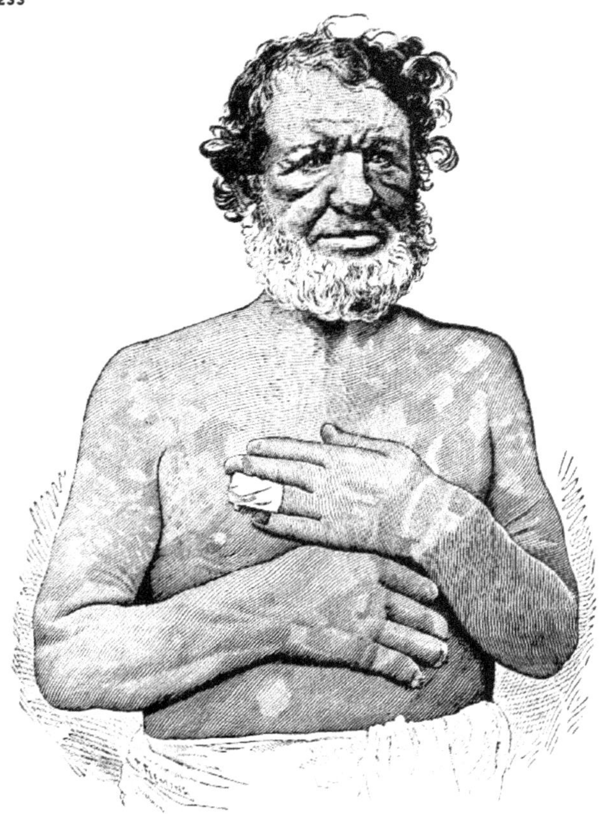

234

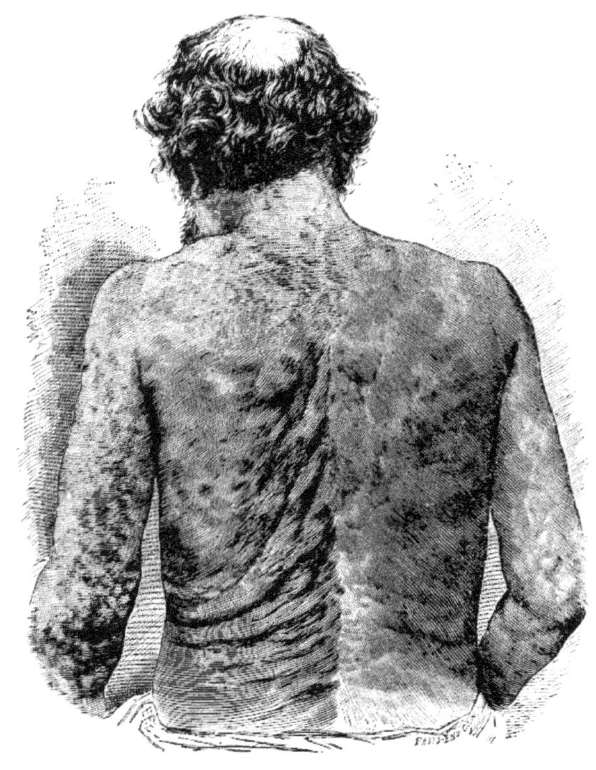

235

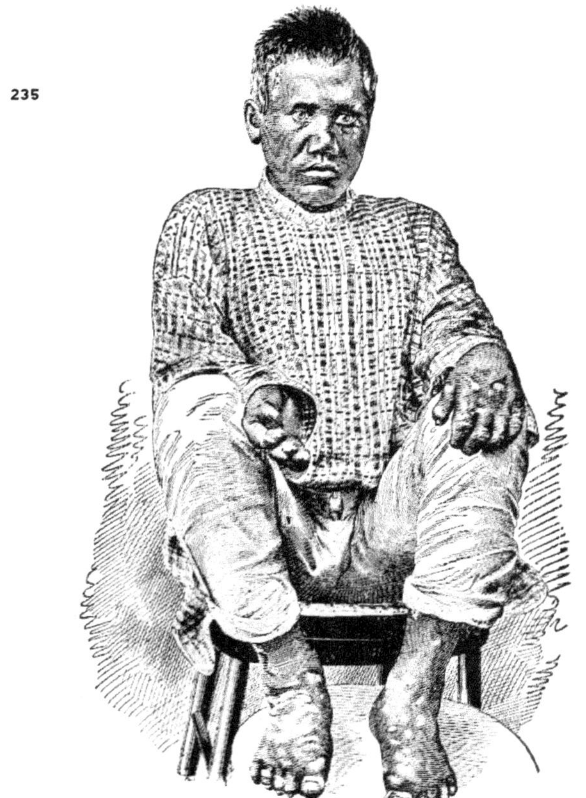

236

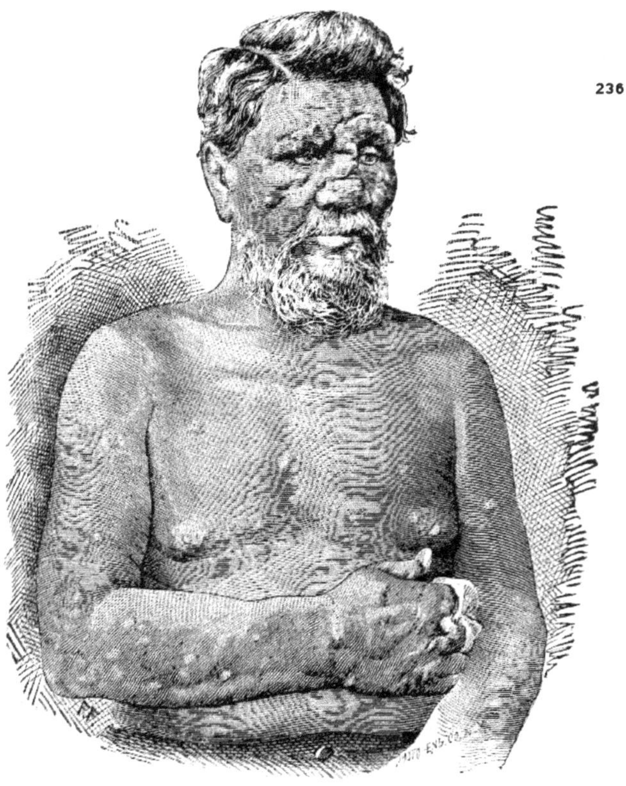

233: Leprosy.

234: Leprosy.

235: Leprosy.

236: Leprosy.

237

238

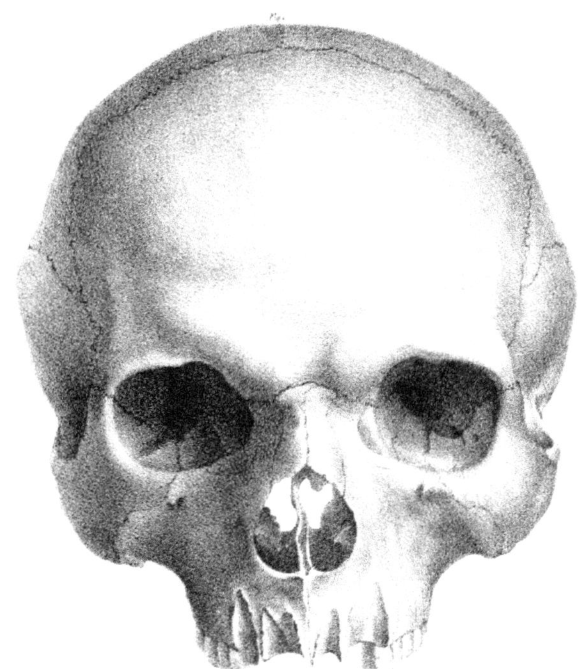

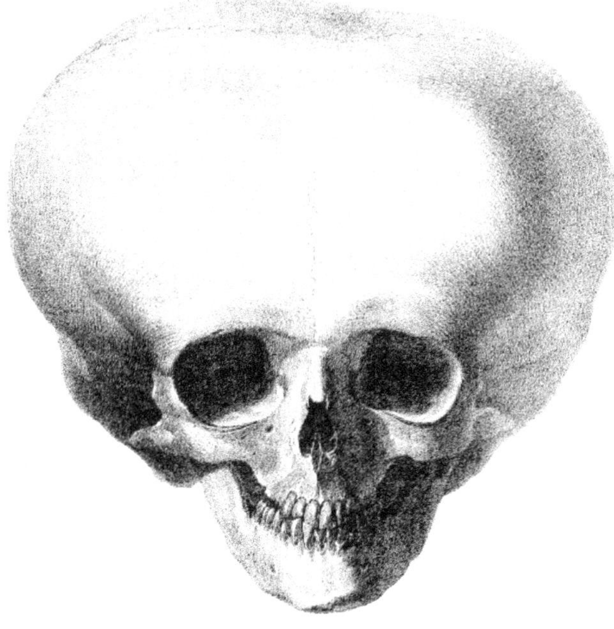

239

240

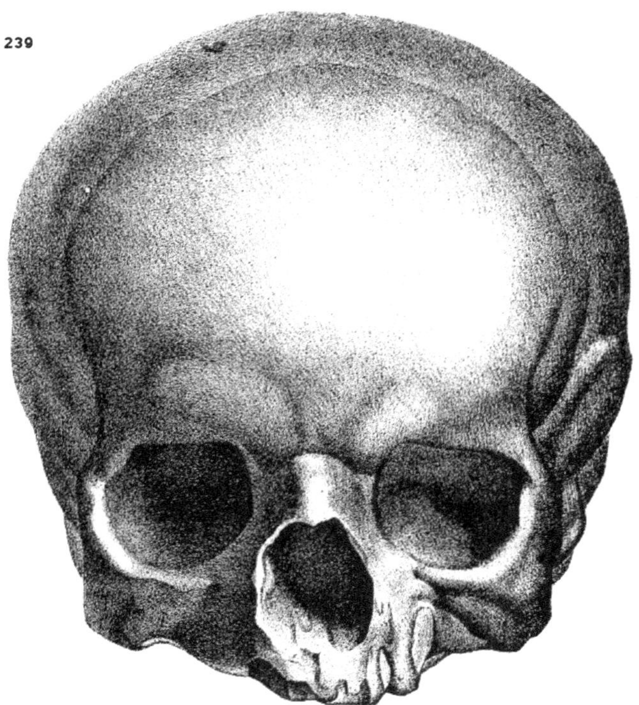

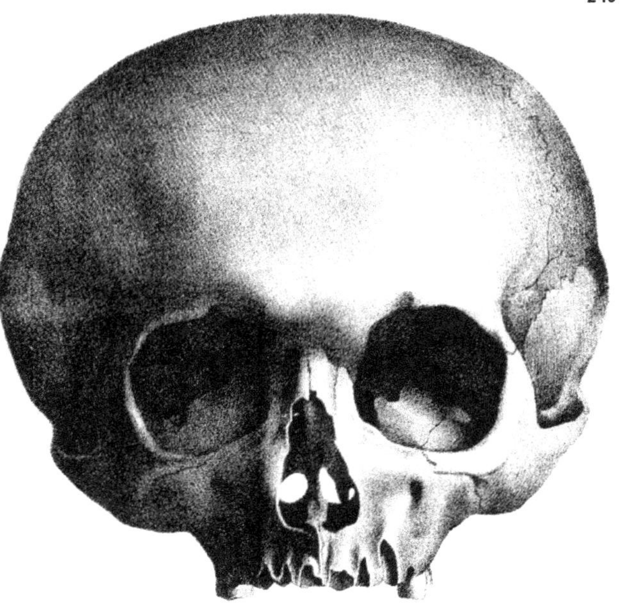

237: Deformity of the skull caused by venereal disease.

238: Deformity of the skull caused by venereal disease.

239: Deformity of the skull caused by venereal disease.

240: Deformity of the skull caused by venereal disease.

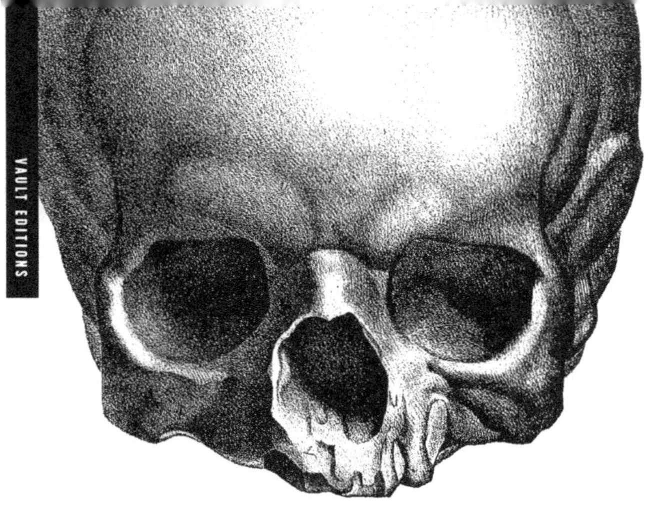

LEARN MORE

At Vault Editions, our mission is to create the world's most diverse and comprehensive collection of image archives available for artists, designers and curious minds. If you have enjoyed this book, you can find more of our titles available at vaulteditions.com.

REVIEW THIS BOOK

As a small, family-owned independent publisher, reviews help spread the word about our work. We would be incredibly grateful if you could leave an honest review of this title wherever you purchased this book.

JOIN OUR COMMUNITY

Are you a creative and curious individual? If so, you will love our community on Instagram. Every day we share bizarre and beautiful artwork ranging from 17th and 18th-century natural history and scientific illustration, to mythical beasts, ornamental designs, anatomical illustration and more. Join our community of 100K+ people today— search @vault_editions on Instagram.

DOWNLOAD YOUR FILES

STEP ONE

Enter the following web address in your web browser on a desktop computer.

www.vaulteditions.com/mad

STEP TWO

Enter the following unique password to access the download page.

mad38579fsdrx3

STEP THREE

Follow the prompts to access your high-resolution files.

TECHNICAL ASSISTANCE

For all technical assistance, please email: info@vaulteditions.com

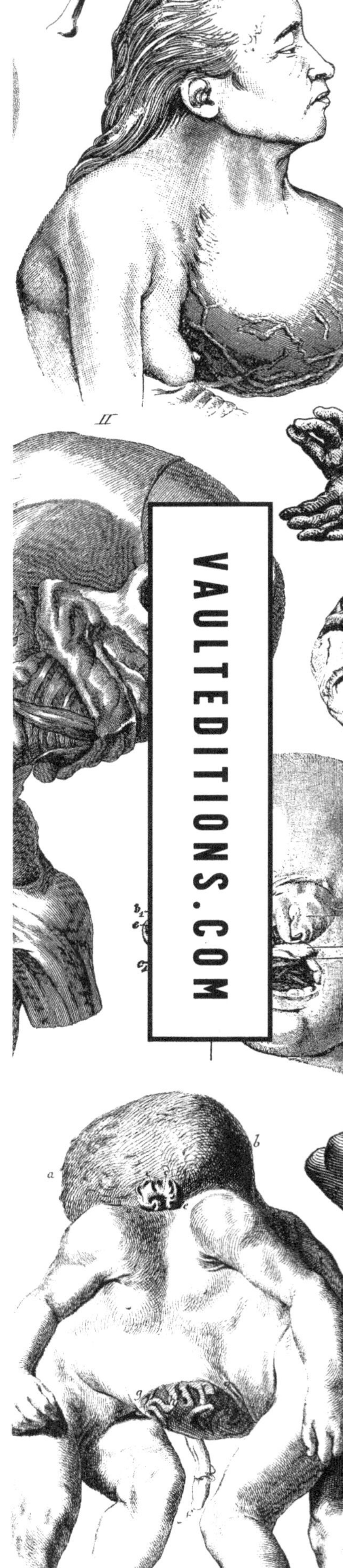

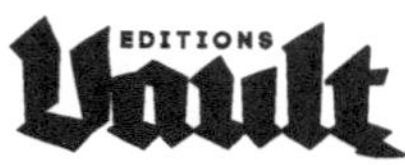